NEW STUDI

Bound for the
Promised Land

Titles in this series:

An index of Scripture references for all the volumes may be found at
http://thegospelcoalition.org/resources/nsbt

NEW STUDIES IN BIBLICAL THEOLOGY 34

Series editor: D. A. Carson

Bound for the Promised Land

THE LAND PROMISE IN GOD'S REDEMPTIVE PLAN

Oren R. Martin

APOLLOS

INTERVARSITY PRESS
DOWNERS GROVE, ILLINOIS 60515

APOLLOS
An imprint of Inter-Varsity Press, England
Norton Street
Nottingham NG7 3HR, England
ivpbooks.com
ivp@ivpbooks.com

InterVarsity Press, USA
P.O. Box 1400
Downers Grove, IL 60515-1426, USA
ivpress.com
email@ivpress.com

InterVarsity Press®, USA, is the book-publishing division of InterVarsity Christian Fellowship/ USA® and a member movement of the International Fellowship of Evangelical Students. Website: www.intervarsity.org.

Inter-Varsity Press, England, is closely linked with the Universities and Colleges Christian Fellowship, a student movement connecting Christian Unions throughout Great Britain, and a member movement of the International Fellowship of Evangelical Students. Website: www.uccf .org.uk

First published 2015

Set in Monotype Times New Roman

Typeset in Great Britain by CRB Associates, Potterhanworth, Lincolnshire

Printed and bound in Great Britain by Ashford Colour Press Ltd, Gosport, Hampshire

USA ISBN 978-0-8308-2635-3 (print)
USA ISBN 978-0-8308-9800-8 (digital)
UK ISBN 978-1-78359-189-3

British Library Cataloguing in Publication Data
A catalogue record for this book is available from the British Library.

Library of Congress Cataloging-in-Publication Data
A catalogue record for this book is available from the Library of Congress.

P	21	20	19	18	17	16	15	14	13	12	11	10	9	8	7	6	5	4	3	2	1
Y	33	32	31	30	29	28	27	26	25	24	23	22	21	20	19	18	17	16	15

To Cindy,
a daily reminder that God's grace
is stunning, undeserved and freely given

Contents

Series preface

New Studies in Biblical Theology is a series of monographs that address key issues in the discipline of biblical theology. Contributions to the series focus on one or more of three areas: (1) the nature and status of biblical theology, including its relations with other disciplines (e.g. historical theology, exegesis, systematic theology, historical criticism, narrative theology); (2) the articulation and exposition of the structure of thought of a particular biblical writer or corpus; and (3) the delineation of a biblical theme across all or part of the biblical corpora.

Above all, these monographs are creative attempts to help thinking Christians understand their Bibles better. The series aims simultaneously to instruct and to edify, to interact with the current literature, and to point the way ahead. In God's universe, mind and heart should not be divorced: in this series we will try not to separate what God has joined together. While the notes interact with the best of scholarly literature, the text is uncluttered with untransliterated Greek and Hebrew, and tries to avoid too much technical jargon. The volumes are written within the framework of confessional evangelicalism, but there is always an attempt at thoughtful engagement with the sweep of the relevant literature.

Theologies of 'the land' of Israel have taken various forms. One thinks of earlier works, such as the magisterial tome by W. D. Davies that was descriptively rich but did not attempt a biblical synthesis. Of course, there have also been many contributions that attempt to tie the various 'land' promises to the re-founding of the nation of Israel more than half a century ago. Dr Martin paints his biblical theology of the land on a grander scale. He argues that the land promises constitute part of a trajectory that begins with the loss of 'land' at the expulsion from Eden and ends, finally, in the new heaven *and the new earth*. The resulting synthesis of the land promises, kingdom promises and eschatology is thought-provoking and sometimes moving.

D. A. Carson
Trinity Evangelical Divinity School

Author's preface

This book is a substantial revision of my dissertation (Martin 2013), and though it bears my name by no means do I claim sole credit. The Lord has brought countless people across my path to encourage me along the way. Most of all, I am thankful for the wonderful opportunity to spend concentrated time mining the riches of his Word for a crucial theme in biblical theology. In this endeavour I have found much delight, and for these blessings I am deeply grateful.

Though it would take another book to thank the inestimable number of people who prayed for and encouraged me, I offer special thanks to a few. I thank my parents, Bob and Nancy Wilson, and in-laws, Lou and Mary Ann Abshire, for their constant support and encouragement. Moreover, I thank friends who have both taught and encouraged me throughout this process and, as a result, have made this work better: Ryan Lister, J. T. English, Matt Hall and John Meade.

I am grateful especially for Bruce Ware, Tom Schreiner and Stephen Wellum, who teach at the Southern Baptist Theological Seminary, not only for their supervision and guidance, but also for their continued encouragement and counsel. It is a privilege to say that I studied with these men and, even more, to call them friends. Thanks also to Clifton Baptist Church in Louisville, Kentucky, where I formerly served as a pastor while writing this book, for the countless ways he has used the saints there to increase our love for God's glory in Christ and his people. Moreover, I am thankful for the men with whom I pastored, especially John Kimbell, Jeremy Pierre, Tom Schreiner and Shawn Wright, who constantly encourage me to be faithful and look to Christ. They are treasured gifts from God.

I am grateful to Philip Duce, senior commissioning editor for theological books at Inter-Varsity Press (UK), for his gracious interaction, encouragement and editorial work that have made this work better. I am particularly grateful for Michael Dietzel, Joseph Pieri and Joel Rosario, who ably assisted me and performed a huge task of editing the bibliography and footnotes. Their labour of love saved me countless hours and I can scarcely thank them for their work. Thanks also to Don Carson, the series editor, for initially accepting this work. Over the years I have developed a deep appreciation for him through his writings and for this series, and I appreciate him even more as a result of his helpful and encouraging feedback. I consider it a great privilege to contribute to a series that has contributed much to my own growth in Christ and understanding of his life-giving Word.

I am dedicating this book to my beloved wife, Cindy, who not only has given us three sweet and beautiful children – Jonathan, Anna and Benjamin – but who also has been my best friend and most trusted counsellor. I love her more than ever and cannot imagine life without her. She is a daily reminder to me that God's grace is stunning and undeserved.

Finally, and most importantly, I am grateful that the gospel is the power of God for salvation to everyone who believes. This work is not a product of my gifts, but of our great God's transforming grace. It is my prayer that God, who fulfils all of his saving promises in Christ and works all things according to the counsel of his will, receives all the glory for any good that comes out of this book, for his glory in Christ and the everlasting joy of his people.

Oren R. Martin

Abbreviations

4QpPs 37	*Pesher on Psalm 37* (Dead Sea Scrolls)
AB	Anchor Bible
AUSDDS	*Andrews University Seminary Doctoral Dissertation Series*
BBR	*Bulletin for Biblical Research*
BDAG	W. Bauer, F. W. Danker, W. F. Arndt and W. F. Gingrich, *A Greek-English Lexicon of the New Testament and Other Early Christian Literature*, 3rd ed., Chicago: University of Chicago Press, 2000
BNTC	Black's New Testament Commentaries
BSac	*Bibliotheca Sacra*
BST	The Bible Speaks Today
BTNT	Biblical Theology of the New Testament
CBQ	*Catholic Biblical Quarterly*
Chm	*Churchman*
ConBOT	Coniectanea biblica: Old Testament Series
DJG	*Dictionary of Jesus and the Gospels*
DOTHP	*Dictionary of the Old Testament: Historical Books*, ed. Bill T. Arnold and H. G. M. Williamson, 2005
DOTP	T. D. Alexander and D. W. Baker (eds.), *Dictionary of the Old Testament: Pentateuch*, Downers Grove: InterVarsity Press, 2002
DTIB	*Dictionary for Theological Interpretation of the Bible*, ed. Kevin Vanhoozer, Grand Rapids: Baker, 2005
EBC	The Expositor's Bible Commentary
ERT	*Evangelical Review of Theology*
EvQ	*Evangelical Quarterly*
Hebr.	Hebrew
IBC	Interpretation Bible Commentary
IBR	Institute for Biblical Research
ICC	International Critical Commentary
Int	*Interpretation*
JAOS	*Journal of the American Oriental Society*

JETS	*Journal of the Evangelical Theological Society*
JR	*Journal of Religion*
JSNT	*Journal for the Study of the New Testament*
JSOTSup	Journal for the Study of the Old Testament, Supplement Series
JTI	*Journal of Theological Interpretation*
LNTS	Library of New Testament Studies
LXX	Septuagint
MT	Masoretic Text
NAC	The New American Commentary
NACSBT	NAC Studies in Bible and Theology
NDBT	*New Dictionary of Biblical Theology*: *Exploring the Unity and Diversity of Scripture*, ed. B. S. Rosner, T. D. Alexander, G. Goldsworthy and D. A. Carson, Downers Grove: InterVarsity Press; Leicester: Inter-Varsity Press, 2000
NIBC	The New International Biblical Commentary
NICNT	The New International Commentary on the New Testament
NICOT	The New International Commentary on the Old Testament
NIDOTTE	*New International Dictionary of Old Testament Theology and Exegesis*, ed. W. A. VanGemeren, 5 vols., Grand Rapids: Zondervan; Carlisle: Paternoster, 1997
NIGTC	The New International Greek Testament Commentary
NIVAC	The NIV Application Commentary
NSBT	New Studies in Biblical Theology
NT	New Testament
OT	Old Testament
PNTC	The Pillar New Testament Commentary
SBET	*Scottish Bulletin of Evangelical Theology*
SBJT	*Southern Baptist Journal of Theology*
SHS	Scripture and Hermeneutics Series
SNTSMS	Society for New Testament Studies Monograph Series
SOTBT	Studies in Old Testament Biblical Theology
SP	Sacra pagina
Str–B	H. Strack and P. Billerbeck, *Kommentar zum Neuen Testament*, 4 vols., Munich: Beck'sche, 1926–8

Them	*Themelios*
TNTC	Tyndale New Testament Commentaries
TOTC	Tyndale Old Testament Commentaries
tr.	translation, translated, translated by
TrinJ	*Trinity Journal*
TynB	*Tyndale Bulletin*
WBC	Word Biblical Commentary
WTJ	*Westminster Theological Journal*
WUNT	Wissenschaftliche Untersuchungen zum Neuen Testament
ZAW	*Zeitschrift für die alttestamentliche Wissenschaft*
ZECNT	Zondervan Exegetical Commentary on the New Testament

Chapter One

Biblical theology and the land promise

Place matters. Just as Genesis begins with creation, where humans live in the presence of their Lord, so Revelation ends with an even more glorious new creation where all of the redeemed dwell with the Lord and his Christ. But the historical development between the beginning and the end is crucial to observe, for the journey from Eden to the new Jerusalem proceeds through the land promised to Abraham. In other words, the Promised Land occupies a special place for God's people after the fall and exile from Eden, because it is the place where they will once again live under his lordship and experience his blessed presence. The Promised Land, then, connects the beginning and the end.

From a broader perspective, Eden is presented as the inaugural kingdom, and the new Jerusalem is presented as the consummated kingdom, where the kingdom of the world is the kingdom of God (Rev. 11:15; 21:1 – 22:5). It is no surprise, then, that the Old Testament focuses the extension of God's kingdom on Israel's land. In other words, God's programme with and through Abraham is to restore the original conditions of God's creational kingdom described in Genesis 1 – 2, which will not finally be accomplished until the former things have passed away and all things are made new (Rev. 21:4–5). Thus the intersection of land and kingdom that commences in Eden will be consummated in the new Jerusalem. Between these historical book? ends, God will re-establish his kingdom on earth through Abraham and his seed living in the land of promise.

The aim of the present study is to demonstrate that the land promised to Abraham advances the place of the kingdom that was lost in Eden and serves as a type throughout Israel's history that anticipates the even greater land – prepared for all of God's people throughout history – that will come as a result of the person and work of Christ. In other words, the land and its blessings find their fulfilment in the new heaven and new earth won by Christ. When each place of God's people is situated within the redemptive-historical framework of God's unfolding plan, the land promised to Abraham is seen to be a progressive fulfilment of God's kingdom on earth. Subsequently, the land promised to and, on more than one occasion, possessed by God's people throughout the Old Testament pointed to something greater that his people throughout all time, in relation to Christ, will enjoy in the new creation for eternity.

To unpack the land promise in the plan of God, we will examine the theme of land as it progressively unfolds across the story line of Scripture. That is, an examination of this theme will take place as it develops from the Old to the New Testament, from promise to fulfilment. This examination will demonstrate that the land promised to Abraham, which was inhabited and lost throughout Israel's history, is important because it picks up the place of God's kingdom that was lost in Eden, thus serving as a subsequent place in God's unfolding plan. Furthermore, from the perspective of Israel's exile, this place anticipates and prepares the way for the coming of Jesus Christ, who wins a new creation for his people. And although those united with Christ by faith in the present era of salvation history enjoy every spiritual blessing in the heavenly places in Christ, they await their final destiny – the new heaven and new earth – to which the land of promise pointed.

The land promise in biblical scholarship

The theme of land in Scripture is an important component in the biblical framework of promise and fulfilment.[1] Remarkably, it has not received a great deal of attention in terms of a whole-Bible biblical theology.[2] The interest in land as a theological theme is relatively recent in the church's history.[3] This observation is not surprising given the focus on Israel since the mid-twentieth century. Even so, exegetically driven, biblically robust and systematically sensitive theologies of land are relatively few. However, on the interest of land from a socio-political perspective, or on the relationship between land/property

---

[1] Martens 1998: 114.

[2] Most treatments of the land promise are embedded in works that cover much broader topics. Furthermore, broader hermeneutical issues such as the Israel–church relationship or the relationship between the covenants are brought into the picture. See e.g. works on theological systems, such as Bateman 1999; Blaising and Bock 1993; Saucy 1993; Feinberg 1988; Robertson 1980; see also works on eschatology, such as Hoekema 1979; Venema 2000; 2008.

[3] Martens 1998: 114.

and ethics, of books there is no end.[4] This section, then, will summarize and briefly evaluate past theological treatments of the land.

The significance of land as a theological theme was described by Gerhard von Rad.[5] Following in his wake, several works have been devoted to the theme of land. Two books published around the same time treated land as a more comprehensive biblical-theological theme – Walter Brueggemann and W. D. Davies – and both cited von Rad's earlier essay.[6] Although these works present comprehensive treatments on the biblical theme of land, both fall short for various reasons. For example, in terms of a 'whole-Bible biblical theology',[7] Brueggemann gives little attention to New Testament texts, which limits his treatment of the development of land across the entire Christian canon. Furthermore, his existential and sociological emphases influence his understanding of the land.[8] For Davies, when it comes to the nature of Scripture, his work is fraught with a dated form-critical view of the Gospels. Also, he concludes that the New Testament spiritualizes the land and relocates it to Christ.[9] As this book will show, this view does not sufficiently present the New Testament fulfilment of what the Old Testament anticipated.

Three additional works examine the concept of land from within the Old Testament. First, Moshe Weinfeld contributes a substantive exegetical piece to the discussion of land.[10] Although helpful in his exegetical work on the relevant Old Testament texts, he fails to

[4] For books on land that focus on the sociopolitical aspects of the Israel–Palestine conflict and conclude with (some) theological/ethical reflection(s), see Ateek 1989; 2008; Barclay 2004; Sizer 2007; Weber 2004; Burge 2004. For books on the relationship of land/property and ethics, see C. J. H. Wright 2004; 1990.

[5] Von Rad 1966; see also Hanson 2005.

[6] Brueggemann 1977; Davies 1974 and, more recently, 1982, which is a summary of his earlier work along with concluding essays by various scholars on the meaning of land and theology in the light of current events.

[7] Carson 2000: 100. A 'whole-Bible biblical theology' is not merely a theology that is biblical, although it is certainly not less than this. The phrase picks up on the discipline of biblical theology, which, as Carson (ibid.) says, 'even as it works inductively from the diverse texts of the Bible, seeks to uncover and articulate the unity of all the biblical texts taken together, resorting primarily to the categories of those text themselves'. See also Rosner 2000: 3–11. This is what James Barr (1999) calls a 'pan-Biblical theology'.

[8] E.g. Brueggemann (1977: 3) says, 'Biblical faith is a pursuit of historical belonging that includes a sense of destiny derived from such a belonging.' A similar perspective is found in Inge (2003), ch. 2.

[9] E.g. Davies (1974: 336), after examining the NT data, says, 'We have discovered in the New Testament, alongside the recognition of the historical role of the land as the scene of the life, death and resurrection of Jesus, a growing recognition that the Christian faith is, in principle, cut loose from the land, that the Gospel demanded a breaking out of its territorial chrysalis.'

[10] Weinfeld 1993.

synthesize it into a coherent theology. For example, when it comes to the varying views of the borders of the Promised Land, he detects redactional activity and concludes that they are contradictory.[11] This lack of coherence is no doubt attributed to his subscription to critical views of Scripture, specifically the documentary hypothesis. Secondly, Norman Habel identifies six ideologies in the Old Testament regarding land: royal, theocratic, ancestral household, prophetic, agrarian and immigrant.[12] But rather than offering a comprehensive biblical theology, Habel aims to connect the land to economic, social, political and religious ideas. Finally, and closer to the approach of this book, Arie Leder treats the land as a coherent and progressive biblical theology.[13] However, he limits his study to the Pentateuch before making application to the church. Thus a more comprehensive biblical theology of the Promised Land is needed.

There are also chapters and articles that treat the theme of land within their overall argument. First, some Old Testament theologies isolate the discussion of land to, at most, a few chapters, which often are limited to Deuteronomy and/or Joshua.[14] Other Old Testament theologies integrate land into one of their central themes; thus giving it greater prominence.[15] Secondly, chapters and articles are devoted to one or more aspects of a theology of land from various theological traditions.[16] While each of these chapters and articles illumines the theme of land in a unique way, they are not comprehensive. Finally, G. K. Beale has provided a chapter in his New Testament theology on the relationship of Israel's land promises to the fulfilment of Israel's

---

[11] Ibid. ch. 3.

[12] Habel 1995.

[13] Leder 2010.

[14] See e.g. House 1998: 197–213, 512–522; Goldingay 2003: 451–528; 2006: 438–449; Preuss 1996: 117–128; Rendtorff 2005: 220–225, 457–469; von Rad 2005: 296–305; Dumbrell 2002: 57–75. Waltke with Yu (2007: 512–587) is a notable exception that offers a more comprehensive treatment of land as it progresses from the Old to the New Testament. Two biblical theologies that also treat land within their overall schema are Kaiser 2008 (90–110), which is based in part on his earlier work (1978: 122–142), and Scobie 2003 (541–567).

[15] See e.g. Dempster 2003; Martens 1998 (the land sections from this work were reprinted in Martens 2004); Alexander 2012; and Dumbrell 1984.

[16] For journal articles, see Miller 1969: 451–465; Kaiser 1981: 302–312; C. J. H. Wright 1993: 153–167; for chapters in books, see Martens 2009, who organizes the land theme around the concept of metaphor; Holwerda 1995: 85–112; Robertson 2000, who presents the land theme from a covenantal perspective; and Horner 2007 (223–252), who presents the land theme from a dispensational perspective. And finally, systematic theologies have not traditionally included in their organization a locus devoted to land; although one exception is Rushdoony 1994 (957–1018).

restoration and new-creation prophecies in Christ and the church.[17] Although similar to the argument of this study, Beale's treatment of the development of the land promise in the Old Testament is brief before he shows the fulfilment in the New Testament.

Other, more recent, works come closer to this study. First, an edited volume by Philip Johnston and Peter Walker is similar in some ways to the present examination of the land theme; especially the first two chapters by Paul Williamson and T. Desmond Alexander.[18] The contributors attempt to provide biblical, theological and contemporary perspectives on the land of promise, albeit from different perspectives.[19] The treatment of land, however, is limited due to the contributors' conflicting views (e.g. Palestinian Christian, Jewish Christian). Secondly, a recent work by Gary Burge holds out even more promise when it comes to the nature and breadth of Scripture.[20] Burge seeks to integrate both Old and New Testament before showing how Jesus and the New Testament reinterpret the land. He argues that Jesus is the 'great rearranger' of the land and that all the properties of the holy land are now relocated in him.[21] However, many will dismiss his conclusions because he does not show sufficient Old Testament warrant for his New Testament conclusions.[22] Thirdly, Craig Bartholomew connects the land promised to Abraham to the broader theme of place.[23] Through a biblical, theological, philosophical, historical and practical investigation, he alerts his readers to the importance of place for humanity as it seeks 'playmaking' in its cities, gardens, homes and a myriad of different types of places. However, the primary purpose of Bartholomew's work is not to examine comprehensively the land promise and its place in redemptive history, but rather to reorient his readers by Scripture and the best of the Christian tradition towards a recovery of place today.[24]

Finally, Peter Gentry and Stephen Wellum have contributed a *via media* between dispensational and covenant theology that examines God's overarching plan to bring about his kingdom through covenant

---

[17] Beale 2011: 750–772.
[18] Johnston and Walker 2000. See also Walker 1994; 1996.
[19] E.g. dispensational, non-dispensational, covenantal and Jewish.
[20] Burge 2010.
[21] Ibid. 41, 129.
[22] E.g. he spends only ten pages on the biblical heritage of land in the OT before moving on to intertestamental literature and the NT.
[23] Bartholomew 2011.
[24] Ibid. 5; see also Inge 2003.

by unpacking in detail each biblical covenant in its own redemptive-historical context and its relationship to the arrival of the new covenant in the person and work of Jesus Christ. The final chapters summarize and apply the theological implications of *kingdom through covenant* to various doctrinal loci, such as the land promise.[25] While my study is in substantial agreement with Gentry and Wellum's *Kingdom Through Covenant*, it aims to go into greater depth by restricting its focus to the theme of land.

Some conclusions can be drawn from this brief survey. First, though a variety of books and articles deal with the topic of land, at many points their theological focus is intertwined with ethics and/or the sociopolitical Israel–Palestine conflict. Secondly, though various theologies study the theme of land, many are restricted to Old Testament theology. Furthermore, Old Testament theologies that treat the theme of land often limit their study to Genesis, Deuteronomy and/or Joshua. Thirdly, because many argue that the New Testament does not advance the promise of land, New Testament theology has not, by and large, examined how the theme of land arises.[26] Hence a theology of land remains problematic for New Testament theology. Finally, further study is needed on the theme of land from the standpoint of a whole-Bible theology. This work, therefore, aims to clarify and complete what is lacking.

Approach and assumptions

Recent studies in biblical theology have tried to argue that no one centre or theme exhaustively captures the rich and multifaceted message of Scripture.[27] Paul House asserts, 'We should give up arguing that one theme and one theme only is the central theme of the Bible and highlight major themes that allow other ideas as subpoints.'[28] This conclusion finds support given the diversity of the

---

[25] Gentry and Wellum 2012: 703–716.

[26] A notable exception is Beale 2011.

[27] Scobie 1991: 178; he repeats the same sentiment in *The Ways of Our God* (2003: 87). For further discussion of this topic, see Martens 1997: 57. For a bold argument for the centre of biblical theology, see J. M. Hamilton 2006a: 57–84; 2010; for a response to Hamilton, see Köstenberger 2012: 445–464.

[28] House 2002: 276. E.g. an attempt to describe some of the major themes in Scripture has been made by Hafemann and House 2007. See also Carson (1998: 810), who in his assessment of the search for a centre concluded, 'pursuit of a center is chimerical'. For more discussion on this topic, see related chapters in Hasel 1991; 2003.

Old and New Testaments. According to James Dunn, a centre for New Testament theology is more easily seen due to its unified focus on Christ and faith in him as Lord, but when the Old Testament is added in the scope of a theological centre, the quest for such a single formulation has never been satisfactorily resolved.[29] This conclusion is often reached because no single centre is broad enough to integrate the multitudinous variety of biblical texts.[30] This does not mean, however, that there is not unity in the diversity. The assumption of an evangelical-theological framework, says Richard Lints, 'ought to be the unity-in-diversity of the Testaments – with unity being prior to the diversity since it is the one God who manifests himself in the diversity of historical epochs'.[31] Hence the continuity between the various parts of Scripture, between Old and New Testament, can and should be anchored in the one triune God who authored it. With these qualifications in mind, a canonical theology can be pursued.

The purpose of this work is not to summarize and engage the debate over a/the centre of biblical theology. If one centre is chosen, it is possible that other central themes that arise from the text will be ignored. At the same time, it is defensible that some themes are better than others at explicating the message of Scripture in so far as they are connected to and incorporate other important themes. J. L. McKenzie states that Old Testament theology should be based on those themes that occur most frequently and that appear to be vital in giving Old Testament belief its distinctive identity.[32] This idea can be broadened to a 'whole-Bible biblical theology',[33] for just as a New Testament theme cannot be examined apart from looking at its Old Testament roots, so also an Old Testament theme cannot be examined apart from its New Testament fulfilment.[34] So themes that progress along the story line of Scripture must be followed to their end, and climax in the person and work of Christ.

For example, various Old Testament, New Testament and canonical-biblical theologies have been organized around central themes such

[29] Dunn 2004: 175.
[30] Merrill 2006: 27.
[31] Lints 1993: 277.
[32] McKenzie 1974: 24–25; see also Scobie 2003: 85.
[33] Carson 2000: 100; Rosner 2000: 3–11.
[34] For a survey of the various approaches to biblical theology, see Klink and Lockett 2012.

as God or kingdom of God,[35] covenant,[36] God's presence,[37] election,[38] Messiah,[39] human viceregency (Gen. 1:26–28)[40] and new creation.[41] Others have focused on some multithemed variation.[42] Works such as these demonstrate that in Scripture there is a unity in diversity – a wholeness in the light of the parts – that displays the richness of God's Word. There are, as Al Wolters writes, 'connections between any given part of the Scriptures and the overall biblical story'.[43] Along with these important interconnected themes, additional themes arise from a careful reading of Scripture that demonstrate the treasures of God's Word and his redemptive plan in history, a plan that has been inaugurated and will culminate in uniting all things in Christ: things in heaven and things on earth (Eph. 1:10). The aim of the present study is to demonstrate that the theme of 'land' is an important one because it shares 'in the complex connections of biblical covenants'.[44]

It is important to note the multifaceted nature of the interpretative process in formulating any particular theme or doctrine. Therefore attention must be given to theological method. First, scholars have rightly noted the relationship between exegesis, biblical theology and systematic theology. It is too simplistic to reduce the hermeneutical process to a series of logical steps (e.g. exegesis, biblical theology, systematic theology). Rather, each discipline informs and checks the others. Secondly, this process takes into account and is informed by historical theology, for every person approaches the text with certain (confessional) presuppositions.[45] Theological method is neither formulated in a vacuum nor merely theoretical. Nor should methodology impose foreign categories on to the text. Rather, the content of

[35] Goldsworthy 1991; 2000; Ridderbos 1962; Kline 2006; Waltke 2007; Schreiner 2013.

[36] P. R. Williamson 2007; Dumbrell 1984; Horton 2002. There is also covenant theology, the theological system organized around the covenant. Covenant theology is traditionally traced back to Johannes Cocceius, the seventeenth-century Dutch theologian. See Van Aselt 2000. On covenant theology's major emphases and the variations within the general system, see Golding 2004.

[37] Terrien 1978.

[38] Preuss 1996: 24–25.

[39] Bateman, Bock and Johnston 2012; Barnett 2009; Alexander 1998.

[40] Merrill 2006.

[41] Alexander 2008; 2012; Beale 2011; 1997; 2002.

[42] See e.g. Dempster 2003; Martens 1998.

[43] Wolters 2004: 261.

[44] Poythress 1991: 70. Brueggemann (1977: 3) says, 'Land is a central, if not *the central theme* of biblical faith. Biblical faith is a pursuit of historical belonging that includes a sense of destiny derived from such belonging. In what follows I suggest that land may be a way of organizing biblical theology' (emphasis original). Brueggemann may claim too much in this statement, though all would agree that land is an important theme.

[45] Osborne 2006: 350.

theology ought to shape its methodology by developing its own intra-systematic categories.[46]

This interpretative and theological process is set forth by Richard Lints, in what he calls the three horizons of redemptive interpretation – the *textual* (immediate context at the grammatical-historical level), *epochal* (context of the period of revelation) and *canonical* (context of the entirety of revelation) horizons.[47] That is, equal study must be given to all texts, rightly interpreted within their respective contexts, with careful attention paid to literary genre in the light of their overall place in redemptive history and the canon to reach sound biblical and theological conclusions.

This theological framework presupposes that Scripture constitutes a unified text with a developing story. God's Word reveals and interprets his redemptive acts, which develop across time, from creation to new creation. 'Biblical revelation', says Lints, 'progresses because it mirrors the progressive nature of redemption.'[48] Theology must keep the redemptive-revelatory and redemptive-historical nature of Scripture in its focus. But not only is God's revelation redemptive-historical; it is redemptive-historical/eschatological. That is, it has a divine *telos*. Horton is correct when he says that when reading Scripture, 'eschatology should be a lens and not merely a locus'.[49] This eschatological permeation of Scripture is rooted in a sovereign God, who is moving history along to his appointed ends.

Another important methodological component for this study is typology, which involves correspondence(s) between persons, events and institutions, and later persons, events and institutions.[50] That is, God's past dealings with his people serve as patterns, or types, for his future dealings with his people. Robert Plummer writes, 'Because God is completely sovereign over history, *all* Old Testament-era saving events, institutions, persons, offices, holidays and ceremonies served to anticipate

[46] Horton 2002: 19; Lints 1993: 270–274.
[47] Lints 1993: 293–311; see also Clowney 1961: 16.
[48] Ibid. 262.
[49] Horton 2002: 5. So also Dumbrell (2002: 9), who further explicates this idea when he says, 'The Bible is a book about the future in light of the human failings of the past and present. In this sense the entire Bible is eschatological, since it focuses upon the ushering in of the kingdom of God, the fulfilling of the divine intention for humanity and society. In very broad terms the biblical sweep is from creation to the new creation. Yet the end is not merely a return to the beginning, for the Bible reveals a great deal more about the divine intention than what is shown at the beginning of Genesis. Regarding eschatology, we must recognize how the Bible develops its theme of God's purpose from the beginning of Genesis to the end in Revelation.'
[50] Ribbens 2011: 81; Hoskins 2006: 19.

the final saving event, the final saving person, the final saving ceremony, etc.'[51] For example, Old Testament prophets anticipated and looked for a new David, a new exodus, a new covenant and a new city of God: the old had thus become a type of the new and was important in pointing forward to it.[52] Subsequently, the New Testament authors saw in Christ and his work the fulfilment, or antitype, of these prophetic hopes.

There are several important components in typology. First, typology pays careful attention to textual and historical/theological correspondences that develop across the canon.[53] These correspondences provide the hermeneutical controls for linking types with their antitype(s). Secondly, typology is prospective and prophetic. That is, God intentionally planned certain persons, events and institutions in redemptive history *in order that* they would serve later redemptive – and Christological – realities.[54] Darrell Bock writes:

> *Typology*, or better *typological-prophetic* usage, expresses a peculiar link of patterns with movement from the lesser OT person or event to the greater NT person or event. . . . God's pattern of salvation is being reactivated in a present fulfillment. This fulfillment takes place both in accordance with messianic hope and promise and in accordance with the pattern of God's activity in salvation.[55]

Thirdly, typology stresses escalation as the Old Testament story line moves forward to its New Testament fulfilment.[56] As a result, God's

[51] Plummer 2010a: 206; emphasis original; see also 2010b: 54–61.
[52] Von Rad 2005: 323.
[53] Baker 2010: 187.
[54] One view of typology is that it is only retrospective. This view has, however, been challenged to see a prospective component because of the nature of Scripture. In favour of the prospective component, Waltke with Yu (2007: 137) rightly says, 'The Bible's unique [divine] Authorship and unity lays the basis for eschatological typology – that is to say, God intended earlier persons, acts, and institutions to present a type or shadow or pattern of future greater fulfillment.' It is essential in this view to tie typology to a dually authored text , for the prospective aspect of the typological connections become clearer at the epochal and canonical levels. Other advocates of prospective typology include Davidson 1981; Goldsworthy 2006: 245–257; Beale 1994: 387–404. Opponents, who favour retrospective typology only, include Baker 1994: 313–330; 2010; France 1998: 39–40. For a brief discussion on this issue, see Marshall 1988: 15–17.
[55] Bock 1987: 49; emphasis original.
[56] In Goppelt's (1982: 18) seminal work on typology, he says, 'If the antitype does not represent a heightening of the type, if it is merely a repetition of the type, then it can be called typology only in certain instances and in a limited way.' Baker (2010: 183), however, does not see heightening between type and antitype as a necessary feature because 'this is simply an aspect of the progression from Old Testament to New Testament'. In any case, there is a pattern of escalation or progression from type to antitype.

redemptive purposes in the Old Testament are unfinished and thus cannot be *fully* understood apart from their fulfilment in the New Testament.[57] Lints notes, 'The Old Testament record of history is prophetic in the sense that it describes a revelation and divine action that are as yet incomplete. And the New Testament points to a consummation of history that now we understand only in part, as through a glass darkly.'[58] Promises in the Old Testament point forward to their fulfilment(s), and the type is fulfilled and surpassed by its antitype.[59] Finally, these typological connections find their terminus in the person and inaugurated-yet-not-consummated work of Christ.[60] In making typological connections – types with their antitypes – promises and fulfilments are linked, which are made clear by textual and historical connections developed both within the Old Testament itself and then from the Old Testament to the New.[61]

By allowing the textual, epochal and canonical horizons and progressive typological connections to illuminate the theme of land, this study will demonstrate how the development of the land promise across the canon provides hermeneutical warrant to see its ultimate fulfilment in the new creation won by Christ. This way of reading Scripture will hopefully help to overcome the impasse of conflicting conclusions concerning the land.

But before embarking upon the task of a biblical theology of land, theological assumptions must first be addressed. There is no such thing as a presupposition-*less* theology. A positive contribution of

[57] Goldsworthy 2006: 243.
[58] Lints 1993: 309.
[59] Scobie 2003: 90.
[60] Davidson 1981: 97.
[61] Seitz (2007: 228) defines intertextuality (or intratextuality) as 'how the Bible relates to itself in its own system of cross-reference . . . it has to do with the way in which parts of the Bible and finally the two Testaments themselves relate to one another'. There are many examples of these relationships, a few of which will demonstrate a pattern in Scripture. Adam was a type of Christ who was to come, as Paul's use of Gen. 1 – 2 in Rom. 5:12–21 makes clear. Jesus links himself with Moses, the representative prophet in the OT (John 3:14–15; 5:45–46; 6:32–35). Similarly, from Heb. 3:1–6 it is clear that Jesus is the ultimate and final prophet like Moses, spoken of in Deut. 18, for he embodies and speaks God's Word perfectly. Other examples include Israel, in which 'son' language is particularly important (Hos. 11:1; Matt. 2:15); the role of leaders as prophets, priests and kings; David, to whom God promised the Messiah and eternal kingship from his line; institutions, such as the temple, Passover and the sacrificial system; and events such as the exodus, which served as a type of the greater redemption that would come in Christ. These examples are not to stand isolated from their place(s) in redemptive history. Rather, they can be fully understood only in their respective redemptive-historical contexts and placement in the canon in relation to the person and work of Christ.

postmodernism has been the raising of the interpreter's awareness that there are no neutral approaches to theology.[62] It is, therefore, essential to recognize presuppositions and evaluate them under the authority of Scripture. To be sure, to defend each one is beyond our scope; nevertheless, these presuppositions are justifiable because they are grounded on the triune God, who has created humans in his image, made himself known in his Word and has graciously and savingly acted on humanity's behalf in history through the person and work of Jesus Christ.[63] These broader assumptions include the commitment to the total truthfulness and reliability of God's Word,[64] the divine and human authorship of Scripture,[65] the possibility of a 'whole-Bible biblical theology',[66] and the unity and continuity of God's saving plan progressively revealed to his people through the Bible's textual diversity.[67]

The plan of the book

This book comprises ten chapters. Following chapter 1, chapter 2 provides the biblical-theological framework from which a theology of land can be canonically understood, and, more specifically, the *framework* for understanding the place of God's people is the kingdom. Chapters 3–6 focus on God's promise of land to Abraham and, subsequently, evaluate the progress of God's fulfilment of his promise in four plot movements across the Old Testament. Chapter 3 considers the importance of Genesis 1 – 11 for the entrance of Abraham into God's redemptive plan and examines the nature and scope of the Abrahamic covenant and the promise of land. Chapters 4–5 look at the progress and fulfilment(s) of God's promise of land throughout Israel's history. Chapter 6 examines the loss of land in exile and the prophetic anticipation of an international and universal restoration brought through a new covenant, which advances God's cosmological

---

[62] See e.g. Grenz and Franke 2001.

[63] See e.g. Feinberg 2001: 37–80; Frame 1987.

[64] See e.g. Beale 2008; Carson and Woodbridge 1986; Woodbridge 1982; Lillback and Gaffin 2013; Frame 2010. This assumption includes the conviction that Scripture is a coherent and established canon composed of sixty-six books, which should be understood 'as a collection of historical texts written over a long period of time, utilizing different literary forms and manifesting diverse perspectives, and as the word of God who spoke and continues to speak through its books' (Schnabel 2000: 36).

[65] See e.g. Ward 2009; Vanhoozer 1998; Goldsworthy 2006; Adam 2008; Carson and Woodbridge 1992; Schnabel 2000.

[66] See e.g. Carson 2000; Rosner 2000.

[67] See e.g. Blomberg 2000: 64–72; Carson 1992: 65–95.

plan from Adam through Abraham, and is cast in terms of an Edenic land, city and temple – all of which are coextensive. These chapters demonstrate, then, that the land is a type of something greater that will come through Abraham's seed and a Davidic son, who will triumphantly bring God's new covenant people into a new creation.

Chapters 7–9 examine the most relevant passages in the New Testament from the Gospels (ch. 6), the epistles (ch. 7) and Revelation (ch. 8). These chapters demonstrate that the land promised to Abraham will finally be in the (physical) new heaven and earth won by Christ. Now, however, the fulfilment is primarily focused on Christ, who has inaugurated a new creational kingdom through his physical resurrection and has made new creations out of those united with him. This united people – both Jew and Gentile – live between the inauguration and consummation of the kingdom, and anticipate the final fulfilment in the new heaven and new earth (Rev. 21 – 22).

Chapter 10 concludes the study by making theological connections and applying the interpretative findings of the previous chapters to theological systems. More specifically, the chapter evaluates how the land promise is interpreted and fulfilled in the theological systems of dispensationalism and covenant theology. In the end, the chapter provides a *via media* in the light of the arguments presented throughout the book.

Chapter Two

The beginning and the end: the land and the kingdom

In the beginning, God created the heavens and the earth. (Gen. 1:1)

Then I saw a new heaven and a new earth, for the first heaven and the first earth had passed away, and the sea was no more. And I saw the holy city, new Jerusalem, coming down out of heaven from God, prepared as a bride adorned for her husband. And I heard a loud voice from the throne saying, 'Behold, the dwelling place of God is with man. He will dwell with them, and they will be his people, and God himself will be with them as their God'. . . .

And he who was seated on the throne said, 'Behold, I am making all things new.' (Rev. 21:1–3, 5)

'A fundamental fact about the Scriptures', according to Richard Lints, 'is that they constitute a text with a developing story. It is a story that clearly progresses toward the accomplishment of specific goals.'[1] 'In the beginning' marks inauguration, but it also anticipates the end. In this eschatological light, Scripture should be read as a text with a beginning, an end and a developing story in between that moves towards a divine goal. One such goal driving the biblical story forward is the establishment of the kingdom of God. That is, fundamental to the story line of Scripture is the notion that God, the Creator and King of the cosmos, has a people who live under his reign. This reality was true in the beginning and will be true at the end.

This chapter will establish a framework for understanding and situating the land promise in redemptive history. More specifically, the land promise will be canonically situated within the biblical story line, from creation to new creation. Moreover, it will show that the land theme is organically related to both the kingdom of God and the covenants as they unfold and progress across the canon. This chapter, then, will consider the beginning (Gen. 1 – 3) and the related

[1] Lints 1993: 262.

themes that subsequently unfold throughout the rest of Scripture, which are essentially eschatological themes that reach their terminus in the end – the new heaven and new earth (Rev. 21 – 22).

The beginning and the end: God's eschatological goal of redemptive history

Crucial to understanding why the canon ends with an Eden-like picture of the eschaton is that Eden is depicted as the prototypical place on earth where God dwells with his people. In short, God's original creation is the archetype of a final – and better – creation to come. That is, God's original creation reaches its eschatological fulfilment in the new heaven and new earth. Put another way, 'Eschatology is like proctology.'[2] The beginning inaugurates the consummated vision at the end, and God's new creation at the end brings to fulfilment his cosmological design from the beginning. But crucial to observing the (dis)continuity between the historical bookends is the historical line that connects them.

Perhaps one of the most prominent features of the beginning and end of the story is the concept of God's kingdom. Jesus' declaration that 'the kingdom of God is at hand' (Mark 1:15) reveals the Old Testament anticipation of the fulfilment of God's saving promises that reach back to Eden, when God promised to undo the effects of sin by triumphing over the serpent. Furthermore, the importance of the kingdom in Jesus' teaching is apparent by the prominence and place of the sayings about the kingdom. When he begins his ministry, Jesus' proclamation of the arrival of the kingdom serves to highlight the fact that it is central to the biblical story line, for he saw in his ministry the fulfilment of Old Testament promises. Mark demonstrates this fulfilment with the announcement 'The time is fulfilled, and the kingdom of God is at hand; repent and believe in the gospel' (1:14–15). Clearly, Jesus did not present a comprehensive biblical theology of the kingdom set within salvation history. However, it is clear from the Gospels that Jesus saw himself acting within and bringing to fulfilment the whole process of salvation history. That is, God's saving promises were being fulfilled in Jesus Christ's life and ministry, from his humiliation to his glorification. Thus the pattern of God's kingdom provides a conceptual approach that spans history from beginning to end.

[2] Levenson 1984: 298.

Although there has been debate on defining the kingdom of God, this concept, when defined with sufficient elasticity, consists of three important components: king/rule, people and place.[3] But to avoid abstraction, the kingdom of God must be tethered to history. God's rule over his people in his place is found on the beginning pages of Scripture and, through many twists and turns, extends to the end. In other words, the kingdom of God is central to the story line of Scripture. As a result, the land promise must be situated in a kingdom-oriented biblical-theological framework.

In the beginning: creation and God's worldwide design

Genesis is about beginnings: the beginning of creation, the world, humanity and the nations, civilization, relationships between God and humans, sin and death, and God's plan in history to make and bless a people for his glory. As the beginning of the story, Genesis introduces the reader to the background, context, main character(s) and themes of the story that will develop. This is the author's chance to show what the rest of the story will be about.[4] As such, Genesis inaugurates the drama of Scripture and is, therefore, foundational. Thus Genesis is the fountainhead of the ensuing biblical story.

Creation and the king of the kingdom

In the beginning God created.[5] He is the *grammatical* subject of the first sentence and the *thematic* subject throughout the creation

[3] Goldsworthy (2000: 53–54) aptly describes the kingdom of God as 'God's people in God's place under God's rule'. Similarly, Bruce Waltke (2001: 18) describes the kingdom in the OT when he writes, 'A nation consists of a common *people*, normally sharing a common *land*, submissive to a common law, and having a common *ruler*' (emphases mine). Debate has surrounded the nature of the kingdom (e.g. external and physical and/or internal and spiritual; reign and/or realm) and the timing of its coming. Concerning the latter, some have tried to propose that the kingdom is either fully present (i.e. 'realized eschatology' [see e.g. Dodd 1935]) or wholly future (i.e. 'consistent eschatology' [see e.g. Weiss 1971, first published in 1892; Schweitzer 1914, first published in 1901]). The position taken in this study as most consistent with the NT fulfilment of the Old is 'inaugurated eschatology', which allows for both a present and future, an already-but-not-yet, dimension to eschatological fulfilment. See e.g. Ladd 1959; 1998; Schreiner 2008: 39–116. For a helpful summary of the debate, see Willis 1987.

[4] Dempster 2003: 45.

[5] For discussion of and arguments for this traditional translation, see Wenham 1987: 11–13.

account.[6] Kenneth Mathews rightly stresses that 'the creation account is theocentric, not creature centered. Its purpose is to glorify the Creator by magnifying him through the majesty of the created order.'[7] God's power and rule are demonstrated in the repeated refrain 'And God said . . . And it was so.' This portrayal of God was (and is) radically countercultural. That God is able to create everything simply by speaking words – and to set limits even on those things (such as sun, moon and stars) that were worshipped as gods – points to the sovereignty and supremacy of God.[8] God is king over creation because, as the Genesis narratives show, the heavens and the earth depend on him for their existence, and not vice versa.

The entire universe is the geographical beginning of God's reign in history, for he is the creator and ruler of all. Creation and history come into existence together through God's speech. Thus the world is not a given, but a gift to display his glory through his dwelling with and ruling over his creatures. For this reason the rule, or kingdom, of God provides a conceptual approach to the commencement of creation. God is the self-existent and self-sufficient creator and king over all that exists, and creation's finitude is displayed in its dependence upon him.

God's kingship is asserted from the beginning, for his first word to his people is a command. They must be fruitful and multiply, fill the earth, subdue it and have dominion over creation (Gen. 1:28). They must also not eat of the tree of the knowledge of good and evil, or else there will be disastrous results (Gen. 2:17). Through his commands and promise, then, God is unequivocally demonstrating his rule over his creation. Furthermore, the rest of Scripture clearly affirms that God is Creator and King. Psalm 95 summons its readers to worship the Lord, the great God and great king above all gods who owns all that is, 'for he made it' (Ps. 95:5). God sits enthroned as king over creation, and his people are to ascribe to him alone glory and strength; indeed, at the sound of his voice creation bursts with life (Ps. 29). Psalm 89 says that all of creation, and especially his people, are to praise the Lord, for he without comparison performs praiseworthy wonders and rules and stills the raging sea (Ps. 89:5–13).

---

[6] Mathews 1996: 113. In fact, God is mentioned thirty-five times in the first chapter alone.

[7] Ibid. 113. This theocentricity, however, does not deny the crucial place of humans in creation, as will be shown below. That is, God is the centre around whom humanity orbits, deriving identity and purpose from the Creator.

[8] Vogt 2009: 63.

Furthermore, he owns the heavens and earth and all that is within them, for he founded them (Ps. 89:11). Thus he dwells in the heavens (Deut. 26:15; 1 Kgs 8:43; Isa. 57:15) and does whatever pleases him (Pss 115:3; 135:6). And finally, God's reign is most fully understood canonically, for Christ shares in this creative and ruling activity – an activity that only God can perform – as he reigns through and over creation by virtue of his triumph over sin and death.[9]

Creation and the people of the king(dom)

In the opening narrative, the climax of creation is humanity.[10] In the beginning of the Genesis narrative, God's creative work shifts from the cosmological to the anthropological. Just as God creates and rules over the heavens and the earth, so also he creates and rules over his people. Humanity, though, is related to yet distinct from the rest of God's good creation. No other created thing, inanimate or animate, has God's own breath breathed in to give it life. Man received breath from God and became a living creature set apart from the rest of creation.

The rare use of 'image' (*ṣelem*) and 'likeness' (*dĕmût*) to describe humanity constitutes it as unique among the created order. Much can be written about these terms, but, as Dempster notes, 'it is clear that they indicate that humanity is uniquely related to both God and the created order'.[11] In relation to God, humanity is endowed with a unique status and commanded to have dominion over every living thing that moves on the earth (Gen. 1:28). Given the commission to govern all living things in creation, God set humanity apart from and

[9] John 1:1–3; 1 Cor. 15:24–28; Col. 1:16–17; Heb. 1:1–2; Rev. 22:1, 3.

[10] The importance of humankind in the divine design does not minimize the theocentric focus of creation. Humans find their existence and role in the created order only in relation to their creator. Numerous literary links support the assertion that humanity is the crown of creation. First, the successive movement through creation follows an escalating order of significance that leads to the creation of humanity on the sixth day. Secondly, there is a noticeable change in style. This creative act is the only one that comes about through divine deliberation ('Let us make', in v. 26). Furthermore, v. 27 is arranged in a poetic chiasm, which highlights the fact that humans are specially created. Thirdly, the verb 'create' (*bārā'*) occurs three times in v. 27. Fourthly, humanity alone is created in the image of God. Fifthly, humanity is commanded to have dominion over creation. Sixthly, the definite article (*ha*) used on the number six is significant. Scholars differ on what the addition of the article precisely means, but at the very least it signifies the uniqueness of the sixth day, especially since it is the only day described as 'very good'. Finally, the significant increase in the number of words allotted to the sixth day demonstrates that the creation of humanity is the 'grand finale' of creation. See Dempster 2003: 57.

[11] Dempster 2003: 58. For an excellent survey of views in the last hundred years, see Jónsson 1988.

gave it a regal standing among all other creatures. In this sense, then, humanity images God by acting as his representative on earth. In other words, to be made in the image of God is to be endowed with a kingly status.[12]

Adam and Eve's image-bearing, though, involves more than just existing as God's viceregents. That is, it entails both what *'ādām* is and what the man and woman do. More specifically, humanity's onto-logical status – the image of God – *results* in ruling the world for God, for humans are his sons.[13] Adam and Eve share a unique role and relationship to the rest of creation. With their royal status, Adam and Eve are to subdue (*kābaš*) and have dominion (*rādâ*) over the earth. This kingly role carries with it the idea of authority and power. For example, Adam is to rule over 'the fish of the sea and over the birds of the heavens and over the livestock and over all the earth and over every creeping thing that creeps on the earth' (Gen. 1:26; cf. v. 28).

Furthermore, Eden was not only their home but also their place of work. This role is often cast in terms of the creational mandate or commission. Given the task, then, to subdue and have dominion, Adam and Eve have a God-given authority over the rest of creation.[14] In other words, this role anticipates a process whereby humanity was to extend this kingship until the entire creation was under the sphere of its rule. Moreover, as the story line progresses, this task takes on eschatological tones and anticipates a day when God will do a new covenant work finally to subdue his people's sins (Mic. 7:19) and, with Yahweh's help, they will subdue their enemies (Zech. 9:15). This task will ultimately come about through an ideal, greater-than-David

[12] Carson (1996: 204–212) notes six implications of being made in the image of God: (1) The image of God can be teased out inductively, (2) humanity is important and dignified, (3) humanity is accountable before God, (4) human beings cannot escape this truth, but can only suppress or deny it, (5) the image of God in man grounds his responsibility towards the rest of creation, and (6) Adam made in the image of God anticipates the last Adam, who is the image of the invisible God.

[13] Image/likeness and sonship come together in Gen. 5:1–3 and Luke 3:38. Concerning this connection, Dempster (2003: 58) says, 'By juxtaposing the divine creation of Adam in the image of God and the subsequent human creation of Seth in the image of Adam, the transmission of the image of God through this genealogical line is implied, as well as the link between sonship and the image of God. As Seth is a son of Adam, so Adam is a son of God.'

[14] This ruling function, though greatly affected, is not lost after the entrance of sin. In Num. 32:22, 29, Yahweh subdues (*kābaš*) Israel's enemies so that Israel in turn will drive them out and possess the land (cf. Deut. 9:1–3). In Josh. 18:1, Israel subdues the land of Canaan before possessing it. Moreover, Israel was commanded to rule (*rādâ*) over their servants, though not harshly (Lev. 25:43), and Solomon had peace-encompassing dominion (*rādâ*) 'over all the region west of the Euphrates from Tiphsah to Gaza, over all the kings west of the Euphrates' (1 Kgs 4:24; cf. 4:21).

messianic king, who will come from Israel, exercise rule over the kingdom(s) and vanquish his enemies until his rule is established to the ends of the earth.[15]

Adam's role, however, extends beyond just being and serving as a king. The words that describe his work in the garden in Genesis 2:15 (*'ābad* and *šāmar*) are the same that are used to describe the priests' work in the temple later in the life and worship of Israel. Beale comments:

> The two Hebrew words for 'cultivate and keep' are usually translated 'serve and guard [or keep]' elsewhere in the Old Testament. . . . When these two words (verbal [*'ābad* and *šāmar*] and nominal forms) occur together in the Old Testament (within an approximately 15-word range), they refer either to Israelites' 'serving' God and 'guarding [keeping]' God's word (approximately 10 times) or to priests who 'keep' the 'service' (or 'charge') of the tabernacle (see Num 3:7–8; 8:25–26; 18:5–6; 1 Chr 23:32; Ezek 44:14).[16]

Therefore Adam's dominion over the land presents him as a type of priest-king, a concept used later to describe God's people as a kingdom of priests.[17] As a result, Adam is to bring the presence of God to the rest of creation.

Finally, Adam and Eve were commanded to be fruitful and multiply and fill the earth (Gen. 1:28). Though Adam and Eve uniquely stand as the forerunners to the rest of humanity, it is significant that they cannot fulfil the creation mandate alone. The expansion of Adam's geographical dominion is connected to the proliferation of his offspring. Adam and Eve's cosmological task will be carried on and fulfilled through their descendants. Through time, then, the whole earth would become a garden-city filled with image-bearing priest-kings, and the earth would be full of the knowledge of the Lord as the waters cover the sea.

Creation and the place of the king(dom)

The third facet of the kingdom triptych is God's place, which is a garden planted by the Lord God. Within this sacred space, Adam and Eve are to be fruitful and multiply, subdue and have dominion over

---

[15] Gen. 49:10; Num. 24:17–19; Pss 72:8; 89:25, 36; 110:1–2; Zech. 9:9–10; cf. Gen. 3:15.
[16] Beale 2004b: 66–67.
[17] Exod. 19:6; Deut. 7:6; 1 Peter 2:5–9; Rev. 1:6; 5:10.

the earth, and enjoy God's blessing (Gen. 1:28–30). This serves as the ideal place for humanity to dwell with and under the Lord God as his viceregents over creation. It is here in the garden where the themes 'kingdom' and 'place' are closely intertwined, for in order for the king to have dominion he must have a domain. This domain is Eden. This sacred space is the archetypal place where God dwells with his people and, through the proliferation of priest-kings, God's glorious presence and rule will expand across the earth.

The importance of Eden does not rest primarily on its being the dwelling place of humans, but on its being the place where God dwells on earth in a unique way and where he has fellowship with his image bearers. It is, as Ezekiel says, the garden of God (Ezek. 28:13; cf. Isa. 51:3).

Thus Eden is the inaugural place where God is with his people. To put it another way, the garden of Eden should be considered as the archetypal tabernacle, temple or sanctuary, a temple-garden, where God dwells with humankind.[18]

Furthermore, the prototypical place where God first dwelt with humans was nothing short of paradise. Commenting on Genesis 2:8, Wenham writes:

> *gān* 'garden' is an enclosed area for cultivation (cf. vv. 5, 15): perhaps we should picture a park surrounded by a hedge (cf. 3:23). This seems to be the understanding of the early versions which

---

[18] Beale (2004b: 66–79) provides multiple textual and theological reasons for this assertion. To summarize his arguments briefly, first, the same Hebrew verbal form used for God's walking in the garden (Gen. 3:8), *mithallēk* (hithpael), is the same form used to describe his presence in the tabernacle (Lev. 26:12; 2 Sam. 7:6–7). Secondly, God put Adam in the garden of Eden to 'work' and 'keep' it (Gen. 2:15). When these two words appear together later in the OT, in every case they carry the same meaning and refer either to the Israelites' serving and keeping God's Word or, more often, to priests who serve God and guard the temple from unholy things/people entering it (Num. 3:7–8; 8:25–26; 18:5–6; 1 Chr. 23:32; Ezek. 44:14; see n. 16 above). Thirdly, the interior atmosphere of the temple was a visible reminder of a garden-like space (1 Kgs 6–7). Fourthly, the entrance and location of Eden, the temple and the eschatological temple or dwelling place of God bear remarkable similarities. Eden and the later sanctuaries faced and were entered from the east (Gen. 3:24; Exod. 25:18–22; 26:31; 36:35; 1 Kgs 6:23–29; 2 Chr. 3:14; Ezek. 47:1). Israel's temple was on Mount Zion (Exod. 15:17), and the eschatological temple is to be located on a mountain (Ezek. 20:2; 43:12; Rev. 21:10). Finally, the river flowing from Eden in Gen. 2:10 is similar to the post-exilic temple (Ezek. 47:1–12) and eschatological temple (Rev. 21:1–2). Indeed, Ezekiel clearly describes the eschatological Mount Zion in ways reminiscent of Eden. Just as Adam was satisfied with every good thing God created, so in the latter days God's people will be abundantly satisfied with his bountiful provision. See also Waltke 2001: 85; Walton 2009: 79–85.

translate *gān* as 'paradise,' a Persian loan word, originally meaning a royal park.[19]

Moreover, later when Eden is mentioned in Scripture, it is described as a fertile area, a lush oasis with vibrant life bursting from it, a desirable piece of real estate in the arid region.[20] This lush territory is a mark of God's presence in and blessing on Eden. When the evidence is cumulatively considered, the garden of Eden is presented as the archetypal and paradisal place where God's people will live in and enjoy his presence.

Finally, through the propagation of Adam's offspring, the boundaries of the garden will expand and extend to fill the whole earth.[21] In the ancient Near East, a growing population would construct a city around the temple. Throughout time, then, the whole earth would become a sanctuary garden-city. While Genesis 2 merely introduces the inauguration of this process, the eschatological outcome will be a sanctified, arboreal temple-city where God will dwell with his people.[22] Had sin, with its devastating effects on humanity and the world, not entered creation, the teleological objectives of Eden would look similar to the picture of the new Jerusalem described in Revelation 21 – 22.

The end of the beginning

The blissful scene at the end of Genesis 2 is followed by the all-too-familiar tragic events of Genesis 3.[23] Rather than fulfil his role as

[19] Wenham 1987: 61.

[20] Isa. 51:3; Ezek. 31:8–9, 16, 18; 36:35.

[21] For ancient Near Eastern parallels to the cosmos as a city and temple, see Niehaus 2008: 83–137.

[22] Alexander 2008: 25–26.

[23] The theological doctrine of 'the fall' has fallen on hard times in critical scholarship. Brevard Childs (1992: 571) writes, 'Some have seen the story as a primitive account of the effects of the growth of human civilization (Wellhausen). Others have interpreted the story as a type of parabolic explanation of human existence as one of limitation and restriction (Westermann). Finally, these chapters have been interpreted philosophically as an ontological description of frailty and finitude which is constitutive of human existence (Tillich).' Despite these objections, says Childs (ibid.), the traditional terminology of the 'fall' should continue to be used because 'both in form and function [Genesis] chapter 3 is at pains to stress the full anthropological and cosmological effects of the disobedience. The aetiological form of the curses makes clear that the events were not simply regarded as entertaining stories from the past, but rather offered a theological interpretation of man's miserable condition, both in the world and before God. Moreover, chapters 2–3 are carefully linked literarily to the larger primeval history of Genesis (1–11), and indeed provide the key for their interpretation.' For a thorough treatment of the doctrine of sin, see Morgan and Peterson 2013.

God's priest-king, fill the earth with his descendants and expand the garden-temple of Eden to the ends of the earth, Adam rebelled against his Lord and forfeited his teleological commission. Instead of ruling creation as God's image-bearing viceregent, Adam pined after deity.[24] By successfully tempting him, the serpent exercised authority over Adam – who named him! – and Adam capitulated in his attempt to usurp God. This rebellion was nothing less than a '"cosmic tragedy" . . . The flagrant rebellion against the divine word by the pinnacle of creation, which has just been invested with the divine rule, is a heinous crime against the cosmos and its Creator'.[25] It is ironic that Adam, who was originally commissioned to guard Eden (Gen. 2:15), was not only expelled from the garden but also relieved of his duty, for now at the east of the garden of Eden God 'placed the cherubim and a flaming sword that turned every way to guard the way to the tree of life' (Gen. 3:24). Paradise gained was now paradise lost.

Now the place God created for his people to live and work became a curse rather than a blessing. The sacred realm of Eden had become defiled. Instead of the land yielding abundant blessing, it would yield hardship and pain. Instead of subduing the land, humans would be subdued by it. Instead of harmonious relationships between humans and nature, and man and woman, conflict would now rule (Gen. 3:17–19). As a result, the creation project was compromised and the global end for humanity to live in God's place under his rule would now have to await its fulfilment by other means.

Against this background, the rest of the biblical story line is interested in how God's kingdom will be restored and extended throughout the entire earth. Will the kingdom of the world ever become again the kingdom of the Lord? Will he ever reign again over his people in his place? The end of the story presents a glorious picture of the restored rule of the sovereign king of the universe, who sits on his throne while the enemy has been subdued and dethroned. But for now, the eschatological outcome depends on a theological response.

The promise of a new beginning

But amid the judgment and announcement of curses, God folds mercy into the middle. Literally, there is a seed of hope for humanity found

---

[24] In contrast Christ, who *is* the image of God, refused to grasp after his divine position for his advantage (Phil. 2:5–11).

[25] Dempster 2003: 66.

in the promise of the serpent's destruction by the offspring of the woman (Gen. 3:15).[26] To be sure, different judgments will befall the man, woman and serpent, but only the serpent will be handed a fatal blow. Though the same word is used to describe the combatants' corresponding action (*šûp*), 'the location of the blow distinguishes the severity and success of the attack'.[27] The serpent will deliver a strike to the heel, but the offspring of the woman will deliver a crushing blow to the head.

The subsequent story in Genesis, and the rest of Scripture, is concerned with resolving this genealogical conflict between the offspring of the woman and the serpent. Dempster writes:

> This battle will determine who will have dominion over the created order – the human or the serpent. The man and the woman have already been told to be fruitful and multiply and to have dominion over the earth. In the immediate context it is clear now that, though this is not a present reality, it will be the future destiny of their progeny. Once the contextual scope is widened, not only to the book of Genesis but to the literary horizon of the canon, there remains no doubt whatsoever of the importance of this genea-logical hope for the human race. The seed of the woman will restore the lost glory. Human – and therefore divine – dominion will be established over the world. The realization of the kingdom of God is linked to the future of the human race.[28]

Hence the story of redemption will be an unfolding of the contents of this conflict and promise. From this point, all of Old Testament

---

[26] Debate centres on whether the text speaks of a specific offspring (singular) or offspring in general (collective), as well as who this offspring is. Collins (2006: 156) argues that the offspring should be taken as singular, for 'in Biblical Hebrew the key signal for a singular or collective offspring is the grammatical number of pronouns that refer to the word: if the author had a specific offspring in view he would have used singular pronouns, and if he meant posterity in general, he would have used plural pronouns. In this text we have two singular pronouns that refer to the woman's offspring, "*he* shall bruise . . . bruise *his* heel". Thus we are entitled to join the Septuagint in seeing an individual as the referent here' (emphases original). See also Collins 1997: 139–148; Alexander 1997: 363–367; J. M. Hamilton 2006b: 30–54.

[27] Mathews 1996: 245. Furthermore, the imperfect verb translated 'bruise' is iterative. Wenham (1987: 80) comments, 'It implies repeated attacks by both sides to injure the other. It declares lifelong mutual hostility between mankind and the serpent race.' This promise, therefore, is eschatologically charged in that it anticipates a long struggle between good and evil, over which humanity will ultimately triumph.

[28] Dempster 2003: 69.

revelation looks forward, points forward and eagerly awaits the promised redeemer.

A new beginning: re-establishing the kingdom through covenant

From a canonical perspective, the eschatological promises completed at the end of history commence in the garden of Eden. However, God's plan was interrupted by the disobedience of humanity and, as a result, sin and death entered the world and humanity was separated from God. But the beginning did not end, for God made a promise that would, in time, undo the effects of sin and restore God's rule. Hence the drama that unfolds focuses on how the kingdom – that is, God's people in God's place under God's rule – will be re-established.[29]

One of the most important ways God re-establishes his kingdom is through the biblical covenants, for they form the backbone of Scripture and are crucial for understanding its overarching story, from creation to new creation.[30] That is, covenant charts a course and serves as a unifying theme for the unfolding kingdom drama.[31] Scripture presents numerous covenants at crucial times in salvation history, all of which serve to reverse the curses of Eden and bring about the escalated re-establishment of the universal expansion of God's kingdom. For this reason, every covenant in some measure involves and advances the promise of God's rule, people and place. Each covenant serves, then, as a (re)new(ed) beginning, a divinely orchestrated means by which the ordained end – a consummated kingdom – will come about.[32]

---

[29] As Alexander (2008: 14) explains, 'The first earth is designed to be a divine residence, for here God intends to coexist with his people. However, the divine plan for this first earth is soon disrupted when the human couple, due to their disobedience, are driven from God's presence. The complex story that follows centres on how the earth can once more become a dwelling place shared by God and humanity.'

[30] I am grateful to Peter Gentry for the category of 'kingdom through covenant'. For a more exhaustive treatment, see Gentry and Wellum 2012; Gentry 2008: 16–42; Martin 2013: 62–98.

[31] Swain 2011: 20.

[32] Defining the term 'covenant' is debated. A covenant involves international treaties, clan/tribal alliances, personal agreements, loyalty agreements, marriage and legal contracts. For heuristic purposes, covenant will be defined as 'an enduring agreement which defines a relationship between two parties involving a solemn, binding obligation(s) specified on the part of at least one of the parties toward the other, made by oath under threat of divine curse, and ratified by a visual ritual' (Gentry 2008: 16; see also Lohfink and Zenger 2000: 17; Niehaus 2008: 56–62).

The kingdom and the covenant at creation

When we turn to Genesis 1 – 2, it is not improper to see it in a covenantal context, though caution should be taken.[33] First, the creation account is framed within a covenantal pattern or framework. That is, there is a title/preamble (1:1), historical prologue (1:2–29), stipulations (1:28; 2:16–17a), witnesses (1:31; 2:1) and blessings/curses (1:28; 2:3, 17).[34] Secondly, although the term for 'covenant' is not contextually found, the essential relational elements of a covenant are present. That is, whether we define this relationship at creation as a 'covenant' relationship or not, the point to be made is that God condescended and initiated this relationship with humanity. God is clearly committed to his image bearers, even after they disobey him. Thirdly, the presence of a covenantal relationship can be shown from later texts. In supporting a covenant with creation, William Dumbrell argues that the way in which the Noahic covenant is introduced in Genesis 6 shows that a previous covenant with Adam was established. In four places God speaks of confirming (*hăqmōtî et-běrîtî*) a covenant with Noah (Gen. 6:18; 9:9, 11, 17), not cutting a covenant (*kārat běrît*).[35] Therefore the covenant with Noah was not initiating something new, but rather confirming for Noah and his descendants God's prior commitment to humanity previously initiated at creation.[36]

[33] There has been much debate over whether a covenant exists between God and Adam/creation. A large focus of the debate centres on the use of the word 'covenant' (*běrît*), since it is not explicitly used in Gen. 1 – 2 and does not appear until Gen. 6. It should be noted, however, that concepts, not merely words, should be looked for in tracing themes through the canon of Scripture. In the past, the study of the Bible's theology has sometimes been reduced to word studies, and in so doing important concepts have been overlooked and missed. The 'word study' method of studying the Bible's theology has been criticized in recent days. Rosner (2000: 6) writes, 'Word studies alone are a shaky foundation upon which to base theology. . . . Sometimes a biblical author will pursue the same concept as another author but with his own vocabulary. Concepts rather than words are a surer footing on which to base thematic study such as that involved in biblical-theological synthesis. In most cases the concept is in fact far bigger than the words normally used to refer to it, even when the words in question appear frequently.'

[34] Niehaus 1995: 144–147; see also J. A. Thompson 1963: 2.

[35] Dumbrell 2002: 16–19; see also Gentry 2008: 19–20; Routledge 2008: 164; Wenham 1987: 175. Contra P. R. Williamson 2007: 52–58. According to Gentry (2008: 20), 'A careful analysis of all the usages of "covenant" shows that the expression "to establish a covenant" means something different than the expression "to cut a covenant."' That is, the language 'to cut' describes the point of entry into a covenant, whereas 'to confirm' is used of ratifying a pre-existing relationship. For an exhaustive study of the usage of the term 'covenant' in Scripture, see Gentry and Wellum's (2012: 717–778) lexical analysis of *běrît*.

[36] Routledge 2008: 164.

However, the absence of the term 'covenant' in Genesis 1 – 2 has caused some to doubt the existence of a covenant relationship.[37] This objection is unsuccessful once a sound lexical and biblical-theological method is employed. To begin with, it is incorrect to conclude that a covenant cannot be present simply because the term is not explicitly used. For example, in 2 Samuel 7 God makes a promise of an ever-lasting dynasty, but by the principle of this objection it cannot technically be considered a covenant, because the term does not contextually appear.[38] Yet when Psalm 89 recounts this promise, it repeatedly uses the term 'covenant' (Ps. 89:3, 28, 34, 39).[39] Secondly, the absence of the term is possibly due to the reality that this time is prior to the entrance of and fall into sin. In other words, it was not necessary at this point in God's relationship with Adam and Eve to demonstrate his commitment to them, for by virtue of his unhindered presence, relationship with and provision for them as their Lord in Eden, his commitment to them was clearly evident. Thirdly, it is important to note that this covenantal context is an original and unique situation that involved, especially in the light of the rest of Scripture, Adam in a representative role on behalf of the human race. Henri Blocher writes, 'The relationship of humankind with God is first determined by the Eden Charter, the creational covenant, made "in Adam".'[40] Moreover, the person and work of Adam establish categories for the person and work of the last Adam, Jesus Christ (cf. Rom. 5:12–21; 1 Cor. 15). The entrances of Adam and Christ at unique and pivotal points in creation and redemptive history, then, have massive effects on them and their posterity. Hence this relation-ship is foundational to all other relationships that follow. Finally, the Noahic covenant clearly alludes to creation themes that were present in Genesis 1 – 3. For example, in Genesis 8:1 – 9:17 there is a 're-creation' of the earth, birds, animals and creeping things, as well as re-establishment of the creation mandate and dominion of humans over the land that was originally given to Adam and Eve. In other

---

[37] See e.g. P. R. Williamson 2007: 52–58.

[38] Interestingly, while acknowledging the absence of the term 'covenant' in 2 Sam. 7, which is the reason why he rejects a covenant in Gen. 1 – 2, P. R. Williamson (2007: 120–121) still argues for a covenant based on the presence of covenantal concepts and terminology (e.g. loyalty, a father–son relationship, protection from enemies, promise of curse). Unfortunately, despite the presence of the same concepts, Williamson fails to see a covenantal relationship in Gen. 1 – 2.

[39] Collins 2006: 113.

[40] Blocher 2006: 255.

words, Noah now carries on the role of Adam and thus fulfils God's purposes in the world. Stephen Dempster writes:

> The covenant with creation after the flood uses language extremely similar to that of Gen. 1–2, even though the word 'covenant' does not occur there. The 'new' covenant with creation is not quite like the old, as there are significant flaws in the post-flood world. It is clearly a post-fallen world, which is graciously preserved from further judgment in spite of human sin.[41]

Therefore, given the context of Genesis 1 – 3 and the covenantal clues therein, seeing a covenantal relationship with Adam/creation is warranted from the beginning.[42]

However, as noted above, this relationship was deeply marred as a result of the fall, which plunged the entire human race into sin. But

---

[41] Dempster 2003: 73, n. 34.

[42] Similarly, Niehaus (2009: 231–233) adduces multiple lines of evidence in support of an Adamic covenant: (1) the apparent conformity of narrative elements in Gen. 1:1 – 2:3 to the pattern of a second millennium BC international treaty; (2) the parallelism between Gen. 1:28 and Gen. 9:1–3; (3) by presenting God as the Creator, Gen. 1:1 also implies that he is Suzerain over all, since creator gods in the ancient Near East were understood to be universal suzerains, from whom all other heavenly and earthly authority derived; (4) the Sabbath ordinance and its root in the creation account (Exod. 20:11) and the concomitant idea that Israel is a new creation by covenant (we note that the Sabbath ordinance is also rooted in Israel's deliverance from Egypt, parallel to the Exodus creation roots, in the renewal covenant, Deut. 5:15); (5) the covenantal terminology echoing Gen. 1 in Jer. 33:20, 25; 31:35–36; (6) there seems to be a parallelism between the first Adam (as covenant mediator) and the second Adam (as covenant mediator); (7) the parallelism of the original heaven and earth (Gen. 1:1) and the new heaven and earth (2 Peter 3:3; Rev. 21:1), the latter being a work and a result of the new covenant mediated by the second Adam; and lastly, (8) Hos. 6:7, which stands as evidence in spite of – and even because of – its ambiguity, and in spite of its many detractors. From these points, Niehaus (ibid.) concludes that 'it should be clear that Gen 1:1–2:3 (and 2:17) and other data (e.g., Ps 47:2, Mal 1:14) display the following facts about God: he is the Creator and Great King over all in heaven and earth; he has provided good things in abundance for those he created; he made the man and woman royalty ("subdue", "rule over") and gave them commands; he blessed them; and he pronounced a curse on them should they disobey his commands. These facts are the essence of covenant: a Great King in authority over lesser rulers, with a historical background of doing good to them, with commands and with blessings, but also a curse in case of disobedience. These facts about the Genesis creation material are the stuff of covenant, and primordially so. Some may not want to say that they constitute a covenant, but the creation data does tell us just what, later in history, would form the constituent elements of a suzerain–vassal treaty in the ancient Near East, and of a divine–human covenant in the Bible. Such things are expressions of God's nature, as that nature comes through to us in the creation data. We know the workman by his work (cf. Rom 1:19–20). God, then, from the beginning showed a nature that could appropriately be called covenantal, and he entered into relationships that could appropriately be called the same.'

God's commitment to humanity after the fall shows that his anthropological and cosmological purposes are not finished. He does not completely eradicate the human race and begin anew. Rather, he calls out one faithful man to continue the line of humanity and thus fulfil the redemptive purposes on the earth. It is precisely out of this human race that the last Adam, when the fullness of time had come, took upon himself humanity in order to bring redemption and deliver his people to a new place, to the kingdom of the beloved Son of God (Col. 1:12–13). All subsequent covenants flow from Eden, and out of fallen humanity God will make a new people with whom he will dwell for ever (Rev. 21 – 22:5).

After the fall, sin increases with each generation. One cannot read Genesis 4 – 5 without an awful sense of God's judgment. Bartholomew writes that 'the effects of sin gather momentum until they become a virtual tsunami in Genesis 6:5'.[43] Indeed, death reigned. An increasing existential awareness of sin and divine judgment escalates from the fall to the time when 'the LORD saw that the wickedness of man was great in the earth, and that every intention of the thoughts of his heart was only evil continually. And the LORD was sorry that he had made man on the earth, and it grieved him to his heart' (Gen. 6:5–6). So the Lord judged humanity in the land in which it was created to know and serve God. But one man found favour in the eyes of the Lord. Thus in the middle of universal judgment is the hope of a new beginning.

The kingdom through the Noahic covenant

The initial sign in the biblical story line of God's reversing the curse is the entrance of Noah. The context is saturated with God's divine promises in the midst of judgment against human rebellion and sin. The initial sin in the garden spread into global rebellion against God. In this context, however, Noah found favour in the eyes of the Lord (Gen. 6:8) and God established a covenant with him (Gen. 6:18; 9:9–17).[44] Noah is the blameless one who will restore God's creation and thus fulfil humanity's role on the earth. Williamson writes, 'The climax of the flood narrative is best understood in terms of a "recreation" covenant – a restoration of the divine order and God's visible kingship that had been established at creation.'[45] God promises that the divine intention of creation will not be lost. He solemnly

---

[43] Bartholomew 2011: 32.
[44] In this context, the term 'covenant' (běrît) is met for the first time.
[45] P. R. Williamson 2007: 60–61.

promises that humanity's creational mandate (Gen. 9:1–7; cf. 1:26–30) will never again be interrupted by a suspension of the natural order. The earth will be inhabited with life, and human beings will know the Lord in an intimate way. In other words, there will come a 'new creation'.[46] This covenant is described as 'everlasting', a term that, in context, appears to signify at least as long as the earth remains (Gen. 8:22). And the promises given to Noah and his offspring point back to God's prior promise of a 'seed' who would come and reverse the effects of sin and the fall.

The Noahic covenant 'reaffirms God's original creational intent, which the flood had placed in abeyance and which humanity's inherent sinfulness would otherwise continue to place in jeopardy'.[47] God is still committed to his fallen creation, especially to those who are created in his image. It is crucial to see this covenant in the light of the overall (post-fall) story line of Scripture. 'Sin came into the world through one man, and death through sin, and so death spread to all men because all sinned' (Rom. 5:12). Adam enjoyed God and his provision in the land, but forfeited it. Nevertheless, God will restore through Noah what was lost by Adam. This new beginning demonstrates advancement in God's redemptive purposes. Noah, like Adam, functions as God's representative on earth who is commissioned to rule the earth, be fruitful and multiply, and bring God's blessing to the world. The biblical story, then, moves towards a new era and a new humanity. But just as Adam failed, so also does Noah (Gen. 9:18–29). Sin and death continue to reign, and once again God judges the nations in the Tower of Babel (Gen. 11). Yet God keeps his promise by calling out another man to fulfil his purposes.

The kingdom through the Abrahamic covenant

The introduction of Abram into the story highlights God's plan to begin anew. To highlight this new beginning, Dempster observes, 'Just as Adam to Noah was ten generations, so is Noah to Abraham. After the arrival of Abram on the scene, a new genealogical formula begins a narrative devoted to this man named Abram, who is described as

---

[46] Dempster (2003: 55) rightly argues that the repeated phrases 'These are the generations of' serve as headings in the flow of Genesis which signal to the reader that God is doing something new (Gen. 2:4; 5:1; 6:9; 10:1; 11:27; 25:12; 25:19; 36:1; 37:2). They appear at key places within the story line of Genesis and indicate that the covenant Lord is not finished with his creation. Rather, as God's image bearers he is committed to work out his new/renewed redemptive purposes for his glory. For further study on the role of the 'toledot' formulas in Genesis and the Pentateuch, see Thomas 2011.

[47] P. R. Williamson 2003: 140.

47

such an inauspicious bearer of promise.'[48] Against the miserable background of the table of nations and the debacle of Babel, the entrance of Abram is clearly an answer to the fundamental problem of humanity. As with Noah, God's promise to Abram initiates a new era of history.[49]

Fallen humanity sought to make a 'name' for itself with the tower of Babel (Gen. 11:4), but for Abram God promises to make a great 'name' (Gen. 12:2). Unlike the story with Noah, however, God does not destroy creation with universal judgment. Instead, God allows the nations to exist and then calls out Abram from them. From this point in the biblical narrative, 'Abraham will provide the redemptive center for those who will be reached through him and his descendants.'[50] The Abrahamic covenant, then, clarifies the way in which God will fulfil for humanity both the blessing promised to Noah for all creation and the promise of a victorious 'seed'. Through God's covenantal dealings with and through Abram, Adam's curse will be removed, dominion will be restored and universal blessing will come to the nations. With Abram, then, the divine telos for humanity – and indeed all creation – finds a new beginning, and with him God begins a process that will be fulfilled in the distant future.

The kingdom through the Mosaic covenant

The Mosaic covenant demonstrates God's determination to advance his kingdom on earth through his people. This covenant furthers the programmatic agenda of the promises given to the patriarchs, for it is the God of Abraham, Isaac and Jacob who delivers his people from the tyrannical rule of Egypt.[51] Therefore, as the biblical story moves from creation blueprint to the final reality, the formation of Israel as a nation ruled by the Lord is an important development. God's deliverance of and covenant with Israel is an advancement of his re-establishment of the Edenic purposes, for through the exodus of the nation his creational plan for the world moves forward. That is, 'in the promised land, as in Eden, the direct presence of God will be encountered in a way which would parallel the condition of man in

---

[48] Dempster 2003: 75.
[49] Furthermore, Dumbrell (1994: 33) notes that the divine speech and command in Gen. 12:1 are structurally similar to the speech and implicit command at the beginning of creation (Gen. 1:3). Thus the call of Abram launches a biblical witness that ultimately leads to a new creation.
[50] Ibid. 33–34.
[51] Exod. 3:6; cf. 2:24–25; Deut. 4:36–38; 1 Chr. 16:15–19; 2 Kgs 13:22–23.

Eden'.[52] This significant advance in God's plan explains the repeated mention of the Mosaic covenant throughout the Old Testament. God fulfils what he promises and, as a result, his cosmological and eschatological objectives for his kingdom in Eden, extended through Noah and promised to the patriarchs, direct the Sinai covenant towards its goal.

The kingdom through the Davidic covenant

The next major covenantal development in the outworking of God's redemptive plan is the Davidic covenant (2 Sam. 7; 1 Chr. 17; cf. Pss 89; 110; 132).[53] 'The chief interest in the rise of the kingdom', says Childs, 'focuses without a doubt on David.'[54] This covenant, like the Mosaic, is built upon the Abrahamic promise that establishes God's people in his place under his rule and blessing.[55] In fact, the chapters in which the establishment of the covenant is described (2 Sam. 7; 1 Chr. 17) are full of allusions to the promises given to Abraham and Moses. For example, David is promised a great name (Gen. 12:2; 2 Sam. 7:9), a special place (Gen. 12:1; Exod. 3:8; 2 Sam. 7:10), victory over enemies (Gen. 22:17; Exod. 23:22; 2 Sam. 7:11), a special relationship between his offspring and God (Gen. 17:7–8; Exod. 4:22; 2 Sam. 7:14) and offspring through whom (international) blessing will come (Gen. 12:3; 22:18; 26:4; Ps. 72:17). Dumbrell writes:

> What God has in store for David is reminiscent of what was promised to Abraham. The establishment of the Davidic empire

[52] Dumbrell 1984: 101.

[53] The Davidic covenant resembles a royal grant covenant, though not perfectly. E.g. it consists of promises to David that are unconditional (e.g. God's promise to raise up a descendant). God's intention to fulfil this promise is repeated in the subsequent history of the Davidic kings despite many acts of disloyalty on their part (cf. 1 Kgs 11:11–13, 34–36; 15:4–5; 2 Kgs 8:19; 2 Chr. 21:7; 23:3). However, the element of a continuous, uninterrupted reign of a Davidic king is not unconditional (see 1 Chr. 28:5–6; 1 Kgs 2:2–4). This is why it is difficult to classify it merely as an unconditional covenant. Certainly, sin can bring disaster on the future offspring reigning on David's throne, as will be seen from Solomon, his son and the future division of the kingdoms of Israel and Judah. Yet this disaster will not ultimately demolish the 'house' (dynasty) of David. Again, like the Abrahamic covenant, 2 Sam. 7 emphasizes the need for obedience by David and his sons, yet the foundation of the covenant is God's unwavering faithfulness to bring about his promises. It becomes clear as the story progresses that although God makes his promises known, the precise details of how he will fulfil them will be revealed later.

[54] Childs 1992: 153.

[55] See Levenson (1985: 209–217), who argues that the Mosaic and Davidic covenants are theologically compatible with, not irreconcilably opposed to, one another. Cf. Anderson 1999: 168–170.

will set the ideal borders of the Promised Land, which the promise to Abraham had foreshadowed (cf. 2 Sam 7:10 and Gen 15:18; note that these borders are defined in Deut 11:24 as Israel's 'place'). At the same time, the foundation of the empire will bring David the Abrahamic great name (cf. 2 Sam 7:9 and Gen 12:2).[56]

Moreover, Beale rightly observes the connection between the construction of the temple and Eden. He writes, 'Second Samuel 7 (cf. 1 Chr 17) closely links the need to build a temple (7:12–13) with the following aspects of Genesis 1:28: (1) ruling and subduing (7:9–16), and (2) a blessing on God's kingly vice-regent (7:29).'[57] Through his commitment to David and his dynasty, then, God plans to accomplish his kingdom purposes set forth in the previous covenants, and ultimately reaching back to Eden, namely to plant his people in his place under his kingship.

It appeared that in David and his offspring, particularly in Solomon, God was fulfilling his covenant promises to re-establish his kingdom (1 Kgs 8:56). His people dwelt peacefully in the land – with God dwelling at the centre – under the wise leadership of the divinely anointed king (1 Kgs 1 – 2). Israel, like Adam, subdued the nations and enjoyed rest from their enemies (1 Kgs 8:56). For instance:

> The narrative describes the uniqueness of this new Israelite king and his superlative wisdom to solve social problems (1 Kgs 3), to promote justice and righteousness (1 Kgs 3:16–28) and to explore and name his Creator's world, in much the same way that Adam did in the garden of Eden (Gen 2:19–20; 1 Kgs 4:32–33 [MT 5:12–13]).[58]

In other words, dominion had been regained. Moreover, in fulfilment of the promises to Abraham, Israel dwelt securely in their land, was a multitudinous nation and experienced God's blessing and presence as well as the blessing of the nations. And, finally, in fulfilment of the Mosaic covenant, Israel enjoyed their status as God's treasured possession, a kingdom of priests who mediated God's rule and presence to the world. At last, it seemed, the Lord was finally fulfilling his teleological objectives through his promise of a Davidic son who would come as God's viceregent to exercise royal rule over God's

---

[56] Dumbrell 1994: 70.
[57] Beale 2004b: 109.
[58] Dempster 2003: 147.

people in his Promised Land, and thus extend God's rule, presence and blessing to the nations.

The kingdom through the new covenant

The previous divine covenants culminate in the new covenant, for this covenant encapsulates the key promises made throughout the Old Testament era (e.g. a physical inheritance, a divine–human relationship, an everlasting dynasty, blessing on a national and international scale).[59] Hence there are certain elements of continuity between the prior covenants. For example, the new covenant is made to the 'house of Israel' and 'house of Judah'; that is, with the whole people of Israel (Jer. 31:31); it emphasizes obedience (Jer. 31:33; Ezek. 36:25–27; Isa. 42:1–4; 51:4–8); it focuses on offspring (Jer. 31:36; 33:22; Ezek. 36:37), particularly on a royal seed (Jer. 33:15–26; Ezek. 37:24–25; Isa. 55:3); and, in the end, it will fulfil the repeated covenant refrain 'I will be their God, and they shall be my people' (Jer. 31:33; cf. 7:23; 11:4; 24:7; 30:22; 32:38; Exod. 29:45; Lev. 26:12; Ezek. 11:20; 37:23, 27).[60] Therefore, though it introduces something new in God's purposes for his people, it must not be viewed in opposition to the previous covenants.

Despite its continuity, however, it is *not* like the previous (Mosaic) covenant (Jer. 31:32). The new covenant will secure the transformation of the heart from the inside out (Jer. 31:33a; Ezek. 36:26), a more intimate relationship with God than ever before, for they shall all know Yahweh (Jer. 31:33b–34; Ezek. 36:27), and an infrangibility unlike the Mosaic covenant (Jer. 31:32).[61] All of these new covenant blessings will come because God will provide full and final forgiveness of sin (Jer. 31:34; Ezek. 36:29, 33).[62] Furthermore, the emphasis of the new

---

[59] P. R. Williamson 2000a: 427.

[60] P. R. Williamson 2007: 152–153.

[61] According to Dumbrell (1994: 99), the newness of the new covenant is also seen in that 'Yahweh will "cut" (i.e., initiate) a covenant. (Note that the word *cut* preserves the traditional language of the beginning of a covenantal arrangement.) And [Jeremiah] describes the covenant as "new," an adjective that carries both qualitative and temporal nuances. Though the word used in the Septuagint connotes qualitative newness, perhaps we should retain both nuances in the Hebrew. That is, the new covenant, while having continuity with the past, will be both a qualitative advance upon the Sinaitic and Davidic covenants and a temporal advance in the course of salvation history.'

[62] Wellum (2006: 142–144) is even more specific in describing the newness of the new covenant. First, he says, there are *structural* changes (Jer. 31:29–30). The previous covenants were structured in such a way that the leaders (e.g. prophets, priests and kings) were representatives of the people. So when the leader sinned, the people also shared in his guilt (see e.g. Achan's sin and Israel's corporate guilt in Josh. 7; 9:18). But now 'everyone shall die for his own sin' (v. 30). The point is that it will no longer be

covenant, described in Jeremiah and Ezekiel, is primarily national.[63] However, both allude to its international significance, and its universal scope is depicted most clearly in Isaiah.[64] Furthermore, the new covenant projects the fulfilment of God's promises, namely to make a worldwide people for God, on to a suffering Servant, an 'ideal Israel', in a new heavens and new earth (Isa. 65:17; 66:22). This fulfilment comes through a covenant enacted on better promises because of the One, the obedient Son, who fulfils it (Heb. 8 – 10).

Israel's Adam-like status, however, was short-lived, as sin devastated David's dynasty until the united kingdom came to a tragic end. And, as a result of the kings' repeated failures, an expectation grew among Israel of the need for God's saving righteousness and of a messianic figure who would deliver the nation from their foreign rulers and usher in God's blessings.[65] Hence prophetic anticipation was building for a new work that would fundamentally change Israel's relationship with God and their place and status in the world.

The king(dom) of God is at hand: the beginning of the end

What begins in the Old Testament is fulfilled in the New. Indeed, all of God's promises come to a head in Jesus Christ, who fulfils God's saving promises. For example, Luke records Jesus' quoting of Isaiah 61:1–2 at the beginning of his ministry:

> The Spirit of the Lord is upon me,
>   because he has anointed me
>   to proclaim good news to the poor.

mediated through human prophets, priests and kings. Rather, each person will have direct access to God through a mediator. Secondly, there are also changes in *nature*. They will *all* know the Lord, from the least to the greatest (v. 34), for all will experience the forgiveness of sins and the law written on their hearts. This reality is different from the previous covenant promises because not everyone in the covenant was regenerate. That is, 'not all who are descended from Israel belong to Israel' (Rom. 9:6). But in the new covenant *all* covenant people are regenerate because *all* will experience forgiveness of sins and will have new hearts regenerated by the Holy Spirit (cf. Jer. 31:33; cf. Ezek. 11:19–20; 36:26–27; Isa. 59:21). The law will be written on their hearts (cf. circumcision of the heart; Deut. 30:6; 10:16; Jer. 4:4; 9:25), and this new heart will lead them to the fear of the Lord. Moreover, they will not turn away from their God (Jer. 32:39–40). Thus the scope of the covenant has changed – everyone will have a circumcised new heart.

[63] Jer. 31:36–40; 33:6–16; Ezek. 36:24–38; 37:11–28.
[64] Jer. 33:9; Ezek. 36:36; 37:28; Isa. 42:6–7; 49:6; 55:3–5; 56:4–8; 66:18–24.
[65] Barker 1992: 309.

He has sent me to proclaim liberty to the captives
and recovering of sight to the blind,
to set at liberty those who are oppressed,
to proclaim the year of the Lord's favour.
(Luke 4:18–19)

Jesus then declares that the time of fulfilment for Isaiah 61 is now, when he says, 'Today this Scripture has been fulfilled in your hearing' (Luke 4:21). Hence the centrality of the kingdom in the New Testament signals that the time of the long-awaited fulfilment has definitively begun.

The signs that the kingdom of God had arrived in the person and mission of Jesus are numerous.[66] For example, Jesus cast out demons (Matt. 12:28; Luke 11:20), demonstrated victory over Satan (Luke 10:18), performed miracles (Matt. 11:2–5), bestowed forgiveness (Mark 2:10; cf. Isa. 33:24; Mic. 7:18–20; Zech. 13:1) and proclaimed that the eschatological promises of the kingdom had come (Matt. 11:5; Mark 1:15). In fact, the position of Mark 1:15 within the structure of the text indicates that the proclamation of the kingdom of God was at the heart of Jesus' preaching.[67] Luke teaches the presence of the kingdom when he recounts how the Pharisees ask Jesus when the kingdom of God is coming. Jesus responds by saying, 'The kingdom of God is not coming with signs to be observed, nor will they say, "Look, here it is!" or "There!" for behold, the kingdom of God is in the midst of you' (Luke 17:20–21). Instead of looking for spectacular outward signs of the presence of a primarily political kingdom, Jesus is saying that the Pharisees ought to realize that the kingdom of God is presently in their midst, in the person of Jesus himself, and that faith in him is necessary for entrance into it.

---

[66] Classic dispensational thought often made a distinction between 'kingdom of God' and 'kingdom of heaven', but in recent years more have attributed Matthew's use of the 'kingdom of heaven' as a reverential circumlocution for God such that 'kingdom of God' and 'kingdom of heaven' are functionally synonymous. However, Jonathan Pennington (2007) has shown that 'heaven' in Matthew is part of a highly developed discourse of heaven and earth language to highlight the tension that exists between heaven and earth, or God's realm and ways versus humanity's, while anticipating its eschatological resolution. This resolution will come as a result of the inauguration and consummation of the kingdom through the life, death and resurrection of Jesus Christ.

[67] Caragounis 1992: 426.

Outside the Gospels, the New Testament also confirms the arrival of the kingdom.[68] In Acts, argues Alan Thompson, though 'there are not a large number of references to the kingdom of God, their strategic placement and contexts indicate an importance that outweighs the number of occurrences of the phrase' (Acts 1:3, 6; 8:12; 14:22; 19:8; 20:25; 28:23, 31).[69] For instance, the references to the kingdom at the beginning and end (1:3, 6; 28:23, 31), the emphasis on the comprehensive teaching of the kingdom attached to these references, the explanation of the kingdom by Jesus to his disciples, and the fact that Luke ends on the subject of the kingdom of God collectively show that these verses frame the entirety of Acts and serve as a hermeneutical lens through which to interpret it.[70] Likewise, Paul demonstrates the in-breaking of the kingdom as a result of the reign of the risen Christ (e.g. Rom. 4:17; 1 Cor. 4:19–20; 15:20–28; Col. 1:13–14), and that those who inherit the kingdom will evidence it in the present (e.g. 1 Cor. 4:20–21; Gal. 5:21; Eph. 5:5).[71] Furthermore, Paul's emphasis on the new creation fits with the already–not yet tension. Believers in Christ are a new creation (2 Cor. 5:17), which has broken into the present as a result of the cross of Christ (Gal. 6:14–15), yet they live in the present evil age (Gal. 1:4; Rom. 8:18–25) and await the resurrection of their bodies in the future (2 Cor. 5:1–10). In Hebrews, believers have presently received the kingdom that cannot be shaken, but a day is coming when things on earth and in heaven will be shaken and removed, and the consummation of God's purposes will be complete (Heb. 12:26–28).

It appears throughout the New Testament, then, that God's kingdom has finally arrived in the person and finished work of Jesus, through whom blessings for the nations come. Yet the fulfilment takes place in a surprising way, for God's saving promises are inaugurated but not yet consummated. That is, the kingdom of God is 'already but not yet'. For example, in Matthew 6:10 Jesus prays to his Father:

> Your kingdom come,
> your will be done,
> on earth as it is in heaven.

---

[68] In addition to the Synoptic Gospels, Schreiner (2008: 27–28, 80–95) argues that the eschatological character of the Gospel of John is expressed by 'eternal life' rather than 'kingdom of God' (e.g. John 3:16, 36; 5:24; 6:40, 47), and his emphasis on the Holy Spirit (John 7:39; 14:26; 15:26; 16:13).

[69] A. J. Thompson 2011: 38; see also his discussion on pp. 38–48.

[70] Ibid. 47.

[71] On the kingdom of God in Paul, see Vickers 2008: 52–67.

In other words, 'the great prophecies of the manifestation of God's powerful saving rule will come to pass'.[72] Also, those who do the will of God will enter into the kingdom (Matt. 7:21), but the ones who do not will enter into judgment (Matt. 7:22–23). The parables of the sower, mustard seed and leaven (Matt. 13; cf. Mark 4; Luke 8) are explicitly presented as revealing a mystery, and how Jesus' kingdom teaching encompasses more than a single catastrophic event. It is here, writes Darrell Bock,

> that Jesus makes his distinctive contribution by foreseeing a long-running program that was declared and initiated in his teaching and work, but that will one day culminate in a comprehensive judgment. It is to this goal that the kingdom is always headed. Thus the emphasis in the kingdom teaching of the Gospels is always aimed toward this fully restorative future.[73]

The kingdom is present because the King-Messiah is present, but his reign will not fully and finally be established until his second coming.

Likewise, Paul depicts the kingdom both as present and future. He is confident that the Lord will ultimately rescue and bring him safely into his kingdom (2 Tim. 4:18). He also believes that the unrighteous will not enter the kingdom of God (1 Cor. 6:9).[74] In 2 Peter 1:11 the readers are exhorted to cultivate godly qualities so that 'there will be richly provided for you an entrance into the eternal kingdom of our Lord and Saviour Jesus Christ'. And finally, while the already character of the kingdom is not absent from Revelation, the book looks forward to the end of history when the triumphant Christ will return, reward the faithful and punish the disobedient. Therefore Christians should be challenged and encouraged to live faithfully in the present (2:1 – 3:22) and run with endurance, even in the face of persecution (1:9; 13:10; 14:12).

The New Testament message of the inaugurated, yet not finally consummated, kingdom as a result of the life, death and resurrection of Christ is crucial in connecting the beginning with the end. It is easy to see, then, why the kingdom is a consistent and unifying theme throughout the biblical story line. The kingdom God created in Eden, and, as a result of sin, advanced through each gracious

---

[72] Beasley-Murray 1992: 24.

[73] Bock 2001: 38; see also Hoekema 1979: 49–50.

[74] The future tense of the verbs in both of these passages indicates that Paul is referring to the future kingdom.

covenant response, has finally arrived in the person and work of Jesus. At the same time, this kingdom awaits its final fulfilment when the kingdom of the world will become the kingdom of our Lord and of his Christ, and he will reign for ever and ever (Rev. 11:15).

In the end: the new creation and God's eschatological kingdom

Scripture begins with creation and ends with a vision of a more glorious creation (Rev. 21 – 22). Between these two accounts lies the history of redemption.[75] The correspondence between the beginning and the end is staggering. Not only is eschatology like protology, but also eschatology escalates protology.[76] That is, the end will echo the beginning – creation as God originally designed it to be. But the end will also bring something qualitatively better. In the description of the new heaven and new earth, no one can fail to see that here primal time and end time correspond to each other. The end time is described as creation made whole again.[77] The book of Revelation vividly reveals God's consummated teleological objectives, which he set out to accomplish from the beginning, and Revelation 21 – 22 gloriously describes the end of history and God's eschatological goal.

New creation and the king(dom)

In the consummative vision of Revelation, John draws attention to the divine throne (Rev. 22:1–3). The divine throne emphasizing God's reign is a central theme throughout Revelation, appearing in a number of visions throughout the book.[78] Perhaps the most comprehensive description of God's rule is found in chapters 4–5, where seventeen of the thirty-four references in the book occur. In fact, Beale calls this glorious vision of God's throne room the 'theological heart' of Revelation.[79] This emphatic cluster testifies to the centrality of God's sovereign rule, for which he is climactically given glory in 4:9–11 and 5:12–13. In these two chapters, a crucial observation to make with regard to God's divine rule is the inclusion of Christ, for Christ clearly

---

[75] VanGemeren 1988: 40.
[76] Beale 2004a: 209.
[77] Westermann 1972: 19.
[78] Rev. 1:4; 3:21; 4 – 5; 7:9–11; 14:3; 19:4–5.
[79] Beale and McDonough 2007: 1098.

shares in the identity of God.[80] In other words, there is progression from the beginning of the biblical story line to its end, for by virtue of Christ's resurrecting blood-bought victory he now shares in his Father's rule.[81] Certainly, Yahweh has set his King, the obedient Son par excellence, to rule over the nations (Ps. 2:6–12). The establishment of God's eternal rule, signified by the prominent presence of his throne, is the fulfilment of God's design from the beginning.

But God's kingship is not new for those familiar with Genesis 1 – 2. The consummation of God's rule in the light of the universal history of human failure, though, serves only to highlight what has been restored. God's ruling presence will fill the city, for 'the throne of God and of the Lamb will be in it' (Rev. 22:3). Furthermore, those who enter the city will serve and worship him (cf. Rev. 7:15). Humanity, then, will once again function as God's kingdom and priests (Rev. 1:6), whom Christ has put in service to his Father, which is to be for his Father's eternal glory and dominion. Therefore the consummation of God's rule in Christ at the end is qualitatively better than at the beginning, for in the new creation nothing or no one will be allowed to challenge his rule, and there will no longer be anything accursed (Rev. 22:3). The King has come, and the kingdom has been restored.

New creation and the people of the king(dom)

Furthermore, the new creation is the fulfilment of God's original intent for humanity and the world, which comes through the redemption of Christ. John teaches that the Lord has in fact created an

---

[80] E.g. in Revelation the self-declaration 'I am the first and the last' (1:17) corresponds to the divine self-declaration 'I am the Alpha and the Omega' (1:8), and this God-Christ pattern continues throughout the book (1:8; 1:17; 21:6; 22:13). Bauckham (1993b: 54–55) concludes, 'A close study of this pattern can reveal the remarkable extent to which Revelation identifies Jesus Christ with God' (see also Bauckham 2008).

[81] Bauckham (1993b: 61) writes, 'The worship of God by the heavenly court in chapter 4 is connected with the acknowledgement of God as the creator of all things (4:11). In chapter 5 the Lamb, Christ, who has triumphed through his death and who is seen standing on the divine throne (the probable meaning of 5:6; cf. 7:17), now becomes in turn the center of the circle of worship in heaven, receiving the obeisance of the living creatures and the elders (5:8). Then the circle expands and the myriads of angels join the living creatures and the elders in a form of worship (5:12) clearly parallel to that offered to God (4:11). Finally, the circle expands to include the whole creation in a doxology addressed to God and the Lamb together (5:13). It is important to notice how the scene is so structured that the worship of the Lamb (5:8–12) leads to the worship of God and the Lamb together (5:13). John does not wish to represent Jesus as an alternative object of worship alongside God, but as one who shares in the glory due to God. He is worthy of divine worship because his worship can be included in the worship of the one God.'

international community of people who will inhabit his new creation.[82] This picture demonstrates the climactic fulfilment of the Abrahamic promises.[83] The promise to Abraham contributes to the larger narrative that Genesis anticipates a future offspring (singular) who will play a central role in establishing God's plan for the earth. Now this seed, Christ (Gal. 3 – 4), mediates God's covenant blessings to the nations (Rev. 21:24; 22:2). For example, John declares, 'Behold, the dwelling place of God is with man. He will dwell with them, and they will be his people, and God himself will be with them as their God' (Rev. 21:3). This declaration echoes the oft-repeated covenant formula sounded throughout the Old Testament.[84] God's covenants with humanity, then, are at last brought to full realization in the new creation populated by the nations.

Furthermore, the presentation of the new Jerusalem at the end of Revelation includes in its symbolism the new people of God. For example, John describes that on the gates of the new Jerusalem 'the names of the twelve tribes of the sons of Israel were inscribed', and 'the wall of the city had twelve foundations, and on them were the twelve names of the twelve apostles of the Lamb' (21:12, 14). In this description, the history of both Israel and the church comes to fulfilment in the new Jerusalem.[85] That is, both the Israel of the Old Testament and the church of the New Testament have their place *as the people of God* in God's final establishment.[86] To consummate God's teleological plan, then, the new creation is established in order to accommodate his multinational people.

Conclusion

From a canonical perspective, the kingdom of God is a central theme in the Lord's redemptive plan of establishing his kingdom on the earth. That is, the beginning, middle and end of the biblical story describe the teleological design of *God's people* in his *place* under his

---

[82] Rev. 21:24, 26; 22:2; cf. Rev. 5:9.
[83] Gen. 12:1–3; 15:5; 17:4–6; 18:18; 22:17–18.
[84] Gen. 17:17; Exod. 6:7; 29:45; Lev. 26:12; Num. 15:41; Deut. 29:13; 2 Sam. 7:24; Ezek. 36:28; 37:23, 27; Zech. 8:8. Furthermore, Beale and McDonough (2007: 1151) comment that 'The reference to "inheriting" the blessings promised in the Davidic prophecy of 2 Sam. 7:14 shows a hint of further inspiration from the promise of Isa. 55:1–3, where God promises those who "thirst" (55:1) that he will make with Israel "an everlasting covenant, the sure mercies of David" (55:3).'
[85] Bauckham 1993a: 312.
[86] Ladd 1972: 281.

rule. Moreover, the biblical-theological structure of the covenants as they unfold across the canon shows how his divinely ordained means will reach his divinely ordained end. But how do we get to the new Jerusalem from Eden? To this question we now turn.

Chapter Three

Making the promise: Genesis

Genesis 1 – 11: the preface to the promise of land

The promises made to Abraham in Genesis occupy a special place in biblical theology. For example, John Murray states that the Abrahamic covenant 'underlies the whole subsequent development of God's redemptive promise, word, and action'.[1] Likewise, Craig Blaising and Darrell Bock state, 'to understand the Bible, one must read it in view of the Abrahamic covenant, for that covenant with Abraham is the foundational framework for interpreting Scripture and the history of redemption which it reveals'.[2] Certainly, many paths to the unity of Scripture exist, but Abraham's role is foundational in that unity.

The events of Genesis 1 – 11, however, are more than simply a prologue to the story of Abraham and Israel. In many ways, these events are paradigmatic, for they reflect the movement from sin to exile to restoration, all of which cycle through the rest of Genesis, the Pentateuch and the Old Testament. That is, the role and experience of humanity progress from the first human couple to the introduction of Abram as a result of what takes place in creation, the fall and the events that unfold. Stephen Dempster writes:

> The world is created by the command of God; the garden of Eden becomes the prime habitat of human beings until their exile from it. Humans are expelled from the earth with the judgment of the great deluge. The postdiluvian human community is dispersed across the face of the earth at Babel. And when Abraham arrives on the historical scene he is promised a commodity that has been in short supply for human beings: a land to call his own.[3]

In other words, Genesis 1 – 11 is crucial for the development of a biblical theology, for Abram is God's response to a problem that emerges from Adam. That is, God's promises to Abram address the

[1] Murray 1988: 4.
[2] Blaising and Bock 1993: 135.
[3] Dempster 2003: 48.

curse of the ground and Adam's expulsion from Eden brought about by sin (Gen. 3:17–19, 23). Though the gracious act of salvation, but not its pattern, is illustrated with Noah, it is with Abram that a new beginning and blueprint are revealed. And a new beginning it is.

God graciously interrupts the escalation of sin and death emanating from and through Adam by promising blessing to and through Abram. This blessing is significant given the story line up to this point. 'Bless' (or derivatives) occurs five times in the call of the patriarch (12:1–3), which is the gracious counterbalance to the five curses against fallen creation and humanity (3:14, 17b; 4:11; 8:21; 9:25).[4] In other words, with the call of Abram God's blessing is resurrected. For example, whereas Adam and Eve experience exile from their homeland (3:24), God calls Abram out of Ur and promises him land that will restore the blessings of Eden. Just as Adam and Eve receive the promise of restoration in the programmatic prophecy of Genesis 3:15, so the promise to Abram clarifies the means through which God will bring his people back from exile into a new place of blessing.

The promise of land in God's plan to redeem humanity from its fallen condition provides an idyllic place from which Adam and Eve had fallen. But this land is not merely a change in location. God's gracious response to the sin and downward spiral of Genesis 3 – 11 is so dramatic and outstanding that it is expressed in language similar to that of a new creation. So, writes Dumbrell, 'as in Gen. 1:3, the form of 12:1 is that of a divine speech which includes a virtual imperative, calling a new phase of history into being, just as the words of Gen. 1:3 had called existence itself into being'.[5] Furthermore, 'the divine speech and command at Genesis 12:1 are structurally similar to the speech and implied command at the beginning of creation'.[6] Through Abram, then, not only will God restore and dwell with his people once again, but he will also restore and dwell with his people in his place – a new creation kingdom on earth.

Genesis 12 – 50: the Abrahamic covenant and promise of land

The covenant with Abraham promises to reverse the curse of Adam and to bring back into reality the advancement of God's kingdom on earth. Of special importance is how God's people will live in his place

---

[4] Mathews 2000: 141.
[5] Dumbrell 1984: 58.
[6] Köstenberger and O'Brien 2001: 28–29.

under his blessing. For Abraham, this place is the land (Gen. 12:1), and this promise runs like a scarlet thread through the rest of the biblical narrative.

The story of Abram begins with God's calling him to leave his home to the land that God will show him. Although Genesis 12:1–3 does not specify which land Abram will possess, the promise that God will make of him a great nation implies promise of the land, for you cannot have a great nation without land.[7] The Lord confirms his promise to Abram (Gen. 15:7; 17:8; cf. 22:17) and to his offspring, Isaac (Gen. 26:3–4) and Jacob/Israel (Gen. 28:4, 13–15; 35:12). Furthermore, the story of Joseph provides an essential link between the patriarchal promises and the exodus from Egypt, for through it the conflict of his exile to Egypt awaits resolution.[8] And although Abraham will taste some of the reality of being in the land, the full reality is delayed four hundred years as he and his offspring live as sojourners and servants in a land not theirs (Gen. 15:13–16). But there is hope, for Abraham's purchase of his burial site guarantees the down payment of his inheritance to come (Gen. 23; 25:9–10; cf. 49:29 – 50:26).

The story of Abraham and his descendants demonstrates the importance of land within the Genesis, and Pentateuchal, narrative. Bruce Reichenbach notes, 'Although the kingdom of God extends throughout the universe (the heavens and the earth), the primary focus in the Pentateuch is on the land.'[9] From the call of Abram the Pentateuch narrates the story of the patriarchs and their descendants, none of whom enters the land to possess it. To explore how the theme of land is developed, important components of the Abrahamic covenant – namely its unconditional and conditional, national and international, regional and global, temporal and eternal dimensions – will be examined.[10] This examination will show that the land promised to Abraham is consistently presented within the Old Testament as a type or pattern of a future and greater reality.

Unconditional and conditional

Crucial to the discussion of Israel's relationship to the land is the nature of the Abrahamic covenant. More specifically, how is the possession

---

[7] Gentry and Wellum 2012: 235. H. G. M. Williamson (1985: 7) writes, 'It is a moot point to what extent one can speak of a nation in isolation from its territory.'

[8] The anticipation of this resolution is reflected e.g. in God's promise to Jacob that he will surely bring him back again (Gen. 46:4), as well as the burial of Abraham, Isaac, Jacob (Gen. 49:29 – 50:14) and Joseph (Gen. 50:24–25) in Canaan, not Egypt.

[9] Reichenbach 2003: 51.

[10] These categories have been adapted from P. R. Williamson 2000b: 15–34.

and fulfilment of the land affected by Abraham's – and by extension his descendants' – (dis)obedience? In other words, while some texts in the Pentateuch apparently promise the land to Abraham and his descendants unconditionally,[11] other texts promise the land with certain qualifications,[12] thus raising the vexed question as to whether the territorial promise is unconditional or provisional in nature?[13]

Some scholars answer this question by suggesting various critical views of the text.[14] However, Williamson rightly notes:

> All such theories ultimately come up against the insuperable problem of why redactors would wish to combine two antithetic traditions, or to qualify the tradition of an unconditional promise on such a selective basis themselves. In any case, if the final redactor was somehow able to harmonize the unconditional and provisional passages, this must also be possible for those who wish to understand the text in its final form. Significantly, even those today who affirm the permanent, unconditional nature of the territorial promise have little difficulty in reconciling this premise with the passages that qualify the promise in some way.[15]

Williamson avoids this dilemma by arguing for two Abrahamic covenants. His proposal, however, does not make the best sense of the biblical data when the covenant is situated in its textual, epochal and canonical horizons. That is, Williamson fails to see the development – a significant development, no less – in God's covenant with Abraham as the story line moves towards its fulfilment, which is seen throughout the Abrahamic narrative.

To begin, the promises in Genesis 12 and 15 are brought together and advanced in Genesis 17. In this pivotal passage, the promises to Abram have been progressively unfolding and gradually building up until here they culminate in a divinely initiated covenant discourse. Despite Abram's attempt to circumvent God's means to obtain a child, God answers Abram's sin by reiterating his promise. God will not only multiply Abram, but multiply him 'greatly' (Gen. 17:2). Moreover, Genesis 17 does more than consolidate God's previous

---

[11] E.g. Gen. 12:7; 13:15, 17; 15:7, 18–21; 28:13, 15; 35:12; Exod. 3:8, 17; 6:8.

[12] Cf. Exod. 20:12; 23:23–33; 34:24; Lev. 18:3, 24–27; Deut. 4:1–5, 40; 5:33; 6:18; 8:1; 11:8–32; 16:20; 18:9–14; 19:8–9; 21:23; 24:4; 25:15; 30:16; 32:47.

[13] P. R. Williamson 2000b: 22–23.

[14] See e.g. von Rad 1966; Weinfeld 1993; Habel 1995. For an overview and critique, see Alexander 2012: 3–110.

[15] P. R. Williamson 2000b: 23.

promises: it extends them. At this point, Williamson and Alexander are correct in observing the national focus of chapter 15 and the international focus of chapter 17.[16] However, rather than viewing them as separate covenants, chapters 15 and 17 develop the promises in the same order in which they were given.[17] That is, Genesis 15 and 17 correlate respectively with the first three promises and the second three promises of Genesis 12:1–3.[18] Byron Wheaton demonstrates from analysing Genesis 12 – 15 and 17 – 22

> the presence of two sections or panels in the narrative with balanced episodes. God's promised solutions to the problems confronting his redemptive action that are introduced in 11:27–32 are given in programmatic fashion in ch. 12. These promises of land and seed are then individually highlighted in the remaining narrative. The land theme is foregrounded in the first half of the cycle, where Abraham's faith is matured and tested, culminating in a divine oath that it will be possessed by the seed. The seed theme, which is foregrounded in the second half of the cycle, traces the development of Abraham's faith in this promise, and it too culminates in an oath that God will fulfill this promise to Abraham. In each case, the oath is the response to a sequence of specific behaviors on Abraham's part to which the promise of land and seed are linked. Each of these sequences climaxes in a noteworthy divine event or word that secures the future. In Abraham, God has created a person who, in the moment of trial, trusts God's Word for his future as it relates both to land and seed. This distinguishes him from his ancestor Adam who through unbelief forfeited the land and corrupted the seed. God's unconditional commitment to Abraham indicates that he can serve as the father of the elect community through whom blessing will come to the world.[19]

In other words, through the nation of Abraham's descendants will come a multitude of nations.

Furthermore, Genesis 22:17–18 thickens the cord of promises. This crowning passage gathers multiple elements from prior Abrahamic promises and expands upon them.[20] First, 'I will *surely* bless you'

---

[16] P. R. Williamson 2007: 89–91; Alexander 2012: 176–179.
[17] Gentry and Wellum 2012: 279; Birch et al. 1999: 79.
[18] Ibid. 268.
[19] Wheaton 2006: 161–162. For a similar reading, see Dumbrell 1984: 75.
[20] Mathews 2005: 298; see also Grüneberg 2003: 228–229.

intensifies the original promise (12:2). Secondly, 'the stars of heaven' recount Abram's God-given vision (15:5) but also includes 'and I will *surely* multiply your offspring' (cf. 3:16). Thirdly, the theme of immeasurable sand brings to mind God's promise to Abraham after his separation from Lot (13:16). And fourthly, although the possession of the 'gate' of his/their enemies is new to the promise, it will be picked up in the blessing of the offspring of Rebekah (24:60). In this passage, God again answers Abraham's failures and questions with bigger promises that advance and escalate the certainty of his plan to bless Abraham and the nations through him.

Finally, when the larger canonical context is considered, there is sufficient ground to conclude that there is a singular Abrahamic covenant. In a later epochal horizon, Nehemiah praises the Lord, the God who chose and brought out Abram, gave him the name Abraham and made a covenant with him to give to his offspring the land (9:7–8). In other words, he conflates chapters 15 and 17 and treats them as two aspects of the Abrahamic covenant, connecting the land grant of chapter 15 with the change in Abraham's name in chapter 17, and regards the Abrahamic covenant as having been fulfilled.[21] Even more, from a canonical perspective, the New Testament never refers to God's relations with Abraham as 'covenants' – *in the plural* (see e.g. Rom. 4; Gal. 3).[22] So the narrative in chapter 17 is reconfirmation by God – to an even greater degree – that he will make good on his promises, especially after Abraham's unbelieving liaison with Hagar in chapter 16. This reassuring promise reveals a surer word in the Abrahamic narrative. Hence Williamson's approach to the Abrahamic covenant(s) is problematic in the light of the biblical data. Another explanation, then, should be given to account better for this divinely intended tension in the text.

One common solution is to appeal to the Abrahamic covenant as unconditional.[23] However, this distinction is not quite accurate, for both unconditional and conditional elements exist. In one sense, the Abrahamic covenant was conditional, for Abraham's obedience was necessary. For example, 'So Abram went' (Gen. 12:4) fulfils the divine command to 'Go from your country' (Gen. 12:1). That is, Abram's

---

[21] Waltke 2001: 263.
[22] Gentry and Wellum 2012: 280.
[23] See e.g. Michael Horton (2006: 23–110), who writes, 'The covenant with Abraham as "the father of many nations" is clearly unconditional (Gen 15), especially as interpreted in the New Testament (cf. Rom 9:6–8; Gal 3:1–29). In contrast, the Mosaic covenant is dependent on Israel's obedience.' It should be noted that there is debate within various theological systems over which covenants are conditional or unconditional.

response was necessary in order that the promise of land, offspring and blessing might be fulfilled. From the outset, then, God's commands are fulfilled in and through Abram's obedience of faith. Though God's gracious promise provides the basis of future fulfilment, Abram's response is necessary to bring it about. To be sure, God's promise engenders the capacity to embrace it by faith, but Abram also shows himself to be an obedient servant when he follows God's commands.[24] Already in Genesis 12, then, a tension exists between God's commands and Abram's response.

Genesis 17 also emphasizes the necessity of Abram's obedience when the Lord commands him to 'walk before me, and be blameless, that I may make my covenant between me and you, and may multiply you greatly' (17:1–2). Furthermore, circumcision is added to the condition of membership within the covenant community. It is important to note, however, that these obligations come after the repetition of the promises and making of the covenant in Genesis 15. That is, they do not constitute a covenant relationship but presuppose one already in place.[25] Gentry rightly demonstrates that the story line leading up to this moment is instructive:

> The circumstances of chapter 16 are important motivation for the covenant confirmation in chapter 17. Genesis 17:2 begins with the verb *wĕ'ettĕnâ*, a form almost certainly to be identified as a first person singular modal, which in direct sequence with the commands of the previous verse marks a purpose or result clause: 'Walk before me and be blameless so that I may make my covenant between me and you.' Obedience is expected of Abram in the covenant relationship. Already in Genesis 12, when Yahweh called Abram and gave him such great promises, there were commands: 'Go' . . . and 'Be a blessing!' Chapter 15 reiterated the great promises and enshrined them in a covenant. Abram has not demonstrated full integrity [in Gen. 16], and so, in chapter 17, God comes to confirm/uphold his covenant and emphasize, among other things, the need for an obedient son in Abram's Adamic role.[26]

Whereas initiating the covenant was an act of God's grace, confirming it involves a human response. In other words, divine grace precedes commands. Indeed, God's grace is evident when, after Abram and

---

[24] Waltke 2001: 205.
[25] Mathews 1996: 195.
[26] Gentry and Wellum 2012: 263.

Sarah sinfully attempt to fulfil the promise through Hagar (ch. 16), chapter 17 begins with the Lord saying, 'I am God Almighty' (17:1). This timely revelation of God's name is significant because of the distance between the fulfilment of God's promise and the barren reality of the situation. As a result, Abram's confidence and faith will be bolstered in God Almighty, who is able to make good on his word. The fulfilment, then, will not finally depend on Abram's ability, but on God, who is powerfully able to do what he has promised.

Perhaps the clearest text that underscores the conditional nature of the Abrahamic covenant is Genesis 22:17–18 (cf. 26:3–5):

> I will surely bless you, and I will surely multiply your offspring as the stars of heaven and as the sand that is on the seashore. And your offspring shall possess the gate of his enemies, and in your offspring shall all the nations of the earth be blessed, because you have obeyed my voice.

This text specifically states that the blessings were given to Abraham 'because' he obeyed the Lord's voice. Wenham holds God's promise and Abraham's obedient response in tension when he writes, 'It could be said that the original promises made in chapter 12 have now been turned into guarantees thanks to Abraham's faithful obedience.'[27] These promises will be fulfilled *because* Abraham has faithfully obeyed God's word. This emphasis on the necessity of obedience appears again in 26:5, where Isaac receives the promises because his father was obedient. Clearly, the emphasis up to this point has been weighted on the faithful promise and performance of God, but it will not come about apart from the faithful obedience of his covenant partner(s). Thus through Abraham's faithful obedience God's blessing will extend to his descendants. Though Abraham's obedience is necessary for the fulfilment of God's oath, it does not function as the basis for God's gracious blessings. This subordination of covenant obedience to promise leads to the other aspect of the Abrahamic covenant.

Genesis 15 powerfully illustrates a clear and profound unilateral-unconditional emphasis as God invokes a curse upon himself if he does not keep his covenant and fails to fulfil his promise.[28] Indeed, God will fulfil his promise concerning Abram's future seed, and Abram receives God's promise by faith (Gen. 15:6). House notes:

[27] Wenham 2003: 43.
[28] Also note, though, the imperatives for Abraham to 'look' and 'number' (Gen. 15:5).

Certainly [Abram's] earlier acts of faith help him believe now, yet this instance is all the more impressive because it occurs years after the original promise is tendered and because it continues to have no evidential basis other than God's word and God's character.[29]

Thus God counts it to Abram as righteousness and then focuses on the land to be possessed (15:7). With the promise of land and offspring in place, then, it appears that in Abram God's plan for history is progressively coming about. Nevertheless, Abram wants to know *how* he will possess the land (15:8). The remainder of the chapter is devoted to God's covenant ceremony with Abram that guarantees the promise. After Abram arranges the animal pieces, God himself passes between them in fiery fashion. In this dramatic act, God is unilaterally obligating himself to Abram and his offspring to the degree that God places himself under a potential curse. Should this God of promise not make good on his word, then may he take the curse on himself.[30] Regarding this ritual, Waltke notes:

> According to extant ancient Near Eastern texts, passing between the slain animals is a ritual that invokes a curse on the participants if they break the covenant. To walk between the carcasses is to submit oneself to the fate of the slaughtered animals as a penalty for covenant breaking. Note that only God walks between the carcasses, signifying that the covenant is not conditioned upon Abraham's future action, but based on Abraham's past faithfulness.[31]

The fact that only God passes between the pieces – as represented by the smoking fire pot and a flaming torch – is astonishing because it shows that the fulfilment of the promise rests on him and him alone. To be sure, God will unconditionally and unilaterally fulfil and meet the conditions of his promise.

[29] House 1998: 74. The force of the construction of this verb indicates that 'the action of faith preceded the vocabulary of faith. That is, by virtue of his earlier obedient response to a word from God, Abram was putting his faith in Yahweh' (V. P. Hamilton 1990: 423; cf. Mathews 2005: 166–167). See also Max Rogland (2008: 239), who argues that the *wĕqatal* form of the verb 'expresses repeated activity (i.e., an "imperfect" situation) and that it would be more accurately translated "and he *kept believing*" rather than "and he believed"'.

[30] On the significance of cutting animals in two as part of covenant ritual, see Jer. 34:18. For further discussion of sacrifices in ancient Near Eastern treatises, see Weinfeld 1970: 184–203.

[31] Waltke with Yu 2007: 319.

Some conclusions can be drawn from above. To begin, the Abrahamic covenant consists of both unconditional and conditional elements and, therefore, is not reduced to one or the other. Thus the common distinction between unconditional and conditional covenants is not quite accurate. Genesis 15 forcefully shows that God will unilaterally fulfil the promise and conditions of the covenant, even if it means taking the curse upon himself. God will keep his promise, and Abram receives the promise by faith. As demonstrated in the covenant ceremony in Genesis 15, Abram can do nothing to enter into the promise. He can only rely on the Lord to fulfil his word.

However, this unconditional emphasis does not remove the necessity of Abraham's obedience. Genesis 17:2 and 22:17–18 demonstrate that God requires an obedient partner in the covenant relationship. God promised the covenant blessings to Abraham, but these blessings are reserved for people who trust and obey the Lord. In other words, the ultimate fulfilment of the covenant is grounded on God's promises, but the means of fulfilment will come through Abraham's – and his descendants' – obedience. Blaising and Bock state that God's commandments to Abraham 'function as the *conditions* for Abraham's *historical experience* of divine blessing, for as he obeys God, God blesses him more and more. But these obligations do not condition the fundamental intention to bless Abraham. They condition the *how* and *when* of the blessing.'[32] This conditionality, therefore, is instrumental to the reception and fulfilment of the promises. This tension between God's promise and the necessity of an obedient partner in the covenant relationship becomes clearer and stronger as the story line progresses.

Ultimately, the grace of God – not the obedience of Abraham or his descendants – remains foundational. To be sure, God will see to it that the demands of the covenant are fulfilled. But if sin is native to fallen humanity, then it is safe to say that the fulfilment of the covenant, and thus the covenant blessing of land, will be brought about by an obedient one who lies beyond Abraham's – and Israel's – horizon. The student of Scripture, therefore, must look forward to an obedient covenant partner who will fulfil the conditions of the covenant in order to bring blessing on himself and, through him, to the nations.

This tension is crucial for understanding the nature and progression of the covenants as they reach their *telos* in Christ, who inaugurates

---

[32] Blaising and Bock 1993: 133–134; emphases original.

a new and better covenant in his own blood. That is, when the larger canonical story line is considered, the conditions are met by God himself when he sends his obedient Son – the true seed of Abraham and Son par excellence – to fulfil the demands of the covenant. Indeed, all of God's promises find their yes in Christ (2 Cor. 1:20), who will win the blessing of a new creation for all of Abraham's offspring.

National and international

Another important aspect of the Abrahamic covenant is whether it is intended to be national (Gen. 12:2, 'nation') or international (Gen. 17:4–6, 'nations'). Williamson considers Genesis 15 as a covenant made between God and Abram and his 'seed', while the covenant in Genesis 17 creates a broadening of the category of 'seed'. Furthermore, God changes Abram's name to Abraham, for God made him 'the father of a multitude of nations' (Gen. 17:5).[33] An intended ambiguity exists in the text, then, for Abraham's 'seed' *both* encompasses a multitude of nations (Gen. 17) *and* relates to an individual descendant (Gen. 22:17b) who will mediate blessing to all the nations of the earth.[34]

When these texts are put together, then, the ultimate inheritors of the patriarchal promises are not restricted to a national entity but extend to an international community. That is, God's programmatic agenda for humanity after Eden begins with the formation of a nation through Abraham and ends with an international people. Thus the promise to and blessing of Abraham reach their goal only when it includes all the families of the earth. This international component comes into focus in the latter prophets (see ch. 6). But for now, it is already difficult to see how the territorial promise could be exhausted by any limited geographical plot, whether Israelite or otherwise, for the multiplication of descendants naturally expands the territorial borders until the earth is filled.

Regional and global

Another issue brought to the fore is whether the land promised to Abraham is restricted to a single geographical plot or is expanded also to include a much broader area. Put another way, from the beginning it seems that the geographical boundaries occupy a considerably larger

[33] P. R. Williamson 2000b: 19.
[34] Alexander 2000b: 770; 1997: 363–367. One can already see hermeneutical warrant for Paul to pick up on this idea when interpreted in the light of Christ (Gal. 3:16, 28–29).

area than the land of Canaan, which will eventually encompass the whole earth as God makes Abraham's offspring as countless as the stars (Gen. 15:5) and into nations (Gen. 17:6).[35] After close examination, then, the land promise(s) may actually support a global, and not strictly regional, fulfilment.

The promise to Abram involves land, but not just any land. This land will be given by God. The boundaries of the land are broad (Exod. 3:8) and there is some flexibility as to its geographical dimensions. John Goldingay suggests that there are at least three ways of determining its boundaries: first, Canaan, the land west of the Jordan, is Israel's heartland;[36] secondly, a territory broader than the land west of the Jordan, which includes land east of the Jordan;[37] and thirdly, a territory broader than the first two that includes land north and east of Canaan that will be part of the area Israel control, but not part of their actual land.[38] Specific geographical boundary markers are given in a number of texts,[39] and the extent of the Promised Land is not identical in each (e.g. the boundaries in Deut. 11:24 are significantly broader than those in Num. 34), which has led some scholars to detect redactional activity.[40] However, Williamson has rightly noted a weakness in this view when he writes, 'The fact that no steps were taken to impose uniformity suggests an element of flexibility difficult to harmonize with rigidly defined territorial borders.'[41] Therefore the interpreter must seek another explanation for the varying accounts of the geographical boundaries.

The various texts that map the territorial borders of the Promised Land indicate that the land was not conclusively defined with geographical precision.[42] One solution is put forth by Goldingay, who says that the boundaries of the land in the Old Testament 'reflect political realities of different periods rather than having significance in their own right'.[43] Or perhaps Williamson is correct when he notes that it can be reasonably inferred that 'the map of the promised land was never seen as permanently fixed, but was subject to at least some

---

[35] P. R. Williamson 2000b: 20.
[36] E.g. Gen. 11:31; 12:5; 17:8; Exod. 6:4; Lev. 14:34; 25:38; Num. 13:2, 17.
[37] E.g. Num. 21:24, 35; 32:39; Josh. 22:9, 13, 15, 32.
[38] Goldingay 2003: 518–519.
[39] E.g. Gen. 15:18–21; Exod. 23:31–33; Num. 34:1–12; Deut. 1:7; 11:24; 34:1–4; Josh. 1:2–4.
[40] Weinfeld 1993: ch. 3; Waldow 1974: 498.
[41] P. R. Williamson 2000b: 20–21.
[42] Martens 1998: 117.
[43] Goldingay 2003: 519.

degree of expansion and redefinition'.[44] For Williamson, such a conclusion is bolstered by texts where the territorial inheritance more generally describes the pre-Israelite occupants,[45] the geographical location of the beneficiaries,[46] and texts that, at the least, implicitly point to a further expansion of the territorial promise.[47] Of particular importance is Genesis 26:3–4, where the unique plural 'lands', when juxtaposed with Genesis 22:17–28, reveals that Abraham's seed will possess or inherit the gate of his enemies. One can already see that Paul is not spiritualizing texts when he says that 'the promise to Abraham and his offspring that he would be heir of the world did not come through the law but through the righteousness of faith' (Rom. 4:13). Rather, Paul is reaching sound exegetical and theological conclusions when he puts all three elements of the covenant together, for he *now* sees Abraham inheriting the world as all people – both Jew and Gentile – come to faith in Jesus Christ.[48]

Therefore, while the Promised Land was primarily a specific territory, there is sufficient biblical warrant to conclude that it was also something more. Williamson writes:

> The fact that the promised land was of more than political significance has often been overlooked, especially by those who still anticipate some sort of future, national fulfillment of the territorial promise. When the global significance of the promised land is taken on board, a future fulfillment in a narrow, regional sense appears largely redundant, and indeed somewhat anticlimactic.[49]

Because the land is not described with geographical precision, then, one might say that it was to some degree an idea[50] – yet it was a

---

[44] P. R. Williamson 2000b: 21.

[45] E.g. a list of ten nations is found in Gen. 15:19–21, whereas most of the other lists in the Pentateuch and former prophets contain only six nations (e.g. Exod. 3:8, 17; 23:23; 33:2; 34:11; Deut. 30:17; Josh. 9:1; Judg. 3:5). Furthermore, there are some lists that add the Girgashites, making a total of seven nations (Deut. 7:1; Josh. 3:10; 24:11), and others that have only five (Exod. 13:5; 1 Kgs 9:20). For more texts, see P. R. Williamson 2000b: 21.

[46] E.g. there are various references to 'this land', 'the land that you see' (e.g. Gen. 12:7; 13:15), 'the land in which they lived as sojourners' (Exod. 6:4) and 'the land on which you lie' (Gen. 28:13).

[47] See e.g. Gen. 26:34; Exod. 34:24; Num. 24:17–18; Deut. 18:8–9. P. R. Williamson 2000b: 21.

[48] Moo 1996: 274; Schreiner 1998: 227; P. R. Williamson 2000b: 22; cf. Gentry and Wellum 2012: 258–266. This passage will be discussed in further exegetical detail in ch. 8.

[49] P. R. Williamson 2000b: 22.

[50] Holwerda 1995: 90.

territory[51] – and this territory would expand with the increase and expansion of its inhabitants.

Temporal and eternal

The last issue to observe concerning the nature of the Abrahamic covenant is whether the territorial promise is temporal or eternal. An important issue in the promise and fulfilment of land is whether to locate its fulfilment in the past – that is, in Israel's history – or in the future. As stated above, God's promise and purpose for Abraham are a reversal of the recurring pattern in Genesis 1 – 11. The land, seed and blessing forfeited by Adam are answered with God's promise of land, seed and blessing to Abraham (Gen. 1:28; 9:1; 17:2, 6). The international scope of the covenant and global dimensions of geography in God's promise suggest that God's solution to humanity's plight is not ultimately limited by physical, geographical or temporal restraints. Moreover, God's promise to Abraham is said to be everlasting.[52] Although the term may not always mean a limitless duration of time, its connection to the blessing of land(s) and nation(s) suggests that the promise will at least be as everlasting as the covenant itself, a covenant that relates primarily to the blessing of the nations through Abraham's seed.

A further indication that the territorial promise is of an enduring nature is its association with rest. This link to rest becomes clearer as the story line progresses and is grounded on the divine rest at the beginning of creation.[53] It is at this point that the anticipatory, or typological, aspect of the Promised Land comes into focus.[54] So

[51] Martens 1998: 117.

[52] E.g. Gen. 13:15; 17:8; 48:4; cf. Exod. 32:13; Josh. 14:9.

[53] E.g. Exod. 33:14; Deut. 3:20; 12:9–10; 25:19; Josh. 1:13; Gen. 2:2–3; Exod. 20:11; Deut. 5:15; Heb. 3:7 – 4:11.

[54] Although at one point P. R. Williamson (2000b: 27) speaks of the promise–fulfilment schema of land in terms of typology, at another point he says that it 'speaks metaphorically of something greater' (25). However, metaphor should be distinguished from typology. Although both make connections between two or more things, persons or events, the difference is found in *how* and *what kind* of connections are made. Paul Hoskins (2006: 19) defines typology as 'the study which traces parallels or correspondences between incidents recorded in the Old Testament and their counterparts in the New Testament such that the latter can be seen to resemble the former in notable respects and yet to go beyond them'. He further elaborates on this definition by saying that 'First, the "correspondences" involved in typology are drawn between "persons, events, and institutions, within the framework of salvation history." Secondly, it is often noted that typological correspondences can already be seen in the Old Testament, especially in works of prophecy like Isaiah and Ezekiel.' So there are identifiable historical and textual connections between the type and antitype that derive from the various texts. Furthermore, typology stresses escalation as the story line moves forward. Leonhard Goppelt

again, while the Promised Land includes the territory occupied by Israel throughout their history, it also encompasses something greater. Such a conclusion grows out of the ways the Abrahamic promise of land, seed and blessing are fulfilled through redemptive history. Thus understood, one finds exegetical basis for the New Testament claim that Abraham looked forward to something greater, 'For he was looking forward to the city that has foundations, whose designer and builder is God' (Heb. 11:10).

Conclusion

Some conclusions can be drawn from above. First, the promise of land in the Abrahamic covenant should be understood in the light of what preceded it, namely Eden as the prototypical place of the kingdom. The land, then, advances through Abraham the place of the kingdom that was lost in Eden. Secondly, the flexibility of the geographical boundaries indicates that, although the boundaries initially delimit territory, the territory anticipates something more. That is, although it begins as a localized geographical plot, its rich theological associations and eschatological horizons actually extend beyond the territory itself. As a result, the patriarchal promise of land anticipates something greater and, therefore, the promise will not ultimately be fulfilled until Abraham's seed fills and occupies the world. The land promised to Abraham, then, is presented as a type or pattern of a greater reality with international and worldwide dimensions.

(1982: 18) writes, 'If the antitype does not represent a heightening of the type, if it is merely a repetition of the type, then it can be called typology only in certain instances and in a limited way.' These connections show that the working out of God's purposes are incomplete until they reach their ultimate fulfilment in Christ and his work.

Chapter Four

Advancing the promise:
Exodus–Deuteronomy

Exodus: bound for the Promised Land

The book of Exodus, aptly named for its key event, resumes and advances the Genesis story line as it opens with 'And' as well as points back to creation and the promises to Abraham.[1] The people of Israel were fruitful, and they multiplied and filled the land. It is difficult to underestimate its significant place in the Old Testament, for it provides the unifying historical and theological basis for subsequent writers to put together Israel's history from creation to the monarchy. Stephen Dempster observes the canonical-shaping language that stems from the exodus and comments:

> Exodus language becomes the grammar used to express future salvation. Whether it is Hosea speaking of Israel going up from the land (Hos 1:11 [2:2 мт]), Isaiah of leading the people through the sea again (Isa 11:15), Micah of Yahweh leading an exodus of crippled and outcasts (Mic 4:6–7), Jeremiah of a new covenant (Jeremiah 31–34.), the Exodus language of salvation is the way Israel construed its understanding of the future.[2]

---

[1] Peter Enns (2000: 146–147) comments, 'English translations routinely leave this word untranslated, perhaps for stylistic reasons. . . . The presence of "and" at the very beginning of the book is striking. Moreover, Exodus 1:1 as a whole cements the connection to Genesis: "These are the names of the sons of Israel who went to Egypt." This verse is essentially a repetition of Genesis 46:8, which announces Israel's journey to Egypt. The same words are now used to announce Israel's departure from Egypt. The fact that Exodus 1:1, including "and," repeats Genesis 46:8 indicates that the story of Israel's departure from Egypt must be understood as a continuation of a story told in Genesis. Israel's presence in Egypt is no product of chance. The Israelites in Egypt are to view their present suffering and oppression in the light of God's larger, unchanging picture. God chose a people for himself and brought them down to Egypt. He will bring them out again.'

[2] Dempster 2008: 4.

It is difficult, then, to overestimate the crucial role that Exodus plays both in the fulfilment of the land promise and the salvation of God's people.

The promise of a recaptured kingdom would be secured through the covenant made with Abraham (Exod. 6:4, 8), a covenant that promised land, seed and universal blessing; and Exodus moves towards the realization of this covenant by showing an increasing Israelite clan bound for the Promised Land. Thus the promise to Abraham and deliverance from Egypt are determinative factors for Israel's future. Exodus, then, may be considered the epicentre of the Pentateuch, especially in view of God's powerful and destination-changing deliverance of his people from foreign rule. Indeed, God will ensure that his people will live in his place under his rule.

Furthermore, the multiplication of a people and movement towards inhabiting a place to live under God's blessing is rooted in his original blessing on humanity. The promises to Israel to plant them in the land are reiterations of a former promise. This connection is forcefully illustrated in Exodus 15:17:

> You will bring them in and plant them on your own mountain,
> the place, O LORD, which you have made for your abode,
> the sanctuary, O Lord, which your hands have established.

At the end of the song sung by Israel after crossing the Red Sea, 'the establishment of Israel in the land of Canaan is pictured as the planting of a tree in a *mountain sanctuary,* exactly the picture of Eden presented in Genesis 2 and Ezekiel 28'.[3] Through their redemption, then, Israel inherit the role of Adam in a new Eden-like land and are the means by which God will fulfil his worldwide purposes.

By the end of Genesis and the beginning of Exodus, however, fulfilment of the patriarchal promises of offspring had hardly progressed. This suspension of the story line is clearly demonstrated in Exodus 1. Genesis ends with the sons of Israel under Joseph numbering seventy people (Gen. 46:27), and Exodus begins with the same fledgling number as they come into Egypt (Exod. 1:5). A new king arises over Egypt who does not know Joseph and who enslaves Israel under the harsh oppression of the Egyptians (1:9–11). And when Pharaoh sees that the people of Israel are 'too many and too mighty' for the Egyptians (1:9), he commands his leaders to afflict Israel to keep them

---

[3] Gentry and Wellum 2012: 227; emphasis original.

from increasing. As a result, Pharaoh, with serpent-like cunning (1:10a), embarks on a policy resulting in hard service, pain in child-bearing, and death, all of which are associated with life outside the garden of Eden.[4] But if these obstacles are not enough, more drastic measures are taken to stop the multiplication of the Israelites when Pharaoh orders the extermination of all Israelite sons (Exod. 1:8–22). These realities serve as vivid illustrations that God's kingdom on earth had not yet come. His people were not living in his place under his rule. Rather, they were living as captives of a foreign king whose rule was opposed to God.

This background sets the scene for God to intervene powerfully on behalf of his people. As the narrative unfolds, it is clear that nothing or no one is able to thwart God's plan. But before Israel's course is drastically changed, there is a sharp turn in the narrative that, for the next four chapters, focuses on one man: Moses. The account of Moses – his birth, preservation and calling to lead God's people out of captivity – marks the promise of a new start. Enns comments:

> The story of Moses' birth is also told in creation language. When his mother looked at the child after his birth, she saw that he was 'good' (*ṭôb*; 2:2). The entire Hebrew phrase is *kî ṭôb*, which is an echo of the refrain in Genesis 1 where God pronounces what he has created 'good.' The birth of Moses is not merely about the birth of one man, but represents the beginning of the birth of the people. The savior of the people is born, and it is through him that God's people will be given a new beginning. Their slavery will end and their savior will bring them safely into their rest, the Promised Land.[5]

This focus on genealogy will set the stage for a change in geography.

But before Israel are delivered, a massive obstacle remains before their eyes: Pharaoh. In Exodus 2:23, the cry of the people went up before God. In chapter 5:15, however, the cry of the people is before Pharaoh. 'It is as if the author wants to show that Pharaoh was standing in God's way and thus provides another motivation for the plagues which follow.'[6] In response to Israel's cry, God commits to deliver them from the hand of the Egyptians to a land flowing with milk and honey (3:8, 10; 6:6–8). As a result of Pharaoh's ordained

---

[4] Watts 2000: 479.
[5] Enns 2000: 147.
[6] Sailhamer 1992: 250.

and willing opposition to God and failure to let his people go, God sends signs that culminate in the death of the Egyptian firstborn (chs. 7–12). Whereas Pharaoh set out to exterminate Israel's firstborn, this great reversal from Exodus 1 reminds the reader that the salvation of God's *son* (Exod. 4:22–23) will come at the cost of the Egyptians' sons. That is, salvation comes through substitution.

Then, in what Elmer Martens calls the programmatic text of the Bible,[7] God says:

> I am the LORD, and I will bring you out from under the burdens of the Egyptians, and I will deliver you from slavery to them, and I will redeem you with an outstretched arm and with great acts of judgement. I will take you to be my people, and I will be your God, and you shall know that I am the LORD your God, who has brought you out from under the burdens of the Egyptians. I will bring you into the land that I swore to give to Abraham, to Isaac, and to Jacob. I will give it to you for a possession. I am the LORD. (Exod. 6:6–8)

Indeed, Israel will now know their creator by a new name: Yahweh (Exod. 6:3).[8] Through the miraculous act of the exodus (ch. 14), an event pregnant with creational overtones, God delivers his people through the chaotic waters of judgment and brings them out as a new creation, free from foreign rule. Though Pharaoh and his men change their minds about freeing Israel and make one last stand against their rival deity, they finally come to know the one true God when they experience total destruction and death in a watery grave.[9] God will get the glory so that they will know that he is Yahweh (Exod. 14:4). Afterward, Moses and the people celebrate in a salvation song affirming Yahweh's lordship and praising him for his unrivalled power and awesome name, for he has become their salvation (ch. 15). At last, Yahweh has delivered his people and promises to plant them in the

---

[7] Martens 1998: 4.

[8] Scholars have noted the problem with God's revelation as Yahweh in Exod. 6:3. Ross Blackburn (2012: 26–28, 60–61) rightly argues that when Exod. 1:1 – 15:21 is situated canonically, what is new is an interpretation of the divine name, not the name itself. More specifically, he says (ibid.), it is 'the revelation of the Lord as Redeemer, the God who, being supreme over all creation, is willing and able to deliver his people. . . . The name that was unknown to the patriarchs, then, was not the label, but rather the character of the Lord as the supreme redeemer, a characteristic of the Lord that Israel had not known, and could not have known apart from being delivered from bondage.'

[9] Dempster 2008: 12.

mountain of his inheritance, where he will live with them as their great king for ever. Now that they have been delivered out of bondage, they have only to go into the land of promise.

The exodus is a momentous event for the fulfilment of God's promises to his people. These promises form the basis of his redemptive work for Israel, and the exodus is the means to bring it about. The spectacular deliverance of Israel out of Egypt constitutes the beginning of a great journey to relocate to a new land – a land 'flowing with milk and honey' (Exod. 3:8, 17; 13:5; 33:3). Israel, it seems, is God's blessed new humanity destined for a new creation from where and through whom blessing to the world will come.

Deuteronomy: the gift of land

While the Promised Land occupies a less dominant role in the previous books of the Pentateuch, Deuteronomy gives the first complete recounting of Israel's story and brings to culmination the theme of God's promise and gift of land. In fact, to speak of the fulfilment of promise in Deuteronomy is, in essence, to speak of the land. Deuteronomy, then, presents a highly developed theology of land.[10]

The idolatrous and unbelieving first generation delivered by Yahweh in the exodus from Egypt failed to enter and settle into the land God had given them. The initial attempt to enter the land of promise proved unsuccessful and, as a result, the exodus generation was sent away into the wilderness. Throughout the Pentateuch, however, the promise of land to the patriarchs continued to form the backbone of God's faithfulness to his people (Deut. 4:31; cf. Lev. 26:40–45). In Leviticus the land 'was understood as a trust from the divine landlord, who is pictured as living in relationship with the Israelites in the land in the same way that he walked with Adam and Eve in the garden (Lev 26:12)'.[11] An inherited problem exists, though – which the provisions of the sacrificial system and the Day of Atonement presuppose – and the only hope for the wilderness generation is the Abrahamic covenant (Lev. 26:42). Likewise, 'Numbers establishes from its very beginning the thematic element of the land as the end to which everything drives, and its matter and movement are consistently oriented toward that goal.'[12] However, the

---

[10] Block 2012: 40.
[11] Dempster 2003: 109.
[12] Clines 1997: 93.

theme of failure continues as the people repeatedly break covenant with Yahweh.[13]

Now, after forty years of wandering in the wilderness, a new generation stands before Moses as he preaches to them, commissioning them to enter the land and instructing them on how they must live in it. Deuteronomy, from beginning to end, exhorts Israel to take possession of the land that the Lord promised to their fathers. At this crucial point in Israel's history – looking back at the failure of the former generation and forward to the land God has given them to possess – the Promised Land becomes a great means of motivation. Gary Millar notes, 'In Deuteronomy, partial fulfilment has already taken place. Yahweh has assured Israel that the land is theirs. In his grace, he has already handed over the deeds to them. This should act as an encouragement to them to go in and possess it.'[14] Thus Deuteronomy narrates the paradox between the Lord's sure promise to his people, which is rooted in his faithfulness in the past, and their response.

The Promised Land is described in a number of ways. First, the land is a gift that Yahweh owns.[15] Although God had every right to destroy Israel for their wilful disobedience and idolatry, Deuteronomy is clear that the land is an underserved gift from him. In fact, variations of the phrase the 'land that the LORD our God is giving' occur nearly thirty times in Deuteronomy and three times in Joshua.[16] Put another way, the land is not earned by Israel. It is neither because of their righteousness that they inherit the land, nor is it for other nations' wickedness that they do not possess it. Rather, God gives it to them in order that 'he may confirm the word that the LORD swore to your fathers, to Abraham, to Isaac, and to Jacob' (Deut. 9:5). Simply put, God's gift of land was tied to his unconditional election of Israel (Deut. 7:6–11).

But in order to keep Israel from receiving the land with closed fists, God reminds them that it ultimately belongs to him.[17] Since God is the creator of the whole earth, the land is first and foremost his land.

---

[13] E.g. the people complained against the Lord (ch. 11), there were sinful problems within the leadership (ch. 12), spies were sent into the land and, instead of trusting God, they feared man (ch. 13), and the people grumbled (ch. 14) and revolted (ch. 16) against Moses and Aaron. The overall progression of the narrative, then, points to the failure of Israel to keep the covenant and to the inevitability of judgment.

[14] Millar 1998: 61.

[15] For more on the land as gift, see Brueggemann 1977: 45–50; Miller 1969: 451–465.

[16] Deut. 1:25; 2:29; 3:20; 4:1, 21; 5:31; 9:6; 11:17, 31; 15:4, 7; 16:20; 17:14; 18:9; 19:1–2, 10, 14; 24:4; 25:19; 26:1–2; 27:2–3; 28:8; 32:49, 52; cf. Num. 10:29; Josh. 1:2, 11, 15.

[17] Habel 1995: 37; C. J. H. Wright 2004: 94.

Thus the people who are Yahweh's inheritance have Canaan as their inheritance (Deut. 4:20–21).[18] God possesses the land, but has granted the use and enjoyment of it to Israel.[19] In other words, his gift comes with conditions, for life in the land requires obedience to God's commands. Though their obedience affects their livelihood in the land, it does not nullify God's gift of the land.[20] Waltke writes:

> Paradoxically, Israel's role in participating in this gift [of land] is conditioned upon their trusting I AM to keep his promises to give them the Land against contrary evidence (Deut 6:18; 8:1; 11:8–9). . . . Here we see the tension of God's prior election of Israel and Israel's subsequent faith-obedience.[21]

Some scholars have attempted to drive a wedge between the conditional and unconditional aspects of the land promise.[22] But the presence of unconditionality does not necessarily exclude conditions, for unconditionality and conditionality concurrently exist in various kinds of relationships, and particularly in sonship (Deut. 14:1; cf. Exod. 4:22–23).[23]

Secondly, the land is described as a new paradise.[24] That is, the description of the land holds out promise of a return to an Eden-like bliss. Waltke calls these extravagant descriptions 'metonymies of effect'.[25] For example, the land is described as being (very) good,[26] having luxurious pasturelands and flowers,[27] and containing abundant fruit.[28] The fruit of the womb and the fruit of the livestock will be

---

[18] Goldingay 2003: 517.

[19] Deut. 6:10–11; cf. Exod. 19:5; Lev. 25:23; Josh. 22:19.

[20] Deut. 4:1, 5, 14, 45; 5:31; 6:1–3; 12:1.

[21] Waltke with Yu 2007: 544.

[22] See e.g. von Rad 1966.

[23] C. J. H. Wright 1990: 15. One can see how this plays out in the NT in places where the reality of who God's people are in Christ ground God's commands for them to obey. Thomas Schreiner and Ardel Caneday (2001: 26) capture this tension by stating that 'biblical admonitions and warnings imply nothing about earning or meriting something from God. Rather, the unconditional promise grounds both the conditional promise and the conditional warning in God's grace, for the biblical testimony is that God's grace and love precedes [sic.] and creates all human faith and obedience (Eph. 2:10).'

[24] Millar 1998: 55, n. 38. See e.g. Deut. 6:3; 11:9; 26:9, 15; 27:3; 31:20; cf. Exod. 3:8, 17; 13:5; 33:3; Lev. 20:24; Num. 13:27; 14:8; 16:13–14.

[25] Waltke with Yu 2007: 512, n. 2.

[26] See Deut. 1:25, 35; 3:25; 4:21–22; 6:18; 8:7, 10; 9:6; 11:17. This language hearkens back to God's 'very good' creation in Gen. 1:31. See also Josh. 23:13, 15–16, and Num. 14:7, which also describe the land in a very similar way to Gen. 1:31.

[27] Millar 2000: 623.

[28] Deut. 7:13; 28:4.

blessed,[29] and no male or female among the people or among the beasts will be barren.[30] The prospect of a rich land in which the people will flourish and multiply suggests a return to Eden-like conditions. At this point in history, then, the second generation stood before God on the edge of a luxurious and bountiful land that offered the nation rest, security and abundance.[31]

Thirdly, Deuteronomy contains numerous references to the creational mandate given to Adam. This task, however, is now passed on to Israel. For example, they will 'multiply' in the land,[32] eventually resulting in filling the earth, which echoes God's teleological design for Eden. Furthermore, the Lord will subdue the land and they must subdue it (Deut. 9:3). Hence the original mandate given to Adam in creation and passed down to Abraham and the patriarchs appears again.[33] The promise of land, then, offers the restoration of relationship with and vocation under God in terms reminiscent of Eden.[34]

Fourthly, recurring themes of 'life' and the 'prolonging of days' allude back to Eden and the life Adam enjoyed before the fall.[35] This blessed and prolonged life is likewise connected to obeying God in the land. Hence Israel, like Adam, must obey God's word in order to live in his place under his rule. And, in a very important passage, Israel must hold fast to Yahweh, 'for he is your life and length of days, that you may dwell in the land that the LORD swore to your fathers, to Abraham, to Isaac, and to Jacob, to give them' (Deut. 30:20). Although this text should not be pressed too far, it is safe to say that, whereas the blessing throughout Deuteronomy is often connected to the land, the blessing is also Yahweh himself. Truly Yahweh is their life.[36]

---

[29] Deut. 7:13; 28:3–5, 11.

[30] Deut. 7:14; 28:4, 11; cf. Exod. 23:26; Lev. 26:9.

[31] Deut. 3:18–22; 6:3; 11:9–12; 26:9, 15; 27:3; 31:20; cf. Exod. 3:8, 17; 13:5; 33:3; Lev. 20:4; Num. 13:27; 14:8; 16:13–14.

[32] Deut. 6:3; 7:13; 8:1, 13; 13:17; 30:16. Deut. 1:10–11 asserts, 'The LORD your God has multiplied you, and behold, you are today as numerous as the stars of heaven. May the LORD, the God of your fathers, make you a thousand times as many as you are and bless you, as he has promised you!' This language is the same as that used in Gen. 15:5.

[33] Beale 2005: 13; Dempster 2003: 79.

[34] Millar 2000: 623.

[35] Deut. 4:40; 5:16; 12:25, 28; 22:7.

[36] This passage is significant because, as one will see in the NT, particularly the Gospels, Jesus is presented as the resurrection and the life (John 11:25; 14:6; cf. Col. 3:4); also, in him is rest (Matt. 11:28). In other words, the life and rest that are often linked to the land will be linked in later revelation to a person, Jesus Christ. These themes will be explored in more detail in chs. 7–8.

Fifthly, inheritance and rest become important aspects of the promise of land.[37] The occupation of the land is associated with rest, adumbrated by the tabernacle while it travels with the people through the wilderness (Exod. 33:14).[38] In Deuteronomy, these connections converge in the land.[39] Indeed, outside the land the people will not experience God-given rest (Deut. 28:65).[40] Each family's inheritance has been given to them by God and is to be protected.[41] Inheritance does not, however, exist only between individual families and God. Land is an inheritance of the entire people,[42] which demonstrates that God views Israel as a son.[43] In other words, land possession is connected to sonship. For example, the Song of Moses in Deuteronomy 32 describes Israel's relationship with God in father–son terms. Inheritance language, according to Millar, 'invests the occupation of the land with greater significance; occupation involves the enjoyment of a filial relationship with God; it is not merely the possession of a piece of real estate'.[44] As in Exodus, the themes of covenant, land and sonship come together. It is because Israel is Yahweh's firstborn son that the land is given as an inheritance.

Moreover, land and rest are mentioned together and are described as gifts from God.[45] God's gift of rest stands in stark contrast to the experience of Israel while they were slaves in Egypt, as well as the subsequent period in the wilderness due to their disobedience. This rest, according to McKeown, 'is not just understood in the negative sense of no longer needing to wander, but also denotes security and safety from one's enemies (Deut. 25:19)'.[46] Rest means freedom from enemy oppression and enjoyment of peace. However, rest is not merely a coincidental by-product of living in the land. Rather, it is a divine gift in its own right (Exod. 33:14; Deut. 3:20).[47]

Finally, Deuteronomy 12:9–11 pulls together the thematic threads of inheritance and rest. When the people of Israel have possessed the land, rest will ensue. As Harris points out, 'The rest that the land

[37] McComiskey 1985: 43.
[38] Harris 2009: 57; McKeown 2003: 489.
[39] Deut. 12:10; cf. 3:20; 25:19.
[40] Harris 2009: 57.
[41] Lev. 25:23–28; Num. 36:6–8; Josh. 19:51.
[42] Deut. 4:21, 38; 15:4; 19:10; cf. Josh. 13:1–7.
[43] Deut. 1:31; 8:5; 14:1; 32:5–6, 18–19.
[44] Millar 2000: 626.
[45] Deut. 3:20; 12:9–10; 25:19; Josh. 1:13–15; 21:43–44.
[46] McKeown 2003: 489.
[47] Alexander 2000a: 36–37.

offers is both rest *from* enemies, and rest *for* God's presence.'[48] That is, rest provides the opportunity for Israel to worship in the place God has chosen to dwell with his covenant people. On this note, Alexander rightly points out that it is impossible to consider the concept of rest without noting its association with the Sabbath.[49] Despite differences in wording, the Decalogue in both Exodus and Deuteronomy associate these two concepts.[50] Whereas Exodus 20:11 contains an explicit connection between the divine institution of the Sabbath and the seventh day of creation, Deuteronomy highlights God's deliverance of the Israelites from the Egyptians (e.g. Deut. 5:15). As a result, Alexander suggests that the deliverance of the Israelites from Egyptian bondage and subsequent settlement in the Promised Land were viewed as in some manner paralleling God's rest following the completion of his creative activity.[51] This textual connection indicates that the rest offered in the land may be tied to the rest of God in creation prior to the fall. 'The acquisition of the Promised Land,' says McKeown, 'while not explicitly described as a return to Edenic bliss, gives Israel the rest and security that was endemic to paradise.'[52] As a result of possessing and inheriting the land, then, Israel would enjoy the gifts of creation in a way that they were originally designed to be enjoyed.[53] Understood in this light, then, possessing their inheritance of the Promised Land typifies entering into God's eternal rest, to which the land of Canaan was the entrance.[54]

The book of Deuteronomy ends with the death of Moses, a unique prophet in the history of Israel (34:10). Despite the fact that Deuteronomy does not close with the patriarchal promises fulfilled, there is a prospect of hope. The great prophet Moses passes on the role of leadership to his servant Joshua – a man full of the Spirit of wisdom (34:9) – and Moses' last words are given to a people poised to enter the Promised Land.

---

[48] Harris 2009: 57; emphases original.
[49] I am grateful to John Meade for his insights into the connection between Sabbath and rest.
[50] Alexander 2000a: 38.
[51] Ibid. 38–39.
[52] McKeown 2003: 489; cf. Beale (2004b: 116), who notes that the Promised Land 'was to be a Garden of Eden on a grander scale'.
[53] Dumbrell 1984: 121–122.
[54] P. R. Williamson 2000b: 27.

Chapter Five

Partially fulfilling the promise: Joshua–Kings

Joshua: the possession of the land

The book of Joshua begins where Deuteronomy ends. It is important, therefore, to see how the theme of land progresses. A major portion of the book of Joshua is devoted to detailing the allotment of inheritances to families and tribes (chs. 13–21). Divorced from its canonical context, these chapters are viewed as an unfortunate break in an otherwise exciting literary narrative that progresses from crossing into the land (chs. 1–5) to taking the land (chs. 6–12) to finally worshipping God in the land (chs. 22–24). However, these chapters clearly demonstrate the fulfilment of God's promise of land in substantial ways.

Three important themes emerge from the text. To begin, there is indication in Joshua that the initial conquest of the land resulted in the fulfilment of the Abrahamic promises. While Deuteronomy anticipates rest from enemies, Joshua concludes with its having been achieved.[1] For example, Joshua 11:23 and 14:15 state that 'the land had rest from war'. This rest was in accordance with all that the Lord had spoken to Moses (11:23). Furthermore, the Lord gave rest to Israel from all their surrounding enemies (Josh. 21:44–45; 22:4; 23:1). Thus the fulfilment of the promises appears to be complete, for 'Not one word of all the good promises that the LORD had made to the house of Israel had failed; all came to pass' (Josh. 21:45; cf. 23:14–15). It appears that God's promise of land has finally been fulfilled.

However, signposts throughout the book of Joshua indicate otherwise.[2] That is, while some texts speak of conquest and rest, others indicate that the land was not fully and finally possessed.[3] As a result, writes Williamson, 'the rather idealistic statements of complete fulfilment are tempered with the more realistic picture

---

[1] Howard 1998: 258–259.
[2] Clarke 2010: 89.
[3] Josh. 13:1, 6–7; 15:63; 24:4–13. Howard (1998: 259) also lists Josh. 11:22; 14:12; 16:10; 17:12–13; 18:2–3; 19:47; 23:4–5, 7, 12–13.

presented elsewhere'.[4] That is, from a broader perspective there was substantial victory over the Canaanites that broke their power and gave Israel the initiative to inhabit the land. However, the details of the conquest concerning every last city and person were left open.[5]

Thus two 'parallel realities'[6] in Joshua regarding the nature and scope of Israel's occupation of Canaan are simultaneously presented, which Waltke labels as both already and not yet.[7] Simply put, a degree of fulfilment had been achieved under Joshua's leadership, yet at the same time it was not finally fulfilled. Walter Kaiser writes:

> [The] promise of the 'seed' to Abraham is 'fulfilled' when Isaac is born and the promise of 'a place' is 'fulfilled' when Joshua takes Canaan. Fulfilled, yes, but only as 'pledges' of the one who can gather up all of the manifold parts of the one promise in himself in their ultimate fulfillment.[8]

As a result, writes Waltke, 'Israel's possession of the Land and rest are expandable themes, for the land was taken "little by little" (Exod 23:30) but never consummately (Heb 4:1–11; 11:39–40).'[9] Furthermore, as one moves from Joshua to Judges, it becomes clear that the comprehensive rest did not last long. Judges describes how the enemies of Israel regain power, bringing an end to the rest that was temporarily achieved under Joshua.[10] Thus, as long as there were pockets of resistance, there could be no final rest. Waltke makes an insightful observation regarding the already–not yet fulfilment presented in Joshua when he writes:

> Future generations must play their part (Judg. 3:1–4). The Chronicler (1 Chron. 13:5) uses Joshua 13:1–7 to present David as greater than Joshua because he rules from Shihor of Egypt to the entrance of Hamath. . . . At any given point along the continuum of fulfillment, it can be said that God fulfilled his promise. Moreover, each fulfillment was a part of the ultimate fulfillment and could be reckoned as such. Isaiah saw the fulfillment of the ideal limits in the messianic age (Is. 11:12–16). The New Testament presents the

---

[4] P. R. Williamson 2000b: 113–114.
[5] Howard (1998: 259) calls these parallel realities 'a stylized summary of sorts'.
[6] Mabie 2005: 318.
[7] Waltke with Yu 2007: 525.
[8] Kaiser 1970: 98.
[9] Waltke with Yu 2007: 525.
[10] Alexander 2000a: 37; Millar 2000: 625; P. R. Williamson 2000b: 30.

same tension regarding the kingdom of God: it is here 'already' but in its fullest sense 'not yet.'[11]

It appears, then, that there remains a greater fulfilment of the promise in the future.[12]

Finally, although the second generation did not obtain ultimate fulfilment of the promise, the text does present their conquest and settlement as an advancement of the Edenic mandate (Gen. 1:28). As some scholars have noted, the structure of Joshua is largely about taking dominion of a piece of land,[13] and in this structure Joshua 18:1 is a central text:[14] 'Then the whole congregation of the people of Israel assembled at Shiloh and set up the tent of meeting there. The land lay subdued before them.' This text brings together two important themes: the subdued land and the setting up of the tent of meeting. It is important to observe in this passage the relationship between rest and the tabernacle. More specifically, the dwelling place of God is set up *after* rest has been achieved. Beale insightfully notes:

> God's rest both at the conclusion of creation in Genesis 1–2 and later in Israel's temple indicates not mere inactivity but that he had demonstrated his sovereignty over the forces of chaos (e.g., enemies of Israel) and now has assumed a position of kingly rest further revealing his sovereign power. Similarly . . . the building of a shrine for divine rest occurs only after the powers of chaos have been defeated.[15]

Thus if the tabernacle is patterned after Eden, signalling another instalment of God's dwelling with his people, then Joshua 18:1 and subsequent fulfilments recall the original Edenic bliss.[16] That is, the setting up of the tent signifies not just the fulfilment of the promise to Israel that God will dwell with them in the land, but also the recovery of the Edenic mission. Israel, then, as God's son, assumes

[11] Waltke with Yu 2007: 525.

[12] Martens (1998: 117) calls them 'degrees' of fulfilment. See also Goldingay 2003: 516; McComiskey 1985: 46–47.

[13] McConville (1993: 101–102) is drawing from a dissertation by H. J. Koorevar (1990). He observes that four leading words signal the basic structure of the book: (1) chs. 1–5 (*'ābar*); (2) chs. 6–11 (*lāqah*); (3) chs. 12–22 (*hālaq*); (4) chs. 23–24 (*'ābad*). For others who have picked up on this work, see Dempster 2003: 126–127; Howard 1998: 358–360.

[14] Dempster 2003: 126–127; Howard 1998: 359.

[15] Beale 2004b: 62.

[16] McKeown 2003: 489.

the role of Adam in exercising dominion over creation in fulfilment of the function of the image of God.[17] Thus this event is a significant fulfilment of God's purposes for his people.

In conclusion, the promises to Abraham respond to the failures of Genesis 1 – 11. Abraham's 'seed' will reign over the earth as God's viceregent, thereby reversing the curse(s) of Genesis 3 and bringing about both a place for God's people and worldwide blessing. The exodus is the means through which God will fulfil his promises to the patriarchs and bring his people into a land to call their own. Deuteronomy and Joshua significantly advance the promise of land and mark how it will be fulfilled. After the wilderness generation, Deuteronomy describes the land as a gift, a new Edenic creation and an inheritance, in which rest will be experienced. Joshua then stands in continuity with Deuteronomy and marks a new beginning that results in conquest, occupation and possession of the land. These results demonstrate further fulfilment of the Abrahamic promises and anticipate a greater fulfilment that will bring Eden-like rest. This fulfilment, therefore, displays a pattern of partial fulfilment, followed by dispossession and subsequent repossession. In other words, God fulfils his promises, but the need for further (re)possession indicates that there was still much work, or obedience, to be done.[18]

David and Solomon: dwelling in the land

A significant advance in God's purpose to plant his people in the land is the arrival of his anointed king, David.[19] Indeed, 'David is seen as the solution to all the problems of Israel's rebellious ways. This can only express an eschatological hope.'[20] In a climactic scene in the book of Samuel after the ark has been brought to Jerusalem, 2 Samuel 7 opens with David in his house enjoying 'rest from all his surrounding enemies'. It is this aspect of the promise 'that provided a key link between the end of the book of Numbers and the time of David'.[21] God's covenant with David involves giving him a great name on an international scale (7:9), appointing a place for his people and securely planting them in it (7:10), and giving him rest from all his enemies

[17] Dempster 2003: 127. See also Goldingay 2003: 512–513.
[18] Dempster (2003: 129) insightfully notes, 'Residence in the land will depend upon obedience, and disobedience will mean expulsion from the land, just as it was in the garden of Eden at the beginning.'
[19] 2 Sam. 7; 1 Chr. 17; cf. Pss 89; 110; 132.
[20] Goldsworthy 2012: 68.
[21] Kaiser 2008: 95; cf. 1973: 135–150.

(7:11). Furthermore, God promises David a future offspring whose kingdom he will establish (7:12–13) and who will be to God a son (7:14). In sum, 'the Davidic covenant contains a total of ten blessings: three fulfilled in David's lifetime, four in the lifetime of his son Solomon, and three in his remote future'.[22] These numerous parallels between the Abrahamic promise and 2 Samuel 7 demonstrate that the Davidic covenant is linked to the Abrahamic covenant in goal and purpose.[23] At this point in Israel's history, then, it appears that God's kingdom is beginning to irrupt centrifugally from the nation of Israel and her land through David and his dynasty.

Furthermore, the exaltation of David as king and the blessing of Israel under his rule marked significant progression in the possession of the land. In fact, for the first time under David, Israel exemplified the people of the Lord living under his lordship in the land.[24] In other words, through David God was continuing to lead his people into the future. For example, 2 Samuel 7:1 echoes the rest God promised to give the second generation (Deut. 12:9–10) and the rest given to Israel under Joshua (21:44; 22:4; 23:1). Moreover, David's final charge to Solomon, like Moses' charge to Joshua to be faithful to Yahweh, reminds the reader that with David there is a return to, as well as a development beyond, the Mosaic era. In fact, David appears in a Joshua-like role and will finally defeat Israel's enemies and give the people rest in the Promised Land. It appears, therefore, that through David's leadership Israel will finally inherit and dwell peacefully in the land.

However, the succeeding narrative blazes an ignoble trail of sin both inside and outside the Davidic house. In David's adultery with Bathsheba, the deceitful and despicable removal of her husband Uriah (2 Sam. 11), and the tumultuous family and national turmoil that ensues (2 Sam. 12 – 20), there is little evidence of the promised divine blessing. Furthermore, David did not have comprehensive rest from his enemies, for he continued to conquer and drive out enemies that remained (2 Sam. 8). Nevertheless, David's desire to build a house for God is monumental because it follows the attainment of rest. In David, still, there is a further advancement and escalation of the fulfilment of the land promises. These promises will find eventual fulfilment in the Davidic dynasty, which Solomon inaugurates. Hence an important question is raised concerning the fulfilment of God's promises after David: Will *šālôm* come with the arrival of *šĕlōmōh* (Solomon)?

[22] Waltke with Yu 2007: 661.
[23] Bock 1999: 181.
[24] Schreiner 2008: 43.

Without question, the succession of Solomon to the throne covers the golden age of Israel, which marked a more comprehensive fulfilment of the territorial promise. To begin, there was a superior quality to Solomon's kingship that provided the kind of rule that God promised would come through the seed of Abraham.[25] Furthermore, multiple promissory threads from the Abrahamic narrative are picked up in Solomon. For example, Solomon's dominion encompassed the boundaries of the land promised to Abraham, and Judah and Israel were as many as the sand by the sea.[26] Dumbrell points out that the Promised Land is secure in Israelite hands, with the very small exceptions of Tyre and Sidon.[27] The prosperity of God's people (1 Kgs 4:20), together with the growth of the kingdom (1 Kgs 4:21), illustrates Solomon's reign as an ideal fulfilment of the very promises to Abraham.[28]

Moreover, in Solomon there is a recovery and advancement of the Adamic commission. When Solomon assumed the throne of his father David, 'his kingdom was firmly established' (1 Kgs 2:12). Solomon possessed superior wisdom, for the Lord gave him 'a wise and discerning mind' according to his request (1 Kgs 3:12). In contrast to Adam, he did not want to know good and evil in order to become like God (Gen. 2:16–17; 3:1–7). Rather, he had a 'proper desire for wisdom, to discern an already existing reality (not to create it) for the purpose of fulfilling the human task of subduing and controlling the creation (Gen 1:26–28)'.[29] In other words, he desired to govern the people of God in order to do justice (1 Kgs 3:9, 16–28). Moreover, the image of vines and fig trees (1 Kgs 4:25) further suggests that Solomon's empire represents a restoration of Eden.[30] Lastly, Solomon acknowledges in his dedication speech that 'Not one word has failed of all his good promise, which he spoke by Moses his servant' (1 Kgs 8:56). Similar to Joshua 21:44–45, then, these fulfilments demonstrate that there was still further advancement of the promises from the time of Joshua to Solomon.

Furthermore, evidence for comprehensive fulfilment of the land promises is seen in Solomon's use of 'rest'. 'Blessed be the LORD who has given rest to his people Israel, according to all that he promised. Not one word has failed of all his good promise, which he spoke by

---

[25] Alexander 2012: 92.
[26] 1 Kgs 4:20–25; cf. Gen. 13:16; 15:5, 18–21; 22:17.
[27] Dumbrell 1994: 75.
[28] De Vries 2004: 72.
[29] Dempster 2003: 147–148.
[30] Harris 2009: 64. See also De Vries 2004; Nelson 1987: 40.

Moses his servant' (1 Kgs 8:56). Under the kingship of the Davidic son, the nation of Israel had achieved rest in the land sworn to the fathers, spoken of through Moses and advanced in Deuteronomy, Joshua and David. David desired to build God a house, purchased the site and built the altar, but Solomon executed the plan and built the temple. Just as the building of the tabernacle involved meticulous detail, so also did the building of the temple (1 Kgs 6:1–38; 7:13–51). But the importance of the temple went beyond the national borders of Israel. Solomon declared that it was designed to be a place where 'all the peoples of the earth may know your name and fear you, as do your people Israel, and that they may know that this house that I have built is called by your name' (1 Kgs 8:43). That is, this temple was to be a conduit of blessing to the entire world (cf. Gen. 12:3).[31]

Finally, the temple was a permanent and visible reminder that the presence of God was in their midst, which demonstrates advancement since Eden.[32] The connection between creation and the temple should not go unnoticed. In fact, Ezekiel explicitly calls Eden the first garden-sanctuary because it is the archetypal temple that will later become central in the life of Israel (28:13–14, 16, 18).[33] The correlation between the land and the temple is important, for the latter is depicted as the dwelling of God 'in a more intensive sense'.[34] Thus the cleansing or defilement of one corresponds to the cleansing or defilement of the other (e.g. Num. 35:33–34). For Solomon, the temple represents a new Eden for the kingdom of God. The subdued land under his reign typifies the incomplete task of Adam to subdue the earth, in Genesis 1 – 3, and the advancement of the Abrahamic promises. Therefore the achievement of the construction of the temple and, consequently, rest, indicate significant advancement of God's promises to dwell with his people in his place.

Life after Solomon: decline and the dispossession of the land

However, troubles soon broke out after the prestige and glory of the reigns of David and Solomon. The narrative immediately moves from the construction and dedication of the temple to Solomon's turning

---

[31] Dempster 2003: 149.
[32] Taylor 2004: 70.
[33] Beale 2004b: 66–80; 2005: 7–12; Alexander 2008: 21–23; 2012: 131–132; Dumbrell 2002: 19–20; Waltke 2001: 57–75; Wenham 1994: 19.
[34] Poythress 1991: 70.

away from the Lord (1 Kgs 11). Moreover, the place where Yahweh had chosen to put his name is no longer part of the story. Hamilton writes:

> Eighteen chapters with no mention of the temple is all the more startling when we realize that the dedication of the temple, with the glory of God filling the temple just as it had done the tabernacle, was the apex of Israel's national prowess. The author takes the reader to the summit of a great mountain at the dedication of the temple, only to drop the reader down the sheer precipice of Israel's plummet into idolatry.[35]

To be sure, the history of the monarchy in Israel had some high points, but on the whole it was short-lived.

In sum, the picture of Solomon that the book of Kings provides is of an Adam-like figure who on the one hand typifies a restoration to Edenic conditions, while on the other hand being responsible, through his disobedience, for the second expulsion from the sanctuary-land and the end of the monarchy. The subsequent chapters of Kings demonstrate 'echoes of exodus', for stunning victory is followed by the idolatrous act of setting up golden calves (1 Kgs 12:25–33).[36] It appears, then, that the path was paved for one of the most traumatic events in Israel's long history.

The death of Solomon and the effects of his disastrous sin eventually lead to the rupture of the kingdom into two parts. In narrative terms, the move from unity to division takes all of one chapter (1 Kgs 12:16–20). Christopher Wright states, 'In the centuries after Solomon the land becomes the focus of constant struggle between the forces of dispossession, greed, exploitation and land-grabbing on the one hand, and the protest of the prophets on the other.'[37]

As the rest of Kings narrates, Israel repeatedly disobeys Yahweh's commands and as a whole is characterized by covenant failure. Furthermore, just as the nation is characterized by unrighteousness, so also the majority of her kings, with few exceptions, show themselves to be covenant-breakers. The focus of these books, therefore, 'shifts from the glories of David and Solomon to the free fall into depravity orchestrated by their progeny'.[38] This vexing problem is what makes the writings of the prophets so important in the fulfilment of God's promises.

[35] J. M. Hamilton 2005: 178.
[36] Dempster 2003: 148.
[37] C. J. H. Wright 2004: 81.
[38] Lister 2010: 238.

Chapter Six

Fulfilling the promise?
Exile and the prophets of
an eschatological hope

The Pentateuch makes clear that the land is the place of covenantal blessing but also provides the potential place of judgment. The latter prophets proclaim the word of Yahweh in the context of the covenant, clearly defined by Deuteronomy, and Israel's disobedience brings to a conclusion the covenantal curses (e.g. Lev. 26; Deut. 28:15–68).[1] Dempster writes, 'The Latter Prophets provide commentary on the grand narrative from creation to exile, showing the just judgment and gracious mercy of God.'[2] Israel – like Adam – lived in Yahweh's place as priest-kings to serve and worship him, yet failed to obey his commands and forfeited their covenantal blessings. Thus the exile marks Yahweh's judgment upon the great sinfulness of both Israel and Judah, against which he had repeatedly warned through his servants the prophets.[3]

Furthermore, the writing prophets mark an epochal onward movement in Old Testament revelation, offering both sobering commentary on Israel's present status and promise of their glorious future.[4] The era of David and Solomon provided a conceptual model for the prophets who predicted the messianic kingdom, but this eschatological kingdom is cast in even more glorious terms. VanGemeren notes:

> On the one hand, the era of the divided kingdom brings to a climax the history of Israel's rebelliousness in the final judgment of God: the exile. On the other hand, this period raises a new hope, focused on God's promises to the prophets. In an era of restoration he will establish his kingdom with a new people, ruled permanently by a Davidic King and richly blessed and restored by the Spirit of God.[5]

[1] McConville 2001: 12.
[2] Dempster 2003: 191.
[3] VanGemeren 1988: 242.
[4] Vos 2004: 185.
[5] VanGemeren 1988: 243.

The prophets, then, offer hope for the future (re)establishment of God's kingdom.

But the promise of restoration goes far beyond what was previously experienced and is described in astonishing realities, for it includes not only the nation of Israel but also the nations, and not only the boundaries of the Promised Land but also the entire earth. The universality stressed in the latter prophets revives the consciousness of the worldwide significance of the Abrahamic promises. As a result, Beale views the prophetic expansion of both Israel's land and God's people as indicators that the words of the prophets have been refracted through the Abrahamic promises.[6] Moreover, 'the prophetic vision of restoration merges king and shepherd images in the Davidic covenant with the promise of international blessing in the Abrahamic covenant'.[7] The robust hope of the prophets, then, advances the covenant promises that extend to something far greater and more extensive than the land of Israel, geographically speaking.

This chapter will present the unified witness and variegated purpose of the prophets.[8] This witness and this purpose are seen through a recurring pattern in the prophetic corpus as a whole – specifically, the latter prophets – as well as within each prophetic book.[9] More specifically, the writing prophets proclaim how Israel had broken the covenant, call her to repentance and pronounce judgment on her as a result of her covenant-breaking and failure to repent, the outcome of which is exile.[10] But in God's word is hope. Rather than a dismal ending, God promises through the prophets restoration to the land that includes both national and international results. This eschatological resolution will be accomplished by the work of the future Messiah, the Davidic king who comes as the Servant of the Lord, whose death will inaugurate

---

[6] Beale 2011: 751, 753.

[7] Pate et al. 2004: 96.

[8] Given the amount of prophetic literature, the following survey will primarily focus on synthesizing the three major prophets – Isaiah, Jeremiah and Ezekiel – though support from the Twelve will be given. Furthermore, more space will be devoted to Isaiah, since, according to Oswalt (1998: 3), 'Of all the books in the OT, Isaiah is perhaps the richest. Its literary grandeur is unequaled. Its scope is unparalleled. The breadth of its view of God is unmatched. In so many ways it is a book of superlatives. Thus it is no wonder that Isaiah is the most quoted prophet in the NT, and along with Psalms and Deuteronomy, one of the most frequently cited of all OT books.'

[9] McConville 2005: 629. In addition to this broad structure, it is also the case that these themes are repeated in sequential order within many of the prophetic books.

[10] Pate et al. (2004: 93), who cite three major types of indictments against Israel: idolatry, social injustice and religious ritualism.

a new covenant and usher in the age of the Spirit, extend his kingdom to the ends of the earth and finally bring about a new creation.

Disobedience and the judgment of exile

Although the exile occurs relatively late in Israel's history, the theological concept is experientially present from the beginning. For example, Adam and Eve's expulsion from the land is the archetype of all subsequent exile (Gen. 3:17–19, 24), and Abraham (Gen. 23:4; cf. Heb. 11:8–10), Jacob (Gen. 31), Joseph and his family (Gen. 39 to Exod. 1) and the wilderness generation (Num. 14) all knew the pain of living away from their homeland.[11] However, none of these examples compared in magnitude to the devastation and loss that occurred when the northern and southern kingdoms went into exile. For this reason, the prophets shared a common prophetic message, though the message is far from uniform.

Throughout Isaiah, and the prophets as a whole, judgment for Israel's sin is a prevalent theme. Judgment takes many forms: natural disaster (24:4–5), military defeat (5:26–30) or disease (1:5–6). But all of these are from the hand of God (43:27–28).[12] Isaiah opens by criticizing and rebuking the nation for their rebellion so that they might return to live under his word. Yahweh, the Creator, calls heaven and earth as witnesses of Israel's covenant-breaking (1:2). There is a scandal to be proclaimed to the entire world, and this scandal is Israel's flagrant sin against the Holy One. But instead of mirroring to the community and world the character of Yahweh in social justice, Israel is characterized by social injustice. One thing is certain: obedience is necessary in order to enjoy God's blessing in the land (Isa. 1:19). The problem, however, is that they have forsaken the Lord and have become foolish (1:3–4; 5:1–30).[13] Dempster writes:

---

[11] Duguid 2000: 475.

[12] Oswalt 1986: 40.

[13] Hosea and Amos, contemporaries of Isaiah, provide commentary on a similar situation as they focus attention on the northern kingdom. In chs. 4–14, Hosea paints a prophetic picture full of doom and hope. McComiskey (1992: 57) comments, 'The catalog of sins is imposing. Oath-taking was false and insincere, people made sworn oaths they did not intend to keep; the society was rampant with killing and theft; adultery was practiced extensively; eruptions of violence took lives with startling frequency. . . . No wonder God has a controversy with this people!' Similarly, Amos, after pronouncing judgment on Israel's neighbours (including Judah) with strategic and rhetorical geographical precision, then sets his sights on Israel. As C. J. H. Wright (1984: 123) says, the effect is 'to throw a kind of geographical noose around Israel and thus to make the climactic accusation against her even more devastatingly powerful'.

The echoes of Deuteronomy are loud and clear. Heaven and earth were called as witnesses to the covenant that was made with Israel (Deut 30:19; 31:28). Moreover, disobedient children were to be disciplined, punished and, if need be, executed if they persisted in rebellion against parental authority (Deut 21:18–21). The pain of Yahweh is profound. He has raised children who do not even acknowledge him anymore, having sunk *beneath* the level of a beast. The text proceeds to describe their immorality – 'a sinful nation, loaded down with guilt, corrupt children with corrupt parents' (Isa 1:4). Their father has tried everything, disciplining them until they have become black and blue, and asking them in frustration, 'Why will you be punished again? Why do you keep on rebelling?' (Isa 1:5). Then the national disaster of an Assyrian invasion is described, in which a remnant living in Jerusalem was spared 'like a hut in a cucumber field' (Isa 1:8). God in mercy did not exercise the death sentence. If he had not spared a remnant, 'we would have been like Sodom and Gomorrah' (Isa 1:9).[14]

Clearly, they have become God's disobedient son. Furthermore, chapters 13–27 demonstrate God's rule over all the nations – when his 'day' comes and he will exert his rule over both heaven and earth – but at the centre of all his operations lies his compassion for his own people. Later texts speak already from the situation of the ruined and forsaken land that is anticipated at the beginning (e.g. 49:17). Therefore, because of their disobedience, sin must be judged.[15] And indeed it will be, for the land will be filled with woe, and the chosen people will be exiled at the hands of a fierce, unsparing foe (5:8–30).[16] Whereas in Isaiah 1:8 the vineyard was associated with the Lord's preservation of a remnant of Zion, now the vineyard is the place where the Lord asks if there is anything more he could have done. Consequently, Isaiah cries out, 'How long, O Lord?' (6:11). John Oswalt comments, 'The answer to his cry is not comforting. There will be no reprieve for Judah. God's justice will be carried out to its full extent until the land is empty. So the prophecies of Deuteronomy would come to fulfilment (Deut. 28:21, 63; 29:28).'[17] The coming desolation appeared certain.

---

[14] Dempster 2003: 172–173; emphasis original.
[15] Isa. 1:15–16, 19–20; 2:5–9; 3:8–9; 5:7; 1:5–6, 24–25; 2:10–11; 3:11; 5:29–30.
[16] House 1998: 277.
[17] Oswalt 1998: 190.

Moving forward, both Jeremiah and Ezekiel are full of condemnation for the virtual apostasy of Israel that has led to their desolation. Rendtorff notes, 'Especially in Jeremiah and Ezekiel, contemporaries of the fall of the kingdom of Judah, the end of the undisturbed life in the land is one of the dominant themes.'[18] Jeremiah offers a glimpse into the most volatile time for Jerusalem, Judah and the surrounding nations. He proclaims the word of the Lord to the people concerning their past failures, which result in utter disaster.[19] They have abandoned the bountiful life-giving blessings of their covenant Lord and instead have gone after things that do not satisfy (2:13). Just as Israel had sinned against Yahweh and was punished, so also Jeremiah named Judah's sin for what it was – covenant treason and failure to know God (11:1–8; 4:22). Citing Deuteronomy, the Lord proclaimed a curse on those who did not 'hear the words of this covenant' (Jer. 11:3; cf. Deut. 27:26; 28:15).[20] Therefore Judah was in danger of following in the footsteps of her sister and suffering her same fate.

Ezekiel, from an exilic perspective, is called to proclaim God's message to the rebellious people of Israel: both the segment that had already been carried away into Babylonian exile and the survivors who still remained in Jerusalem (2:1 – 3:11). In two graphic pictures, Ezekiel 16 and 23 portray Israel as an abandoned girl whom the Lord found in an open field, compassionately cleansed and purified, and brought into covenant with himself (16:4–14). Yet she rejected the covenant care and provision of her Lord and entered into adulterous religious practices (16:15–34; 23:1–21), thus proving that she is no better than the pagan nations. Likewise, Judah is no better than her older sister Samaria and her younger sister Sodom (16:46). In fact, she is worse (16:47–52). She has become an object of reproach to all those around her (16:57). This powerful and tragic picture describes the pollution that precipitates Yahweh's judgment. As a result, God abandons the temple in Jerusalem (10:1–22), the land is defiled (6:1 – 7:27) and his glorious presence departs (11:22–25).

The latter prophets repeatedly demonstrate that God's punishment for Israel's disobedience to the covenant – and, more importantly, her covenant Lord – is exile and loss of land. This does not, however,

---

[18] Rendtorff 2005: 467–468.

[19] Jer. 2:1 – 3:5; 5:20–31.

[20] J. A. Thompson (1980: 343) argues that 'this covenant' refers to the Mosaic covenant, not the Josianic covenant, 'which was so prominent in the minds of Jeremiah's hearers', for 'the pronoun "*this*" points forward to vv. 4–5, which deal with the Sinaitic covenant at the beginning of Israel's history' (emphasis original).

negate the prophets' call to repentance.[21] Nevertheless, neither Israel nor Judah as a whole repented, and the prophets acknowledge their obstinacy and proclaim the certain judgment of exile away from the land and away from Yahweh's presence. Perhaps none saw, expressed and lamented this land loss more than Jeremiah, the poet of the land par excellence.[22] VanGemeren writes:

> Jeremiah loved God's people and wanted to intercede for them (14:7, 20), but his was a mission of death. He had to speak of starvation, death, exile, and alienation. The prophet could not escape experiencing the pangs of exile before it happened . . . Jeremiah's loneliness was heightened by the prohibition against marriage (16:2–4).[23]

Although he announced the same message of doom as his prophetic predecessors, he identified with his message and with his people in a more personal way than any other prophet.[24] In the prediction and experience of exile, then, the promises of Israel's and Judah's past hope and election are called into question by the prophets' certain message of inevitable judgment.[25]

As a result, the period of the exile was the most traumatic in the nation's history. There were various reactions among those who went into exile. Some prospered materially, adapted and assimilated themselves to their new environment, and even intermarried and lost their covenant identity. Others repented and were devoted to the Lord, and, even though they were away from the land and the temple, they drew near to the Lord and remembered his promises. God's judgment, then, did not necessarily imply his total absence. However, the grief of exile was profound and is reflected in certain psalms such as Psalm 137, where every line is alive with pain and the people could only weep for Jerusalem when their captors taunted them to sing the songs of Zion.[26]

If the glorious part of Israel's history is her reception of the land, the tragedy is that this gift was forfeited.[27] In Israel's history, then,

[21] See e.g. Isa. 1:16–17; Jer. 7:3; 18:11; 26:3; 35:15; Ezek. 2 – 3; 14:6; 18:30–32; cf. Amos 5:1–17; Zech. 3:1–4.
[22] Brueggemann 1977: 107.
[23] VanGemeren 1990: 295.
[24] Anderson 1986: 392.
[25] Von Rad 1965: 103.
[26] Kidner 1973: 459; see also Ross 1997: 598.
[27] Martens 1998: 231.

just as the exodus served as the paradigmatic event of redemption, so the exile represented the paradigmatic event of judgment. But rather than moving the nation's experience of redemption forward, expulsion from the land appeared to call into question all the gains made up to this point. At this point in the story, it appears that the end of Israel in the land had come. Bartholomew and Goheen write:

> For the Israelites being marched off as slaves to Babylon, it certainly must seem like the end. What has come of God's great promises to Abraham, of his covenant with Israel at Sinai, of his vow that David's house would go on forever? The house of the Lord himself has been destroyed! Where was the Lord while Babylon triumphed over Israel? Have God's purposes for his family run into the sand. Worse, have God's purposes to redeem the creation through Israel failed?[28]

So it seemed that Israel has walked the path of the promise of land, through its fulfilment, and on to its loss.[29]

The eschatological hope of the prophets

Nevertheless, God's last word is not judgment. Throughout the prophetic message, comfort and hope often emerge even in the midst of discipline. Routledge notes, 'The theme of the prophetic books is the death and rebirth of Israel: death, in the form of defeat and exile; rebirth in the return from exile, resettlement in the land and the recovery of Israel's status as a nation.'[30] In fact, 'Of the sixteen canonical writing prophets, ten (Amos, Hosea, Isaiah, Micah, Zephaniah, Jeremiah, Ezekiel, Obadiah, Zechariah, Joel) write about a future restoration of Israel.'[31] This message transforms judgment into hope. As a result, judgment and salvation are the two great poles between which the prophetic proclamation moves.[32] Amazingly, God not only promises to restore the faithful exiles (Jer. 24:1–10; 29:10–14; Ezek. 36:8–15; Isa. 40), but will also be a 'scaled-down sanctuary' for them in the midst of it (Ezek. 11:16). Indeed, the exile was God's

---

[28] Bartholomew and Goheen 2004: 104.
[29] Rendtorff 2005: 467.
[30] Routledge 2008: 266.
[31] Saucy 1993: 223, n. 6.
[32] Rendtorff 2005: 662; see also Davies 1974: 39; Bartholomew 2011: 82. For a proposal that explains the logical relationship between these two themes, see J. M. Hamilton 2010.

fatherly process of saving a remnant for himself who would inherit the promises.[33] Thus a thread of hope remained.

The ground of this hope is God and his gracious promises that look back to Eden, Abraham and David. According to Richard Schultz, the

> prophetic depictions of the future are richly intertextual in nature and warrant close textual comparisons, while offering a further illustration of the integral relationship and striking continuity between the Torah, the Former Prophets, the Latter Prophets, and the New Testament.[34]

As a result, God will crush the enemy through the seed of the woman and bring about the covenant promises of land, seed and international blessing. Moreover, God will bring these blessings through a Davidic son who will accomplish a greater exodus for his people. To be sure, just as God has fulfilled his promise in the past, so he will do in the future also. These themes resound throughout the prophets.

To begin, if Isaiah opens by confronting the sinful nation, within this same context of judgment a glorious future is also predicted. Dempster notes, 'Juxtaposed to such bleak images of land and people is the temple mount, which grows to be the highest mountain, dominating the landscape of not only Israel but the world (2:1–5). Zion has become Everest.'[35] From beginning to end, this alternation of motifs throughout Isaiah presents a glorious vision of a return

---

[33] VanGemeren 1988: 299. See e.g. Isa. 1:9; 11:10–12, 16; 46:3–4; Jer. 23:1–4; 31:7–8; Joel 2:32; Mic. 2:12; 4:6–7; Zech. 8:11–13.

[34] Schultz 2012: 354. Beale (2012a: 39–40) notes, '[Intertextuality's] original meaning and its ongoing typical definition is the synchronic study of multiple linkages among texts that are not the result of authorial intent but are considered often only from the readers' viewpoint. Accordingly, intertextuality associates at least two texts (and their contexts), which creates a new context in which to understand a text (often the earlier text); this also means that texts are open to the influence of past texts and to the contexts of present readers. According to many, intertextuality entails that the reader and the reader's new context are what give the most meaning to these linkages. . . . In biblical studies, "intertextuality" is sometimes used to refer to the procedure by which a later biblical text refers to an earlier text, how that earlier text enhances the meaning of the later one, and how the later one creatively develops the earlier meaning. In this respect, "intertextuality" may be seen as a procedure of inner-biblical or intrabiblical exegesis, which is crucial to doing biblical theology and for understanding the relation of the OT to the NT. . . . Therefore it may be better to use the phrase "inner-biblical exegesis" or "inner-biblical allusion" instead of "intertextuality," since the former two nomen-clatures are less likely to be confused with postmodern reader-oriented approaches to interpretation, where the term "intertextuality" had its origin.' See also Kevin Vanhoozer 1998.

[35] Dempster 2003: 173.

presented in terms of a restored and renewed city. Barry Webb observes:

> The vision of the book moves, in fact, from the historical Jerusalem of the eighth century (under judgment) to the new Jerusalem of the eschaton, which is the center of the new cosmos and symbol of the new age. To this new Jerusalem the nations come (66:18–21; cf. 60:1–22) so that ultimately the nations find their salvation in Zion.[36]

But crucial to Isaiah's vision is the *development* within the book concerning this transformation.[37]

Isaiah's prophecy describes Israel's return from exile in both imminent and distant ways, and in language reminiscent of the exodus. This return will result in an ideal community established under messianic leadership, followed by a transformed new age brought about by a greater exodus.[38] The first return from exile is a physical release and return to the land (42:18 – 43:21) that will be accomplished by Cyrus, who will permit enslaved Israel to return to their homeland (44:24 – 45:1; cf. Ezra 1:1–3). This restoration was a sign of God's faithfulness to his promise. But this (partial) fulfilment of God's promised restoration in no way compares to the prophets' final vision, for the returning remnant was far from the holiness that the Lord promised would come with the age of the Spirit. VanGemeren notes, 'they did not give freely to the priests but kept for themselves whatever they could; they failed to give the best sacrifices to the Lord (Hag 1; Mal 1). Even the priests were not fully devoted to the Lord, for they did not teach the full implications of the law (Mal 2:1–9).'[39] The announcements of return, then, suggest developments on a larger scale than represented by the diminutive community in Jerusalem.

A deeper captivity kept Israel from being fully restored. Oswalt comments, 'as deliverance from physical bondage demanded the servant Cyrus, so deliverance from spiritual bondage calls for the Servant, One who will be what Israel is not, so that she may have the possibility of becoming what she is to be'.[40] To put it another way, though the people are taken out of Babylon, Babylon needs to be taken out of

[36] Webb 1990: 71.
[37] Gentry and Wellum 2012: 468.
[38] Isa. 11:1–16; 35:1–10; 51:9–11; 52:11–12.
[39] VanGemeren 1988: 305.
[40] Oswalt 1998: 59.

the people.[41] Just as Isaiah's reference to Babylon 'goes beyond the historical empire as a symbol of the epitome of collective human glory and pride in opposition to the purposes of God',[42] so also Isaiah's reference to Israel's glorious restoration extends beyond the nation and includes an international community. In other words, the restoration involves the remnant and the nations: all who trust in Yahweh and his promises of salvation. Therefore a subsequent – and greater – return will be when they are fully and finally forgiven for their sins (43:22 – 44:23). This deliverance will be accomplished by God's Servant-King, who will bring back Israel so that God's salvation may reach the nations (49:1 – 53:12).[43] That is, forgiveness will come through Yahweh's (individual) Servant who will deliver his (corporate) servant Israel (42:1–9; 49:1–6), suffer with his people (7:14–17), redeem his people (9:2–7), rule over his people (11:1–5), and atone for sin by suffering, dying and taking upon himself the punishment they deserve (42:1–9; 49:5–6; 50:4–9; 52:13 – 53:12).[44] The status of the Servant is of such a nature that neither corporate Israel nor any mere human representative can perform such a task. Moreover, Oswalt rightly notes that the Lord's 'task of restoring Israel to himself is not a large enough task for the Servant. He is of such a nature, calling and preparation that he should be given a larger task: saving the world!'[45] Indeed, this one is Yahweh's Servant par excellence.

The Servant's substitutionary atonement will, in effect, initiate a new covenant (55:1–5) that offers waters of life and enjoyment of the blessings of both the Abrahamic and Davidic covenants for Israel *and* the nations (54:1 – 55:13; cf. 19:19–25).[46] Such an international programme was the intention of God all along.[47] Moreover, by means of the Servant in Isaiah 52:13 – 53:12 whose substitutionary offering for sin and whose resurrection enable him to bring to fulfilment the

[41] Gentry and Wellum 2012: 437–438.

[42] Saucy 1993: 224.

[43] The sequence of redemption is important, for it marks the fulfilment of the Abrahamic promise that through Israel the nations will be blessed (Gen. 12:1–3).

[44] Oswalt 1998: 41.

[45] Ibid. 293.

[46] Zechariah buttresses these themes when he discloses a sanctifying fountain opened for the house of David and the inhabitants of Jerusalem. This Davidic king shall speak peace to the nations, rule from sea to sea and from the river Euphrates to the ends of the earth, and bring reconciliation to God and his people, which includes the nations (Zech. 9 – 14; cf. 2:10–12; 8:20–23), through his death.

[47] The result that 'your offspring will possess the nations' (Isa. 54:3) appears to advance the promise to Abraham that his 'offspring shall possess the gate of his enemies' (Gen. 22:17).

promises of Yahweh in the Davidic covenant, a Davidic king will bless and rule the nations because Yahweh has made him leader and commander of the peoples (55:4–5).[48] This work, then, is the basis for the new covenant. As a result, not only is the remnant called the Lord's servants (Isa. 54:17; cf. 65:13–25), but so also are foreigners (Isa. 56:6).[49]

That is, though the new covenant is directed towards Israel, Gentiles will be included.[50] Likewise, Amos anticipates the coming of a Davidic king who will

> raise up
>   the booth of David that is fallen
> and repair its breaches,
>   and raise up its ruins
>   and rebuild it as in the days of old,
> that they may possess the remnant of Edom
>   and all the nations who are called by my name.
>   (Amos 9:11–12)

Astonishingly, this restoration and rebuilding will not be limited to the divided kingdom of Israel, but will extend to the Gentiles (cf. Acts 15:15–17). Finally, in fulfilment of the Abrahamic covenant, the Lord will give his *name* and *blessing* to his servants in the land.[51] The result of the Servant's saving work, then, creates *servants.*[52] And all – Israel as well as foreigners and eunuchs[53] – will go to Jerusalem, God's holy mountain, in a pilgrimage of worship (Isa. 2:2–4; 27:13; cf. Mic. 4:1–5).

But Isaiah does not stop with the emergence of a Davidic king who ushers in a new age. Instead, Isaiah proceeds to describe the result of this new covenant age and the glories awaiting the Lord's servants. Isaiah 65:17 – 66:24 is a cumulative summation of the eschatological themes that occur throughout Isaiah and enlarges the hope of restoration to the city of Jerusalem and the land in otherworldly language that describes astounding realities.[54] Motyer comments:

---

[48] Gentry 2007: 294.
[49] Gentry and Wellum 2012: 465.
[50] Ware 1992: 73.
[51] Isa. 65:13–16; cf. Gen. 12:3; 17:5; 22:18; 26:4.
[52] Motyer 1993: 451.
[53] Isa. 56:3–5; contrast with Deut. 23:1.
[54] Isa. 2:1–4; 4:2–6; 9:1–16; 11:1–10.

Like all visionaries Isaiah largely furnished the future from the present. But his development of the 'city' theme shows that he was consciously thinking beyond the geographical Zion/Jerusalem to the ideal it embodied. Thus, for example, in 11:6–9 the Lord's 'holy mountain' has become the whole redeemed creation; also in 65:17–18 the easy way the prophet moves from the 'new earth' to the newly created Jerusalem speaks to the same point. In the Bible the 'city' began (Gen 11:4) as humankind's attempt to achieve its own salvation without reference to God, and when Isaiah looks forward to the End, he sees the fall of the 'city' humankind has built (24:1–10), Babel on a worldwide scale. . . . In a word, Isaiah's vision is of the Mount Zion to which the redeemed have already come (Heb 12:22) and which is also yet to be revealed from heaven (Rev 21:2).[55]

These eschatological themes have appeared throughout Isaiah. In fact, 'the "container" of this earlier prophecy (11:1–10) is exploded in superabundance'.[56] What is new, however, is the joining of these earlier prophecies into one consummate vision. This vision provides an interpretation of the earlier prophecies as part of the one eschatological goal: the creation of a new heaven and new earth.

When the various strands are drawn together, Isaiah's vision of final restoration involves new heavens and a new earth (65:17; 66:22), a new Jerusalem (65:18–19; cf. 4:2–6) and a holy mountain, Zion (65:25; cf. 2:1–4; 4:2–6). Moreover, in fulfilment of the promises to and covenant with Abraham, God will give them a new *name* and they will receive *blessing* in the *land* by the God of truth (Isa. 65:15–16). Finally, this new creation city-mountain calls to mind Eden, 'the holy mountain of God' (Ezek. 28:13–14), where his people lived in his presence and under his lordship. By the end of Isaiah, then, this temple-mountain-city is coextensive with the new heaven and new earth.[57] They are one and the same.[58] The final vision resounds with astonishing realities cast in terms of God's kingdom coming to and filling the earth. Thus God will save his people through the work of the Servant-King and make the place where they will live. The order is crucial, for it is reversed from that in the old creation. In the old creation, God first created the place and then created and put his

---

[55] Motyer 1999: 27.
[56] Dempster 2003: 181.
[57] Gentry and Wellum 2012: 468.
[58] Alexander 2008: 54.

people there to live. In the new creation, however, God first makes his people and then will make the new creation where they will live.[59]

Complementary pictures of a hopeful restoration to the land emerge in Jeremiah and Ezekiel. Though Jeremiah announces that Israel has become God's stubborn and rebellious son (3:19, 22; 5:23; cf. Deut. 21:18, 20) and, as a result, will be uprooted from the land (4:23–26; 24), there is still hope for a renewed people in a renewed place.[60] Yahweh promises to take back his people – but only if they repent – and if they return to him:

> then nations shall bless themselves in him,
> and in him shall they glory.
>
> (4:2)

The reference to the nations blessing themselves in him indicates that the promises to Abraham will be realized if Israel repents and glorifies Yahweh.[61] Like Isaiah, then, the nations are in view in the restoration of Israel and Judah, and this cosmological and teleological goal is in fulfilment of the Abrahamic promises.[62] Furthermore, Jeremiah proclaims that Israel will return from exile in terms of a new exodus (16:14–15). In fact, this exodus will be so great that the former exodus will no longer be spoken of.

[59] Gentry and Wellum 2012: 467–468. See also Bartholomew 2007: 173–195.

[60] J. A. Thompson (1980: 112–113) lists several significant passages that indicate Jeremiah's hopeful views: 'When [Jeremiah] purchased the field of his cousin Hanamel in Anathoth, with the Babylonians already overrunning the land having only recently lifted the siege of Jerusalem and with every prospect of renewing it, he wanted to demonstrate his faith in Yahweh's plans for future restoration. "Thus says Yahweh of hosts the God of Israel: Houses and fields and vineyards shall again be bought in this land" (32:15). Again, his letter to the exiles in Babylon (ch. 29) contains a promise that when seventy years had been completed Yahweh would visit his people and bring them back to their land and restore their fortunes. Part of that vision saw Israel seeking Yahweh with all their heart (29:10–14). Other passages appear in 31:2–6, 15–22, both of which seem to have been directed to Northern Israel, possibly from the early years of Jeremiah's career. These views breathe a spirit of hope.' He also lists other passages where hope for the future is expressed, though some are disputed by scholars (cf. 3:15–16; 4:9–10; 12:14–17; 16:14–15; 23:3–4, 7–8; 30:8–11, 16–24; 31:1, 7–14, 23–28, 35–40; 33:6–26).

[61] J. M. Hamilton 2010: 215.

[62] Also see Jer. 12:14–17, which speaks of an exile, not just for Judah but also for God's evil neighbours, 'who touch the heritage that I have given my people Israel to inherit' (v. 14). Astonishingly, writes Gentry and Wellum (2012: 488), 'according to verse 15, *each land* and *people* will have a return from exile. And when all the exiles are brought home, if the nations learn from Israel to swear by the God of Israel, then they will be "built up" or established in the midst of the restored Israel. If they do not, each will be permanently eradicated as a nation' (emphases original).

Then, in Jeremiah 30 – 33, Jeremiah unfolds the great promises of salvation and offers hope beyond the exile that will come in the form of a new covenant and return to the land. Of particular importance is 31:38–40, which concerns the rebuilding and expansion of Jerusalem. In addition to the restoration of Davidic leadership (30:8–11), priest-hood (31:14) and people (31:31–34), the restoration of the city brings to completion the glorious reversal of Jeremiah's pronouncements of judgment. Though the city has been destroyed, the future age of redemption will see its restoration – *and more*. Derek Kidner comments:

> In [31:38–40] the promise is 'earthed' not merely in this planet but in the familiar details of Israel's capital, naming rubbish dumps and all. . . . As for these details, the prophecy is again using the known and the near to project an image of the ultimate. The city would indeed be rebuilt, and we read in Nehemiah 3:1 of the tower of Hananel as situated near the starting-point of that operation, as Nehemiah's account works its way westward from the northeast corner, turning south at presumably the Corner Gate, eventually to come northwards up the east side, via the Horse Gate (Neh. 3:28) to complete the circuit. But the vision outruns that exercise, in scale and in significance. *The measuring line shall go out farther* (39), not turning at the Corner Gate; and the places that were once unclean *shall be sacred to the Lord* (40). Added to these things, the promise that the city would never again be overthrown (40c) is a further sign that we must look beyond 'the present Jerusalem' to 'the Jerusalem above' (Gal. 4:25–26): the great company of saints and angels which is already our home city, as seen in, e.g., Hebrews 12:22–24; Revelation 21:1–22:5.[63]

The new Jerusalem, then, will be both different and expanded from the old, and the rebuilt city will become the centre of God's presence among his people (3:14–18; cf. Isa. 65:17; 66:12; Rev. 21:3).[64]

Like Isaiah and Ezekiel, Jeremiah describes the restoration of both people and place in the future and pins these hopes on a Davidic leader, a righteous branch, who, interestingly, in Jeremiah is a com-bination of both king and priest.[65] This King-Priest will secure a new covenant for his people as certain as Yahweh's covenant with day and night, make the people dwell securely in the land and multiply the

---

[63] Kidner 1987: 111; emphases original.
[64] Huey 1993: 288–289.
[65] Jer. 33:14–18; cf. Isa. 9:6–7; 11:1–10; 53:1–3.

offspring of David to be as numerous as the immeasurable sands of the sea in fulfilment of his covenant with Abraham (33:14–26).[66] Moreover, Jeremiah 31:35–40 indicates that the new covenant age will operate within the contours of a new creation, as Isaiah and Ezekiel also make clear. Accordingly, Jeremiah looks forward to an idealized return to an expanded land.

However, subsequent history proved differently. The post-exilic return to the land failed to live up to its promise. Yet it marks the inauguration of God's eschatological programme. When would Yahweh 'build and plant' his people in the land?[67] Jeremiah describes the return in eschatological language of the 'latter days', but also describes Israel as having to spend seventy years in exile before Yahweh will rebuild and replant them in the land (29:10; cf. 25:11–12). Dempster rightly notes:

> While not giving a precise timeline for the working out of all the individual details of the future complex of eschatological events, the expression 'seventy years' is certainly important. The end of exile would be the sign that building and planting would begin.[68]

This return from exile – aimed at Israel and Judah – will also include the nations who 'shall be built up in the midst of my people' (Jer. 12:16), and they shall dwell securely in the new Jerusalem whose borders encompass the land.

[66] P. R. Williamson (2007: 74) argues that this passage refers to the covenant with Noah rather than creation, when he writes, 'While some scholars have pointed to Jeremiah 33:20–26 for further support [that Jer. 31:35–37 refers to Gen. 1 – 2], the references here to a covenant with inanimate created things seem to allude more to dimensions of the Noahic covenant reflected in Genesis 8:22–9:13 (esp. Gen. 8:22) than to an implicit "covenant with creation" in Genesis 1–3. Admittedly, the somewhat similar analogy drawn in Jeremiah 31:35–37 may indeed allude to the fixed order established at creation, although this appears to build an argument from silence.' In response to Williamson, however, given that Gen. 1:14–16 establishes the fixed order at creation, it seems more natural not to restrict the reference to Gen. 8:22 – 9:13 (esp. Gen. 8:22) only. Moreover, if one accepts a covenant relationship with/at creation that is reaffirmed and upheld in Gen. 6 – 9, then it further confirms the reference to creation in Gen. 1 – 3.

[67] According to Martens (1998: 302), the terms 'build' and 'plant' (e.g. Jer. 24:6) are 'theologically colored', for they 'attempt to present salvation history in picturesque language and to capture the familiar tones of Yahweh's saving acts. One should add more specifically the expression deals with land.' The final appearance of these verbs in the prophets is found in Amos 9:11–15, which focuses on both people and place. God is going to rebuild his people, making a new humanity that includes the nations, and plant it in a new creation.

[68] Dempster 2003: 167.

Finally, Ezekiel contains glorious prophecies of restoration. Alongside hopes of ingathering are prophecies that the renewed people will be purified in heart and spirit, and they will be one flock under a new David (34 – 37).[69] As a result, 'the nations will know that I am the LORD who sanctifies Israel, when my sanctuary is in their midst forevermore' (37:28). Whereas Yahweh had been a sanctuary to the exiles 'for a while' (11:16), his presence will be with them for ever. Thus Yahweh's sanctuary in the midst of his covenant people will finally convince the nations of his sanctifying power.

Furthermore, the divided kingdoms of Israel and Judah will return from exile through a new exodus and be joined once again as one people (36:24–38; cf. 37:15–23). God will make a new covenant (36:16–38), which will deal with their sin and finally fulfil his covenant so that he can say, 'They shall be my people, and I will be their God' (37:23; cf. v. 27). In order for this restoration to come, however, Yahweh must create a holy people from nothing. And that he will do by bringing life from the dead. Indeed, Ezekiel resurrects (new) creation language to illustrate vividly that new life will come to Israel from their deathlike existence in exile. In other words, their restoration to the land is related to their resurrection from the dead. The dead will be brought to life so that they too may participate in the restoration. But Ezekiel's vision of restoration does not stop with Israel, for other nations are included in Yahweh's everlasting covenant (16:59–63). Gentry notes:

Careful readers will draw the conclusion from what has preceded in Ezekiel 16 that the renewed Israel is no longer based on ethnic parameters, but defined by those who are reconciled to the Lord and believing in him: 'Jerusalem will be given both Samaria and Sodom,

---

[69] On this point Dempster (ibid. 170–172) notes, 'Even the divided kingdom of exiles is reunited under a new leader, who is said to be "my servant David" (37:24–25; cf. 34:23–24). But he is also described as one who will come to power through relative obscurity. In a remarkable allegorical passage, a Davidic descendant is compared to a tender shoot (*yōneqet*) plucked from a tall tree, taken to Mount Zion and planted there to grow into a huge tree, bearing fruit and providing shade for all the birds of the forest (17:22–24). Thus all the trees of the forest (peoples of the world) will know that "I the LORD lower the tall tree and raise the low tree. I dry up the green tree and make the dry tree flourish" (17:24). Later, this "David" who will come to power is remembered for his humble origins as a shepherd (34:23); he will provide true leadership, as opposed to past leaders, who are symbolized as corrupt and destructive shepherds. Both these motifs of Davidic rule (a tender shoot and a shepherd) echo Jeremiah's prediction of a "plant growth" from the line of David, which will bring good shepherds – justice for the nation (Jer. 23:1–8). Ezekiel states that it is during this period of time of future Davidic leadership that a covenant of shalom will bring a flourishing prosperity and fertility to the land (34:23–31), which will be a new Eden (36:35).'

but not on the basis of the Israelite Covenant' (16:61). In the New Covenant, the old divisions in Israel are healed and the Gentiles are included. Only faithful human partners (i.e. believers) constitute the covenant community. And the Davidic Messiah is ruler over all.[70]

Hence Ezekiel, like similar passages in Isaiah and Jeremiah, indicates that the restoration will have international significance.

Ezekiel continues in chapters 40–48 with his programme by envisioning a rebuilt temple with revitalized worship. That is, a new humanity is (re)created (ch. 37) and then placed in a new Eden. The climactic vision in chapters 40–48 describes the fulfilment of the promises of chapters 1–39. In a significant passage, Ezekiel 37:25–28 pulls together various strands of the new place for God's people and prepares the way for even more glorious promises in chapters 40–48:

> They shall dwell in the land that I gave to my servant Jacob, where your fathers lived. They and their children and their children's children shall dwell there for ever, and David my servant shall be their prince for ever. I will make a covenant of peace with them. It shall be an everlasting covenant with them. And I will set them in their land and multiply them, and will set my sanctuary in their midst for evermore. My dwelling place shall be with them, and I will be their God, and they shall be my people. Then the nations will know that I am the LORD who sanctifies Israel, when my sanctuary is in their midst for evermore.

Beale notes, 'That both passages are part of the same promise is apparent from noticing that twice in 37:25–28 and twice in 43:7, 9 occurs the phrase "I will dwell among the sons of Israel for ever" (with minor variations in wording).'[71] It is significant, then, that Ezekiel ends with a vision of a purified land with boundaries situated around a new temple complex.[72]

Moreover, from another angle Ezekiel 47:1–12 contains an abun= dance of Edenic imagery and describes a paradisal temple that extends to encompass the entire land. It can be said, then, that the new temple is the new creation and restores the consummate state of paradise.[73] Taylor comments:

---

[70] Gentry and Wellum 2012: 481.
[71] Beale 2004b: 329.
[72] Dempster 2003: 171; Beale 2004b: 350.
[73] Lee 2001: 15.

The commentator is justified in looking for parallels to and antecedents for this kind of symbolism, and most turn to the creation narrative in Genesis 2. The former paradise which was watered by the four-streamed river (Gen 2:10) is here paralleled by the new creation which also has its rivers and its trees (7). If we add to this the fact that Ezekiel [in 28:1–19] seems to have known of a paradise tradition linked to a 'holy mountain of God' (28:14, 16) as well as a 'garden of God,' the parallel to our present passage is almost complete.[74]

Significantly, Ezekiel uses the same language as Jeremiah regarding a measuring line extending the boundaries outward (Ezek. 47:3; Jer. 31:39; cf. Zech. 2). Thus the promise concerning the renewed Israel's living in the land under a new David is fulfilled in the vision of the temple, recreating Edenic conditions, the boundaries of which are coterminous with the land. From a canonical perspective, then, Revelation presents this worldwide temple as the new heaven and new earth – the new Jerusalem – in the light of the fulfilment of Christ, the true temple.[75] According to Walker, for the New Testament writers

[74] Taylor 2009: 270–271. Symbolism should not be equated with spiritualizing, for 'the Lord retains his interest in the physical environment . . . and when the human race is finally reconciled to him, all of creation will reap the benefits (Rom 8:18–25)' (Block 1998: 702).

[75] It is beyond the scope of this chapter to provide a detailed discussion of all the allusions of Ezek. 40 – 48 in Rev. 21 – 22. Nevertheless, a brief overview is in order. Admittedly, there is some discontinuity between the visions of Ezekiel and John. Block (ibid.), for these reasons, contends that Ezekiel's temple is not fulfilled in Rev. 21. First, the two cities have different names ('The LORD Is There' [Ezek. 48:35] versus 'new Jerusalem' [Rev. 21:2]). Secondly, Ezekiel's city is square and composed of common stones, whereas John's is cubic and composed of precious stones. Thirdly, Ezekiel's temple is at the centre of everything, whereas the temple's existence is denied in Rev. 21:22. Fourthly, Ezekiel portrays a parochially Israelite city, whereas Rev. 21 describes a cosmopolitan place of Jews and Gentiles. Fifthly, sacrificial animals are at the heart of Ezekiel's temple, whereas the sacrificial Lamb is at the heart of John's temple. Finally, in Ezekiel's temple the clean and unclean are distinguished, whereas John makes no such distinction. Nevertheless, Beale (2004b: 348–353) provides a convincing response to Block's criticisms. First, the concepts of both names are true of both cities. In fact, Rev. 21:2 develops 3:12 and recalls Ezek. 48:35, where the names are mentioned together, which actually bolsters the links between Ezekiel and John. Secondly, Ezekiel's square and John's cube are a matter of perspective, for both are similar in shape and John even uses the word 'foursquare' in 21:16, which combines Ezekiel's vision with an allusion to the cubic shape of the holy of holies from Solomon's temple (1 Kgs 6:20). Furthermore, Ezekiel does not comment on the kinds of stones making up the foundation and walls. Thirdly, John does not deny the temple's existence; only its *physical* existence. The true temple, that is, God and the Lamb, is now central (Rev. 21:22), which comes close to the essence of Ezekiel's temple that culminated in

this prophecy became a brilliant way of speaking pictorially of what God had now achieved in and through Jesus. Paradoxically, therefore, although Ezekiel's vision had focused so much upon the Temple, it found its ultimate fulfillment in that city where there was 'no Temple,' because 'its Temple is the Lord God Almighty and the Lamb' (Rev 21:22).[76]

Indeed, the temple had necessarily been transformed and expanded from Ezekiel to Revelation in the light of the true temple – Jesus Christ – who became flesh and dwelt among us (John 1:14). Ezekiel, then, in line with the prophets' manifold message of restoration, describes astounding hope for the future that includes transformed land and human nature – a new Eden

> that has been enlarged to include the entire land of Israel with one immense river of life and many trees of life. The transformation of the Dead Sea into a body of water teeming with vitality shows the radical impact of God's presence in the land (Ezek 48:35).[77]

the Lord's glorious presence (Ezek. 48:35). Fourthly, Ezekiel does picture Gentiles in the new Jerusalem (47:22–23), though this probably would have been understood as Gentiles who convert to the faith of Israel. Actually, Revelation depicts Jews and Gentiles who have been made one people, kingdom-priests, by the firstborn of the dead, the ruler of the kings of earth (1:5–6). Fifthly, a solution to Ezekiel's animal sacrifices and John's living sacrificial Lamb is a matter of perspective. In other words, Ezekiel's vision employs language and imagery in terms that the Jews of that day would understand. This picture is not, however, a spiritualization of the promises, for the sacrifice of Christ was no doubt the physical fulfilment of the sacrificial system. Both the OT promise and the eschatological fulfilment are physical, and hence literal, but the form of the sacred containers is different. What appears in Ezekiel to be animal sacrifices, which formerly could give only incomplete and temporary covering for sin, find escalated fulfilment in Christ's sacrifice, which provides eternal covering for sin. Therefore to say that Christ typologically fulfils Ezekiel's sacrifices as the Lamb sacrificed for sin is not a figurative or spiritualizing use of the OT, but the eschato-logical reality to which the sacrificial system pointed (Heb. 8 – 10). Finally, in response to Block's critique concerning Ezekiel's ongoing need to distinguish between the clean and unclean, Beale's answer is that Ezekiel depicts an inaugurated but not yet consummated eschatological temple. Paul understands the inaugurated temple described in Ezek. 37:26–28 to be the church, yet there is still the ongoing need to 'touch no unclean thing' (2 Cor. 6:17) and to cleanse oneself 'from every defilement of body and spirit' (2 Cor. 7:1; cf. 1 Cor. 6:18–19). Yet in the consummated city-temple, sin and death will be no more, neither will there be mourning nor crying, nor pain anymore, for the former things have passed away (Rev. 21:4). Therefore Rev. 21 – 22 further interprets the yet-future fulfilment of Ezekiel by collapsing temple, city and land into one end-time picture, and describes the fulfilment of God's covenant promises.

[76] Walker 1996: 313.
[77] Dempster 2003: 171.

Conclusion

The prophetic texts interpret Israel's exile in the light of prior promises of judgment and blessing. Instead of ending on a note of judgment, however, the prophets end on a note of hope in language 'which becomes increasingly extravagant'.[78] God will make a new covenant and renew the people and the land – and indeed all nature. Jerusalem will become the centre of the world, the highest mountain, where all the nations will go to receive blessing. Through the substitutionary work of a Davidic Servant-Shepherd-King, God will make a new creation that is reminiscent of the idyllic conditions of Eden, where his people will dwell securely. The land, writes Wellum, 'will be God's temple sanctuary and its borders, like the rule of the king, will extend to the entire creation (Ps 72:8–11, 17–19)'.[79] It appears from the prophets, then, that the long-awaited kingdom lies just over the horizon.

---

[78] Clements 2004: 167.
[79] Gentry and Wellum 2012: 712–713.

A concluding summary of the Old Testament

The Promised Land in the Old Testament – when situated within the kingdom and covenantal framework of Scripture as it progressively unfolds – was designed by God to serve as a type or pattern of a greater, future reality. Every fulfilment is followed by failure and, although the promise is fulfilled at various points, it anticipates a greater and final fulfilment. That is, the fulfilments under Joshua, David, Solomon and the return from exile demonstrate that, although Israel enjoyed blessing and rest at each point, there still remained a greater fulfilment and final rest for the people of God.

Therefore the promise of land to the nation of Israel is understood within the broader context of God's programmatic agenda that begins with Adam, progresses from Abraham to Israel, and culminates in an international community living in a new creation. In other words, the national dimension involving the geographical territory of Israel should be viewed as a transitional stage in the outworking of God's redemptive plan, a plan that spans from creation to new creation and ultimately includes people from every nation filling the entire earth. This goal seems apparent since Abraham's multitudinous descendants require a much larger territory than Canaan. Indeed, Abraham's offspring will inhabit the earth and thus fulfil the Adamic commission. But the history of Israel shows that in order for God's covenant promises to be fulfilled, a new humanity is necessary; and for a new humanity, a new Adam must come.

As a result, the inheritance of the land of Canaan was designed to recapture what was lost in Eden: a temple-mountain-city where God would dwell with his people. In other words, the land of promise aimed to be God's local manifestation of his kingdom. This was hardly the picture of Israel in exile. However, Israel did return under Cyrus, who gave permission to the people to return to the land. Furthermore, under the leadership of Ezra and Nehemiah, and the words from prophets such as Haggai and Zechariah, the temple was rebuilt and God promised prosperity and peace (Zech. 1:16; 8:1–13).

The temple, however, lacked the glory it once had prior to its destruction and the exile. Its less-than-glorious existence helped to galvanize the meager remnant into a surviving community. Moreover, the post-exilic accounts of temple rebuilding do not mention the return of Yahweh's presence (e.g. Ezra, Haggai), and the people do not enjoy promised peace and rest. Rather, they were slaves once again in their own land (Neh. 9:36). The relative safety and peace they did enjoy lasted only as long as their masters permitted it.

Therefore what was ultimately needed to return from exile was obedience that flowed from new hearts (e.g. Deut. 30; Jer. 31; Ezek. 36). That is, righteousness was needed for Israel to enjoy God's covenant blessings (Ezek. 33:12). As a result, the prophets advance the typological trajectory of God's promise by portraying the return from exile in various ways and stages, including both a physical and spiritual return with national and international results. That is, not only will there be a return to the land, but the people will also return in heart through God's gracious work in the new covenant brought about by his Davidic Servant-King. Furthermore, this return will include incredible realities that transcend the old covenant forms. That is, the return will be so glorious that it is described as a new Jerusalem coextensive with the new creation that is filled with the people of God from every nation.

However, the Old Testament ends with none of these realities in place. Still, God is faithful and in his word of promise is hope. But *how* and *when* would he fulfil his promises? The New Testament answers these questions.

Chapter Seven

The fulfilment of the promise inaugurated: the Gospels

The land promise in New Testament theology

According to Bruce Waltke, 'The trajectory of the land motif into the New Testament is the most difficult biblical motif to track.'[1] This is so because the term 'land' is rarely found in the New Testament.[2] Naim Ateek notes, 'In the Old Testament the word or words designating the "land" appear more than 1,600 times, but in the New Testament fewer than fifty times.'[3] Another problem arises when discovering how the land promise is fulfilled, or begins to be fulfilled, in the New Testament. When Christ comes, announces the arrival of the kingdom and performs his saving work, he does not return believing people to a physical land as a mark of their redemption.[4] Moreover, there is no mention of or emphasis on Christians migrating to Israel's land. It appears, then, that the New Testament is silent when it comes to the Promised Land.

However, despite the relatively rare occurrences of the term 'land' in the New Testament, Gary Millar rightly notes that 'the formative influence in biblical theology of the relational ideas associated with land must not be underestimated'.[5] It is for this reason that concepts, not just words, in the New Testament are examined to synthesize the biblical data into a coherent theology of land, for in most cases the concept is far bigger than the words used to refer to it.[6] As a result, the New Testament demonstrates the fulfilment of land in ways that are both similar and dissimilar to those found in the Old Testament.

---

[1] Waltke with Yu 2007: 559.
[2] Walker 2000: 82.
[3] Ateek 2000: 209. Martens (2009: 225) broadens his count by including other words associated with land when he writes, '[In contrast to the OT], NT words such as *gē* "land," *chōra, chōrion* "region," and *agros* "field" are found in the NT some 325 times.'
[4] Beale 2011: 750.
[5] Millar 2000: 627.
[6] Rosner 2000: 6.

Furthermore, it is not quite accurate to conclude that the New Testament has little to say about the land. Stephen Wellum writes:

> First, the order in producing the new creation is reversed from that used in producing the old creation. In the old creation, God first made the place where we live, and then he made the creatures to live there. In the new creation, however, God first will make his new people, and then he will make the home where they will live. The priority of the New Testament is on how God is making a new people, and the land theme is secondary to this, even though it is clearly taught, especially in Revelation 21–22. Second, once the subject of land is placed within the larger discussion of the covenants, the New Testament has much more to say about the land than some may think.[7]

In addition, the primary focus of the New Testament is on Christ and the inauguration of the kingdom. If the New Testament centres on the fulfilment of God's saving promises in which

> the Lord would reign over the whole earth, the son of David would serve as king, and the exile would be over. . . . The Lord would pour out his Spirit on all flesh, and the promise to Abraham that all nations would be blessed, to the ends of the earth, would become a reality,[8]

then its focus is rightly on the King who brings this kingdom. Indeed, the New Testament makes clear from the beginning that God's promises in the Old Testament reach their *telos* in Christ. Therefore a biblical theology of land that somehow bypassed Jesus Christ would be a contradiction in terms.[9] To derive a coherent theology of land from the New Testament, then, one must also examine the general nature of the fulfilment of God's promises in Christ.

The following chapters will examine the most relevant passages in the New Testament and argue that it presents an already–not yet fulfilment of the Promised Land in the Old Testament.[10] More

[7] Gentry and Wellum 2012: 713.

[8] Schreiner 2008: 45.

[9] Walker 2000: 81.

[10] Although each NT book contributes in its own unique way to the fulfilment of God's promises and the inaugurated, yet not consummated, arrival of the kingdom, each book does not explicitly link this fulfilment to the Promised Land. Therefore only programmatic texts from the NT that contain clear, exegetical and theological

specifically, the New Testament presents the land promised to Abraham and his offspring as finally fulfilled in the (physical) new creation, as a result of the person and work of Christ. At this time in salvation history, however, the fulfilment is focused primarily on Christ, who himself has inaugurated a new creation through his resurrection and has made new creations out of those united with him.[11] That is, in Christ God's covenant presence and blessing is found, and those united to him by faith in his death and resurrection receive their inheritance, rest and indeed every spiritual blessing in the heavenly places in him (Eph. 1:3). In the present, believers live as exiles (1 Peter 1:1; 2:11) between the inauguration and consummation of the kingdom and anticipate the final fulfilment and enjoyment of these covenant blessings in his presence in the new heaven and new earth won by the Lord Jesus Christ (Rev. 21 – 22).

Fulfilment in Matthew

The canonical shape of the New Testament provides a helpful link regarding the relationship between the Old Testament expectation of restoration and its fulfilment. Hamilton writes, 'From the beginning, Matthew's genealogy and narratives of the early life of Jesus establish

connections will be examined. For a different approach, see Burge (2010: 39), who suggests that Matthew's use of 'earth'/'land' in 25:14–30 'could refer to the soil or the ground; but for some, it may refer to the land. If this is the case, it refers to the cautious, preservationist instinct in first-century Judaism to preserve the land in a world rapidly overwhelmed by pagan life. Rather than risk investments, the third servant hid his money *inside the land*' (emphasis original). Burge, however, admits that this reading is speculative, for 'such an interpretation is far from certain since it requires an allegorizing of the story that is foreign and arbitrary to the story itself. This may be an innocent account of a man putting money in the ground.' Burge and France also argue that Jesus' relative silence concerning, or negative view of, historically important cities such as Jerusalem justify the conclusion that 'Jesus is the great re-arranger of the land' (Burge 2010: 35, 41) and that Jerusalem 'is now superseded by the kingdom of heaven' (France 2008: 126). Although Burge and France are correct in observing a shift in focus to Jesus Christ, a better solution would be to view the ultimate fulfilment – not replacement or supersession – of the nation, land, city and temple in a consummated new (physical) city-temple-creation inhabited by an international people, which the rest of the NT confirms.

[11] I came to this conclusion on my own when preparing a paper for a doctoral seminar on eschatology (spring 2010), but later found it substantiated in Beale (2011: 751), who writes, 'This "two-stage fulfilment" can be termed an "installment fulfilment," wherein the initial spiritual stage is "literal" in that the OT promise also had a literal spiritual dimension. E.g. the promise of resurrection in the OT includes a person's spirit also being resurrected along with the body, though the NT sees this spiritual resurrection occurring first. Accordingly, the land promises and their fulfilment are a crucial part of the storyline dealing with Jesus's resurrection as the already-not yet end-time new creation.'

connections between Jesus and the story of Israel at both prophetic and typological levels.'[12] Matthew begins, 'The book of the genealogy [*biblos geneseōs*] of Jesus Christ, the son of David, the son of Abraham' (1:1).[13] Matthew's genealogy is significant because the phrase *biblos geneseōs* (Hebr. *seper tōlĕdôt*) is found in only two other places in the Old Testament LXX (Gen. 2:4; 5:1). Thus Matthew opens by intentionally linking his own plot into the larger narrative that reaches back to the beginning. These two occurrences in the biblical story line, then, are important to consider in order to understand Matthew's use of *biblos geneseōs* in 1:1.

Genesis 2:4 gives the account of God's creation of the heavens and the earth, and Genesis 5:1 begins a new genealogical tree after the fall that emphasizes the continuation of humanity and a re-creation through the Noahic covenant. Thus it is momentous that Matthew 1:1 is only the third place in the canon where this phrase is used. Beale rightly notes:

> That Matthew is, indeed, alluding to Genesis 2 and 5 is enhanced by observing that these are the only two places in the entire Greek OT where the phrase *biblos geneseōs* occurs. Matthew's point in using this phrase is to make clear that he is narrating the record of the new age, the new creation, launched by the coming of Jesus Christ and ending in his death and resurrection.[14]

[12] J. M. Hamilton 2010: 358.

[13] There is some debate as to how this verse should be translated and how it functions in Matthew. The debate revolves around the phrase *biblos geneseōs*. Allison (2005: 158) points out that most translations consistently render this phrase as 'book of genealogy' or some equivalent. This seems simple enough until one gets into the vast amount of literature. The common views are that Matt. 1:1 introduces (1) the genealogy only (1:2–17; e.g. Hagner [1993], Nolland [2005]), (2) all of ch. 1 (e.g. Turner [2008]), (3) the infancy narrative (1:2 – 2:23; e.g. Carson [1984]), (4) the first main part of the Gospel (1:2 – 4:16), (5) the heading for the entire Gospel, and (6) a combination of all of the options listed above, which is Allison's (2005: 158–159) view. For a good survey of these views, see Davies and Allison 2004 and Luz 2007: 69–70. After surveying the various options, Fenton (1977: 36) concludes that Matthew intended his words to have more than one evocation: '1:1 is telescopic: it can be extended to include more and more of what Matthew is beginning to write about. First, it can cover *the genealogy* which immediately covers it; then, it can refer to the account of the *birth* of Jesus; thirdly, it can mean "history" or "life story;" finally, it can refer to the whole new creation which begins at the conception of Jesus and will be completed at his second coming.'

[14] Beale 2004b: 171. See also France 2007: 26–28; contra Nolland 2005: 71 and Luz 2007: 70. Beale (2004b: 171–172) may strengthen his point when he notes, 'Perhaps, also mention of the Holy Spirit in conceiving Jesus (1:18–20) points further to him as the beginning of the new creation, just as the Spirit was mentioned in Genesis 1:2 as forming the first creation,' though this point concerning the role of the Holy Spirit in creation is disputed.

In other words, Matthew's introduction connects Jesus to the first creation, the post-fall re-creation where the image of God is proliferated, and now to the commencement of a new beginning – a new creation. This point leads Davies and Allison to translate Matthew 1:1 as 'Book of the New Genesis wrought by Jesus Christ, son of David, son of Abraham'.[15] In effect, writes Luz, 'Matthew sets out with a new "book of origins", with a new *Heilsgeschichte*, or history of God's actions in the world and in humanity's salvation. It is as if he were writing the Bible anew.'[16] Through his genealogy, then, Matthew is weaving together key threads from the Old Testament. That is, he advances new creation themes through the genealogy of the Messiah and indicates the inaugural fulfilment of Old Testament promises.

However, Matthew does not include an exhaustive list of Jesus' genealogical history, and the fact that Matthew is making Jesus' history fit into a pattern indicates that this is not so much a statistical observation as a theological reflection on the working out of God's purposes. It shows that the period of preparation is now complete, and that the stage is set for the dawning of the time of fulfilment in the coming of the promised Messiah. Moreover, it should be read in the light of two pivotal connections – he is the son of David and son of Abraham. That is, as the son of Abraham Jesus brings to fulfilment all God's covenant promises and, even further, as the son of David Jesus brings God's messianic rule as the one sent to establish God's kingdom. The rest of Matthew will demonstrate how and through whom God has remembered his covenants to bring his kingdom promises to fulfilment.

Furthermore, Matthew paints a complete picture, from the beginning of Israel's history to its end, or goal, by the way he frames his genealogy of the Messiah in three balanced periods of fourteen generations each.[17] Hence Matthew points his readers to the arrival of the

---

[15] Davies and Allison 2004: 153. This wording would certainly have a profound effect on readers familiar with the OT. France (2007: 28) writes, 'The effect on a Jewish reader is comparable to that of John's opening phrase, "In the beginning." . . . The theme of the fulfilment of Scripture is signaled from the very start, and these opening words suggest that a new creation is taking place.'

[16] Luz 1993: 24.

[17] The three sets of fourteen generations have generated much debate. Carson (1984: 68–69) cites several suggestions for why Matthew structured his genealogy in this way. The most common proposals are that (1) fourteen is the numerical value of David in Hebrew, (2) three sets of fourteens equals six sets of sevens, and the sequence of six sevens anticipates the seventh seven, which is understood to be the climax of history, and (3) the intentional omission of some kings and addition of others highlight the royal Davidic dimension, which finds its culmination in the coming of Jesus. In any case, the common denominator is that kingship is highlighted in a way that points to the goal of all that preceded in Israel's history: the coming of the promised Messiah.

Messiah who has come in fulfilment of the Davidic promises of a kingdom and the Abrahamic promises of international blessing (cf. Matt. 3:9; 8:11). But Matthew goes further and includes the unexpected: the exile. Wright notes:

> This is not so regular a marker within Jewish schemes, but for Matthew it is crucial. . . . Until the great day of redemption dawned, Israel was still 'in her sins,' still in need of rescue. The genealogy then says to Matthew's careful reader that the long story of Abraham's people will come to its fulfillment, its seventh seven, with a new David, who will rescue his people from their exile, that is, 'save his people from their sins.' When Matthew says precisely this in 1:18–21 we should not be surprised.[18]

It appears that the long-awaited return from exile has dawned.

It is difficult to imagine, then, that for Matthew and his audience the fulfilment of the promises to Abraham and David, and the promised return from exile, do not include the land. Joel Willitts notes:

> When one has references to the kingdom of God and *Eretz Israel* contained in a context that stands within the [Davidic/Israelite] restorative stream of tradition, it is likely that the hope for the restoration of the Promised Land is not far off.[19]

Therefore Matthew's references to the kingdom of God and the land should be seen within the 'Land-Kingdom' motif.[20]

The first connection with land is found in Matthew 2:15 (cf. Hos. 11:1). In the context of Hosea, God is recalling the history of Israel, God's son (Exod. 4:22–23), when he delivered them out of Egypt. This was in fulfilment of God's promises of calling out a people and giving them their own land. But Hosea 11:2–7 goes on to lament how Israel has wandered away from the Lord and to predict the future return to exile (11:5).[21] In other words, another exodus was needed. This exodus event became central in the life of Israel, to which later revelation would attest. As God's revelation progressed through

---

In other words, Matthew is presenting this greater Davidic king, as will be demonstrated throughout the rest of his Gospel.

[18] N. T. Wright 1992: 385–386.
[19] Willitts 2007: 171.
[20] Kim 2001: 83.
[21] Blomberg 1992: 7.

Israel's successes and failures, an even greater exodus began to be anticipated.[22] Within this typological milieu, then, Hosea is looking for a saving visitation from the Lord. Derek Bass writes, 'The passage flows from retrospect to prospect, recalling the first exodus to the promise of new exodus. To be sure, the Exodus from Egypt forms the type or pattern of the promised salvation to come.'[23] This point is important, for what Matthew sees was already something Hosea himself had seen.[24] That is, Matthew is not reading into Hosea what is not there; rather, he is rightly putting together God's organic and progressive revelation in chronological order to demonstrate that God's true Son has arrived to accomplish a greater exodus in fulfilment of his promises. Carson notes:

> Hosea, building on existing revelation, grasped the messianic nuances of the 'son' language already applied to Israel and David's promised heir in previous revelation so that had he been able to see Matthew's use of Hosea 11:1, he would not have disapproved, even if messianic nuances were not in his mind at the time.[25]

As a result, Matthew now sees Jesus as the locus of true Israel, which he goes on to show in Jesus' testing in the wilderness, the giving of a 'new law' in the Sermon on the Mount, and his further use of 'son' language for Jesus.

It is at this point that one comes into contact with typology in Matthew. Blomberg notes:

> That Israel had been delivered from Egypt, that Israel would again be exiled there but again restored, and that the child believed to be the messiah also had to return to Israel from Egypt formed too striking a set of parallels for Matthew to attribute them to chance.[26]

Jesus is the typological fulfilment of Israel, for he is the true Israel who fulfils the promises made to Abraham and David.[27] Hence the

---

[22] Isa. 43:16–21; 51:9–11; Jer. 16:14–15; 31:31–34; Hos. 2:14–15; 11:10–11.

[23] Bass 2008: 218.

[24] Beale 2012b: 699.

[25] Carson 1984: 92; so also France 2007: 81.

[26] Blomberg 1992: 8.

[27] Schreiner 2008: 70–75. That Jesus himself is the locus of true Israel does not mean that God has no further purpose for ethnic Israel. What it does mean, however, is that 'the position of God's people in the Messianic age is determined by reference to Jesus, not race' (Carson 1984: 93).

Messiah, God's obedient Son, has come to perform a new and greater exodus for the people of God and restore them from exile (Hos. 11:10–11).[28] In this greater exodus, not only will God bring his people out of bondage to sin, but he will also finally bring them into abundant blessing, something that Israel did not lastingly enjoy. Whereas Israel made it out of Egypt, they did not permanently enter into the land of blessing. Unlike the exodus under the leadership of Moses, then, through the liberating work of Jesus God definitively brings his people out of captivity and into the place of redemptive blessing. This new locus of blessing becomes clearer through the rest of Matthew's Gospel.

The first appearance of 'land' is in Matthew 5:5, 'Blessed are the meek, for they shall inherit the earth.' The verb 'inherit' in the Old Testament (Hebr. *yāraš*; LXX *klēronomeō*) is often linked to Israel's entering into and possessing the land (e.g. Deut. 4:1; 16:20; Isa. 57:13). In this context, the specific reference is to Psalm 37:11:

> But the meek shall inherit the land
> and delight themselves in abundant peace.

A few observations are important for interpreting Matthew 5:5 and the use of Psalm 37. To begin, Psalm 37 is eschatologically oriented (vv. 18, 29). That is, the familiar theme of inheriting the land is projected forward and promised as a future hope to those who wait for the Lord and keep his way (v. 34). This motif is threaded throughout the entire psalm, to which appeal is made as a longed-for ideal.[29] This eschatological orientation is further confirmed by the fact that Psalm 37 was already recognized as messianic in Jesus' day (4QpPs 37).[30] Likewise, the Beatitudes are framed within the eschatological context of the kingdom, which is both already and not yet. This inaugurated eschatology is evidenced by the repetition of the present blessing in verses 3 and 10 ('for theirs is the kingdom of heaven') and the future blessings that are framed between these bookends ('for they shall' in vv. 4–9). The tension between 'now' and 'not yet', threaded through the rest of the New Testament, also runs through the promises of Matthew 5:3–10.[31] Hence Matthew is picking up and advancing the eschatological trajectory of Psalm 37.

[28] Bass 2008: 224.
[29] Ps. 37:3, 9, 11, 18, 22, 29, 34.
[30] Carson 1984: 133.
[31] France 2007: 164.

It is unlikely, then, given the typological nature of the land promise in the Old Testament that Jesus is referring strictly to the geographical territory initially promised to Abraham and possessed – and lost – by Israel. That is, he appears to be interpreting the eschatological land inheritance of the psalm through the lens of other universalized texts in the Old Testament.[32] As the Old Testament repeatedly demonstrates, the anticipation of entering into the land 'ultimately became a pointer towards entrance into the new heaven and new earth (cf. Isa. 66:22; Rev. 21:1), the consummation of the messianic kingdom'.[33] It is understandable, then, that Jesus interprets the fulfilment of these land promises in an eschatological light.[34]

However, the fulfilment should not be spiritualized into some kind of non-territorial space. France heads in this direction when he writes, 'There is a general tendency in the NT to treat the OT promise about "the land" as finding fulfilment in nonliteral ways, and such an orientation seems required here too.'[35] But for Matthew the culmination of God's promises will result in the renewal of all things. For example, in response to Peter's question concerning a reward for the disciples, Jesus replies, 'Truly, I say to you, in the new world, when the Son of Man will sit on his glorious throne, you who have followed me will also sit on twelve thrones, judging the twelve tribes of Israel' (19:27–28). The word translated as 'new world' or 'renewal' (*palingenesia*) is used only one other time in the New Testament (Titus 3:5),[36] and here it has to do with the consummation of the kingdom. Turner comments:

> Cosmic eschatological renewal is linked to Jesus's previous stress on the priority of the created order in Matt. 19:4, 8. The moral disorder of the present world is contrary not only to God's past

[32] Beale 2011: 756.

[33] Carson 1984: 134.

[34] Contra Burge (2010: 35), who concludes that Jesus 'reinterpreted the promises that came to those in his kingdom'. Rather, Jesus correctly interpreted the stream of texts in the OT, which progressed and escalated through time and reached their fulfilment in him and his work.

[35] France 2007: 166–167; see also Davies: 1974: 362. Interestingly, Nolland (2005: 202) also heads in the same direction when, after affirming that the Beatitudes weigh in favour of Matthew's intending *gē* to refer to Israel as the land of covenant promise, he comments, 'This, of course, is in the first instance a judgment about imagery and not about a literal referent.'

[36] For an extensive list of its use in Greco-Roman literature, see Derrett 1984: 51–58; see also Sim 1993: 3–12.

creation but also to God's future renewal of that creation. The end will renew the beginning; eschatology restores protology.[37]

Earlier in Matthew, Jesus taught his disciples to pray that God's (heavenly) kingdom would come to earth (Matt. 6:9–10). The hope for Jesus' followers, then, is not an ethereal, non-physical existence, but the consummation of spiritual realities coming into effect on the earth. Likewise, in Matthew 19 the future place of Jesus' disciples is not described as a destruction of the earth or a spiritual, non-physical kingdom, but a *palingenesia*, a new world (19:28).[38] Thus the earth has a territorial connotation and the Beatitudes an eschatological dimension. When put together, Matthew describes an eschatological reborn earth for those in the kingdom. Amazingly, the 'blessed' in Matthew will inherit the earth (Matt. 5:5) – the kingdom of heaven (vv. 3, 10) – and though they mourn in the present, they will reign with Christ in the new earth.[39]

Finally, in a passage laden with Old Testament imagery, Jesus lays claim to what was experienced, albeit temporarily, in Israel's life in the land. Matthew records Jesus as saying, 'Come to me, all who labour and are heavy laden, and I will give you rest. Take my yoke upon you, and learn from me, for I am gentle and lowly in heart, and you will find rest for your souls. For my yoke is easy, and my burden is light' (11:28–30). Jesus has chosen by his Father's gracious will to reveal his kingdom truths, not to the wise and understanding of the world but to little children, the unlearned (vv. 25–26). Perhaps even more astonishing, however, is his gift of rest (*anapausō*). Rest, once promised and given by God to obedient Israel in the land, is no longer centred in a geographical territory. Rather, it is now bound up in and given by Christ, which testifies to his divine identity. Significantly,

---

[37] Turner 2008: 475. See also Nolland (2005: 799), who surveys the various uses of *palingenesia* in extra-biblical literature and concludes that the use of this Greek term 'locates this material in a Hellenistic context, but the idea of a remaking of the world is well rooted in the OT (Isa 65:17; 66:22)'.

[38] Pennington 2007: 326–327. See also Betz 1995: 128.

[39] Others have noted the connection between Matt. 5:5 and Isa. 60:21; 61:7. See e.g. Luz 2007: 195, n. 94; Nolland 2005: 201, n. 40; France 2007: 166; Beale 2011: 757. Blomberg (1992: 20) points out that 'the poor mourners of Isaiah 61:1–2 are also described as inheriting the earth in 61:7, at least in the LXX'. Also, notes Beale (2011: 757), 'In the context of Isa. 60:21, the "land" refers to the "city of Zion" (v. 14), its "gates" (vv. 11, 18), and the "land" of Israel (v. 18). Isaiah 65:17–18 and 66:20–22 inextricably link end-time Jerusalem with the coming new creation. That Israel will "possess the land for ever" (in the second line of Isa. 60:21) must refer to the initial mention of the "world to come" and not merely the localized promised land.'

'you will find rest for your souls' echoes Jeremiah 6:16, where it is the reward Yahweh offers to those who search for the good way and walk in it. Furthermore, the rest promised to David (2 Sam. 7:11) that was experienced under the temple-constructing reign of his son Solomon (1 Chr. 22:9) – only to be forfeited as a result of sin – is now given under the yoke of the true Davidic Son. It is now Jesus who invites others to enjoy his gift of rest. France rightly comments:

> That Jesus now issues the same promise [of rest] under his own authority says much for the Christology underlying this extraordinary pericope. As in the beatitudes of 5:3–10, there is no doubt an eschatological dimension to the rest which Jesus offers, but that does not mean that the offer has no relevance to the problems encountered by disciples in this life; it is for the present as well as for the future, just as the 'sabbath rest which still remains for the people of God' in Hebrews 4:1–11 is nonetheless one which its readers are exhorted to enter into 'today.'[40]

Jesus now takes on the role of God in giving and fulfilling the promises of rest, which certainly brings to mind God's rest after creation and Israel's Sabbath rest.[41] Jesus offers divine rest to the citizens of the kingdom of God, and will give it.

Now, at last, the burden and toil experienced in the garden after the fall (Gen. 3:17–29), under Israel's slavery in Egypt (Exod. 6:6) and presently under the demands of Rome are relieved under 'the gentle Revealer' to whom the Old Testament rest pointed.[42] This rest is given to and experienced by those who are related to Jesus.[43] Hence the rest previously promised and enjoyed in the land is connected typologically in relation to Christ, who will give his rest in his eternal kingdom to those who come to him.

The end of Matthew (28:18–20) returns to the theme introduced at the very beginning (1:1). The blessings promised to Abraham and in him to all peoples of the earth are now to be fulfilled under the authority of Jesus the Messiah. As a result of Jesus' definitive work, he now exercises his divine authority, given by his Father, in heaven

---

[40] France 2007: 450.

[41] Gen. 2:2; Exod. 20:10–11; 31:15; 35:2. It is no coincidence that immediately following this passage is another where Jesus is shown to be greater than David and the temple, and to be Lord of the Sabbath (Matt. 12:1–14).

[42] Carson 1984: 278–279.

[43] See also Heb. 3 – 4; Rev. 6:11; 14:13.

and on earth by sending his disciple-making disciples 'as an eschatological marker inaugurating the beginning of his universal mission'.[44] This transnational mission has cosmic, eschatological implications. When people from all nations are discipled, a new humanity is formed. Obedience to Jesus' mandate, then, fulfils the original creation mandate God gave to humanity's first parents in the garden of Eden. Whereas Adam failed his commission, Jesus obediently fulfilled his. As a result, those now related to Jesus pray for God's kingdom to come on earth and wait for their future inheritance of rest in the new world. In fulfilment of God's covenant promises, then, the disciples will enjoy the Lord's presence in their mission to possess all the nations of the earth, for Jesus will be with them always, 'to the end of the age' (v. 20). In other words, Jesus is Lord over both the land and his people.

Fulfilment in John

According to Gary Burge, John 15:1–6 is the 'most profound theological relocation of Israel's holy space'.[45] Scholars have noted the prominence of the fulfilment motif in John, which permeates his Gospel leading up to this text. For example, Jesus is now the true dwelling place of God, the one who became flesh and dwelt (*skēnoō*) among us (1:14; cf. Exod. 25:8–9).[46] He is the true temple (*naos*), so that now the resurrected Lord is the place where the glory of God is revealed, where his forgiveness and new life are experienced, and where fellowship with God is for ever enjoyed. Andreas Köstenberger notes:

> [John's] fulfillment Christology entails the recognition that physical locations of worship are inadequate (esp. 4:19–24) and leads to the conclusion that Jesus is now the focus of worship (9:38; 20:28). As the proper focus of worship, Jesus replaces any temple, implying that the Jerusalem temple is obsolete (11:48–52; 13–21). The silence regarding the temple in John 13–21 is a rhetorical device pointing to Jesus as its permanent replacement.[47]

Furthermore, Jesus fulfils the Jewish Feasts (e.g. Tabernacles, Dedication, Passover). Hoskins notes:

[44] Carson 1984: 595.
[45] Burge 2010: 53.
[46] Carson 1991: 127.
[47] Köstenberger 2009: 424–425.

Jesus' fulfillment of the Jewish Feasts and the Temple dwells upon the nature and content of God's provision for all his people. Jesus is and gives the true food and true drink that delivers believers from thirst and hunger. He demonstrates this by offering his flesh and blood for the life of the world and sending the Spirit to enrich believers with the salvific benefits of his sacrificial death.[48]

He is also the true shepherd, in contrast to God's unfaithful shepherds, whose role is patterned after God's good shepherd, David (1 Sam. 17:34–36). In later revelation, this shepherd is identified with both David and Yahweh (Ezek. 34). Simply put, Jesus is the fulfilment of God's saving promises and is now the holy place where God can be found.

Now, in John 15, Jesus says, 'I am the true vine' (v. 1). Vineyard imagery was common in the ancient world, and one familiar with the Old Testament would certainly understand the connection Jesus was making.[49] The vineyard or vine was a symbol for Israel, God's covenant people, and consistently stressed Israel's disobedience and failure to bear fruit no matter how much God tended to and cultivated them. Thus God would judge Israel by the hands of other nations (Isa. 5). Surprisingly, though, in this 'extended metaphor' it is not a nation or people that fulfil Israel's purpose; it is Jesus.[50] Beasley-Murray comments:

It is striking that in every instance when Israel in its historical life is depicted in the OT as a vine or vineyard, the nation is set under the judgment of God for its corruption, sometimes explicitly for its failure to produce good fruit (e.g., Isa. 5:1–7; Jer. 2:21). . . . It seems likely therefore that the description of Jesus as the *true* vine is primarily intended to contrast with the failure of the vine Israel to fulfill its calling to be fruitful for God. That the vine is *Jesus*, not the church, is intentional; the Lord is viewed in his representative capacity, the Son of God – Son of Man, who dies and rises that in union with him a renewed people of God might come into being and bring forth fruit for God.[51]

[48] Hoskins 2006: 181.
[49] See e.g. Isa. 5:1–7; 27:2–6; Ps. 80:8–16; Jer. 2:21; 12:10–13; Ezek. 15:1–8; 17:1–21; Hos. 10:1–2. The OT background is strongly favoured by the majority of commentators because of the number of OT references, allusions and recurrences of the replacement/fulfilment motif. See e.g. Carson 1991: 513; Brown 1970: 669–672; Morris 1995: 593; Ridderbos 1997: 515.
[50] Carson 1991: 513.
[51] Beasley-Murray 1999: 272; emphases original.

Indeed, Jesus is the true vine – the true Israel – and his disciples are now the branches, participants in Jesus.

For John 15, according to Carson, 'perhaps the most important Old Testament passage is Psalm 80, in that it brings together the themes of vine and son of man'.[52] This psalm is a prayer for the restoration of Israel, a vine that God brought out of Egypt, planted and blessed in the land (vv. 8–9).[53] Just as God had delivered and planted his people in the past, so the psalmist is praying for salvation in the future, which certainly included restoration to the land. However, John 15 indicates that a redemptive-historical shift has taken place. The true vine *now* is not apostate Israel but Jesus himself, and the place of blessing is in him. Now, if exiled Israel want to be restored, then they must be rightly related to Jesus and planted in him. Gary Burge comments:

> [The people of Israel] cannot be rooted in the vineyard unless first they are grafted into Jesus. . . . Branches that attempt living in The Land, the vineyard, which refuse to be attached to Jesus will be cast out and burned (John 15:6). . . . God the Father is now cultivating a vineyard in which only one life-giving vine grows. Attachment to this vine and this vine alone gives the benefits of life once promised through The Land.[54]

Thus the answer to the psalmist's lament to be delivered and replanted has come through the true vine. Whereas blessing once flowed from the land, now blessing flows from Jesus, who enables his people to bear fruit and who goes to prepare a place for them (John 14:2). Significantly, the rest of the New Testament builds on these themes for the church, as God's people live between the ages and await their final destination.

[52] Carson 1991: 513.

[53] The date of this psalm is uncertain. Because the psalmist mentions 'Israel', 'Ephraim', 'Benjamin' and 'Manasseh', one view is that Israel had not yet fallen to Assyria. Another view, however, is that the post-exilic psalmist from the southern kingdom is familiar with the events of the northern kingdom and, therefore, prays that the same events will come to Judah. In either case the theme is the same, for the psalmist's lament is for God's restoration to come in the light of his judgment by exile.

[54] Burge 1994: 393–394.

Chapter Eight

The fulfilment of the promise inaugurated: the epistles

Fulfilment in Paul

The fulfilment of the land promise in relation to Christ is further confirmed in Paul. One clear text, for example, is found in Romans 4:13. Romans 1:18 – 3:20 demonstrates the solidarity of humanity in sin and the inevitability of judgment on the basis of God's righteous character. All people are guilty because, although they have a knowledge of God based on his revelation in nature, they suppress the truth in unrighteousness (v. 18), 'exchange the glory of the immortal God for images resembling mortal man and birds and animals and creeping things' (v. 23), 'exchanged the truth about God for a lie and worshipped and served the creature rather than the Creator' (v. 25) and 'did not see fit to acknowledge God' (v. 28). In 2:5–16 Paul describes the day of judgment, when God will judge every man according to his works (2:6). The standard of this judgment is God's law, which is either explicit in the Torah for Jews, or implicit in the conscience of Gentiles (2:12–25). The result, then, is that only the law-keepers will be justified in God's sight (2:7, 10, 12).

However, herein lies the problem: there is no perfect law-keeper, neither Jew nor Gentile, for every person is under the power of sin and no one is righteous before God (3:10–18). The prospect for humanity, then, is universal judgment, for Torah-breaking Jews are no more acceptable to God than Gentiles, whose conscience accuses or excuses them. As a result, all are doomed and no one will be justified by the works of the law, since through the law comes knowledge of sin (3:20).

But *now*,[1] in Romans 3:21–26, Paul takes a sharp turn in his argument by presenting the solution to the universal plight of

---

[1] The adverbial expression that begins Rom. 3:21–26 indicates a sharp contrast in the flow of Paul's argument, which began in 1:18. *Nyn de* may indicate a logical connection (cf. 7:17), but here it most likely denotes a temporal one (cf. 6:22; 7:6). In other words, whereas God's judging righteousness was primarily manifested under the old era (Rom. 1:18 – 3:20), his saving righteousness is now manifested in the advent of

humanity. This passage deals with how people are saved from God's judgment on sin through the work of Christ. Paul proclaims that the righteousness of God[2] has now been revealed apart from the law[3]

the person and work of Christ. In other words, there is now a salvation-historical shift that marks the solution to the problem revealed in 1:18 – 3:20. This solution has now been manifested 'apart from the law'. Most commentators agree that this is a salvation-historical shift in the flow of Paul's argument. See e.g. Cranfield 1975: 201; Dunn 1988: 164; Morris 1988: 173; Moo 1996: 221; Schreiner 1998: 180; contra Jewett 2007: 272. Also see Byrne 1996: 123, and 129, n. 21, and Murray 1965: 108, who take it as both logical and temporal but emphasize primarily the temporal. However, Carson (2004: 122) is correct in stating that this temporal contrast should not be pressed too far, as though the era under the old covenant should be characterized as only consisting of condemnation, but the era under the new covenant is one only of grace. He notes, 'just as the portrait of God as a God of justifying grace is ratcheted up as one moves from the old covenant to the new, so the portrait of God as a God of holy wrath is ratcheted up as one moves from the old covenant to the new'. Moreover, in this very paragraph, the *earlier* period is characterized as the time of God's forbearance.

[2] In context, the 'righteousness of God' (*dikaiosynē theou*) should not be understood as God's moral attribute of being righteous, but rather his justifying activity. So Murray 1965: 30; Morris 1988: 103; Moo 1996: 222; Schreiner 1998: 180. Furthermore, debate surrounds the meaning of this phrase. The righteousness of God is commonly understood to mean the believer's status before God and/or God's saving power. Also, it is viewed as either forensic (i.e. God *declares* one to be innocent or guilty), transformative (i.e. God *makes* one innocent or guilty), or both. Moo (1996: 70–71) describes three options: (1) an attribute of God; (2) status given by God; and (3) an activity of God. These positions have come to be divided into either forensic or transformative categories. Moo opts for a forensic understanding of righteousness, while Schreiner earlier opted for a both-and view in his commentary on Romans but has since changed to a forensic view. Cf. Schreiner 1998: 62–67 with Schreiner 2001: 192–217. Paul's use of the 'righteousness of God' is pregnant with meaning given its usage in the OT (see e.g. Judg. 5:11; 1 Sam. 12:7; cf. Mic. 6:5; Ps. 98:2–3; Deut. 25:1; cf. 2 Sam. 15:4; 1 Kgs 8:31–32; 2 Chr. 6:23; Prov. 16:15). This phrase, in the light of its context and other places where Paul uses it, is best understood as forensic (see e.g. 1:17, 21–22; 4:3, 5–6, 9; 9:30; 10:3–4, 6; Phil. 3:9; Schreiner 2001: 203–209). It predominantly refers to God, who justifies, declares righteous and acquits the guilty, and to human beings who have this action pronounced on them (the only exception being in 1 Tim. 3:16, where Paul says that Christ was 'vindicated by the Spirit'). In the context of Romans, this righteousness is seen as God's 'vindicating act of raising Christ from the dead for us' (Seifrid 2000: 47). Seifrid also points out that 'the biblical themes of God's deliverance of the oppressed, his vindication of his Servant, his faithfulness to Israel and his salvation of the world are implicitly present' (ibid). Furthermore, there are other places in Romans that help clarify Paul's understanding and use of 'righteousness' (see e.g. Rom. 2:13; cf. 3:20, 24, 26, 28, 30; 4:5; 5:1; 8:33–34; see also 'account' or 'reckon' [*logizomai*] language: 4:3–6, 8–11, 22–24; 9:8; cf. Gal. 3:6).

[3] The 'law' without the article (*chōris nomou*) often refers to the Mosaic covenant, which failed because of humanity's inability to keep it (Lev. 18:26; 19:37; 20:22; Deut. 4:1–2). The adverbial phrase *chōris nomou* modifies *pephanerōtai*, which most take as another way of saying *ex ergōn nomou* (3:20), meaning 'apart from doing the law', 'apart from the works of the law' or modifying the law-covenant, which would reiterate the salvation-historical shift in Rom. 3:21. See e.g. Calvin 1998: 134; Murray 1965: 110; Cranfield 1975: 201; Schreiner 1998: 180. This phrase, then, emphasizes the new era inaugurated by the work of Christ in which God justifies sinners. So Schreiner 1998: 180; Moo 1996: 223; Carson 2004: 123.

through faith in Jesus Christ[4] for all who believe, whether Jew or Gentile. All have sinned and fall short of God's glory, but God is patient and merciful. Indeed, he has fulfilled his saving promises of redemption[5] to those who place their faith in him by judging sin in the bloody death of his Son,[6] whom he set forth publicly as a propitiation, or sacrifice, of atonement.[7] In this way, then, God demonstrated his justice *even* in justifying the one who has faith in Jesus.[8]

[4] There has been much debate in recent years concerning how the phrase *pisteōs Iēsou Christou* should be understood. Two representatives for the subjective genitive reading are Richard B. Hays (1997: 46–47) and Luke Timothy Johnson (1982: 77–90). Their most compelling arguments are (1) the subjective reading is more consistent linguistically; and (2) it makes better sense in context, namely that it avoids the redundancy of what immediately follows (i.e. 'faith in Christ . . . to all who believe'). See also Wallace 1996: 114–116. Most scholars agree that a choice cannot be made on the basis of linguistic evidence alone. Therefore context is crucial in deciding which of these options is more faithful to the text. Schreiner (1998: 181–186) sets forth four lines of evidence in support of the objective genitive reading: 'Paul often refers to the faith of believers, he never refers to the faith of Christ, he writes specifically of Christ as being the object of the believers' faith, and the flow of thought in Rom. 3–4 supports the idea of faith in Christ' (so also Moo 1996: 224–226). Furthermore, two additional arguments can be offered. First, ch. 4 follows 3:21–26, where the emphasis is not on Christ's obedience but on Abraham's believing. Secondly, the 'redundancy' of *eis pantas tous pisteuontas* (for all who believe) emphasizes something very important, namely the universality of God's righteousness for *all* who believe, whether Jew or Gentile, 'For there is no distinction' (3:22b). This theme is very important for Paul in Romans (1:16; 2:10).

[5] There has been much debate surrounding the *lyt-* word group. Paul can describe redemption in various ways to denote adoption (Rom. 8:23), forgiveness of trespasses (Eph. 1:7; Col. 1:14), and a ransom or price paid. This context supports the idea of a price paid. But not only does it denote a price paid; it also looks back to the deliverance of Israel from the Egyptians and of exile from the Assyrians and Babylonians. In agreement with the Gospels, then, Israel's liberation has ultimately come through the finished work of Christ to those who believe in him (cf. Isa. 35:10; 51:11). So Schreiner 1998: 189–190; Moo 1996: 229–230; Carson 2004: 128. See also the classic works by Morris 1965: 11–64; 1983: 106–131.

[6] Most likely *en tō autou haimati* modifies *hilastērion*, so that Christ's blood is the means by which God's wrath is propitiated. It is through the blood, or death, of Christ that salvation and its benefits come to the individual by faith (Rom. 5:9; Eph. 1:7; 2:13; Col. 1:20). So Schreiner 1998: 194; Moo 1996: 236–237; Murray 1965: 120–121; Morris 1965: 182.

[7] There is debate over the meaning of propitiation (*hilastērion*). The most common view is that it means (1) expiation, (2) propitiation or (3) mercy seat. However, one does not have to opt for an either/or answer. The terms 'blood', 'righteousness', 'sins' and 'set forth publicly' demonstrate the expiatory, propitiatory and sacrificial aspects of Christ's atonement. The idea of substitution is also brought into the picture since this concept was clearly in the OT and anticipated the coming Messiah (e.g. Isa. 52:13 – 53:12). Therefore the sacrifice and substitution of Christ on behalf of sinners includes both the removal of sin and the satisfaction of God's wrath.

[8] I take the *kai* joining the last two phrases (*auton dikaion kai dikaiounta ton*) as concessive. So Schreiner 1998: 198; Moo 1996: 242; Cranfield 1975: 213.

In Romans 3:27–31, Paul draws some conclusions from verses 21–26. First, because righteousness is based on faith in what God has accomplished in Christ (vv. 21–26), and not on human obedience, boasting is excluded (vv. 27–28). Secondly, the oneness of God demands that every person, whether Jew or Gentile, is justified in the same way: by faith (vv. 29–30). And thirdly, Paul concludes that faith does not nullify the commands of the law, but rather obedience will flow from those who have faith in Christ (v. 31).[9] As confirmation that righteousness is attained only through faith, Paul introduces Abraham in Romans 4 to demonstrate that justification is by faith alone, not by works, and that this salvation promise is for *all* people who believe (vv. 1–25).

Romans 4:13, then, builds on Paul's previous argument, defines the content of the promise to Abraham and explains what it is, namely that Abraham and his offspring would be heir (*klēronomon*) of the world.[10] In the Old Testament, inheritance was almost exclusively connected to the land and was a fundamental part of Israel's covenant relationship with God.[11] Burge notes that the land is a 'by-product of the covenant, a gift of the covenant. It is not a possession that can be held independently.'[12] While there is no explicit statement in the Old Testament that Abraham would become heir of the world, the idea is there.[13] That is, while the land initially promised to Abraham and his descendants extended to the borders of Canaan, both the typological pattern and trajectory of the Old Testament show that as his offspring multiplied and filled the earth, so also would the boundaries of the land encompass the earth. Of particular importance is Genesis 26:3–4, where the unique plural 'lands' (*hā'ărāṣōt*), when read in conjunction with the oath to which it alludes in Genesis 22:17–18, makes clear that Abraham's seed will possess/inherit the gate of his enemies.[14] This, together with Genesis 22:17, provides firm exegetical

---

[9] Schreiner 1998: 208.

[10] Moo 1996: 273–274; Schreiner 1998: 227; Murray 1965: 142.

[11] Dunn 1988: 213. Gen. 12:7; 13:15–17; 15:7, 18; 17:6–8, 19; 22:17–18; 26:3–4; 28:13–15. See also Harris 2009: 31–103.

[12] Burge 2010: 4.

[13] Schreiner 1998: 227; so also Moo 1996: 274. Contra Cranfield (1975: 239), who argues, 'Nowhere in the OT is the promise to Abraham couched in terms at all close to *to klēronomon auton einai kosmou*. What is promised in the various Genesis passages is a numberless progeny, possession of the land of Canaan, and that all the nations of the earth shall be blessed (or shall bless themselves) in Abraham or his seed. But Judaism came to interpret the promise to Abraham as a much more comprehensive promise.'

[14] So Moo 1996: 274; P. R. Williamson 2000b: 22.

warrant for Paul's assertion that Abraham would inherit the world.[15] Paul, then, is demonstrating sound biblical exegesis, informed by Scripture's redemptive-historical story line, by putting all three elements of the covenant together.[16] Therefore in the light of Christ – Abraham's (singular) seed (Gal. 3) – Abraham and his (corporate) offspring will inherit the world as people, both Jew and Gentile, come to faith in Jesus Christ.[17]

[15] On this point, Dunn (1988: 213) writes that for Paul, 'The concept had been broadened out from Canaan to embrace the whole earth. . . . Our passage therefore is a good example of the extent to which Paul's own thinking reflects ideas which were widespread in other strands of Jewish theology at that time (cf. Matt. 5:5; Heb. 1:2).' Dunn (ibid.) lists Ecclesiasticus 44.21; *Jubilees* 17.3; 22.14; 32.19; *1 Enoch* 5.7; Philo; *De Somniis* 1.175; *De Vita Mosis* 1.155; cf. *4 Ezra* 6.59; *Apostolic Constitutions* 8.12.23; rabbinic references in Str–B, 3.209; the world to come – *Syriac Apocalypse of Baruch* 14.13; 51.3. See also Burge 2010: 15–24; Moo 1996: 274, n. 18. Burge (2010) argues that the dispersal of Jewish life into non-Jewish cities in the Roman Empire raised questions about the integrity of Jewish identity. How would Jewish life and identity remain intact outside the land? Burge's answer is Israel's commitment to their identity markers (e.g. Sabbath, dietary laws, circumcision, the temple). In other words, they were ceremonially committed to the land while separated from it. The result was a redefinition of the land, such that for many the reality of life in the land took on eschatological tones. For others, such as Philo and Josephus, the land was allegorized or completely neglected. Thus this entire redefinition of land deeply influences the formation of Christian thinking in the NT. It should be noted that this 'redefinition' or 'allegorizing' raises important methodological questions for a theology of land. E.g. how and to what extent should extra-biblical literature be consulted and incorporated into theological formulation? Although Paul was certainly familiar with the literature, what remains to be proven is *what* he derived from these texts that he did not derive from the OT itself. In other words, when the various texts are put together from the OT to the NT, redefining or allegorizing the land promises is unnecessary, for the OT points to Abraham's 'inheriting the world', and the NT reveals both how and when it is fulfilled.

[16] Schreiner 1998: 227.

[17] Moo 1996: 274; Schreiner 1998: 227; P. R. Williamson 2000b: 22; Hester 1968: 77–78. The same could be said of Eph. 6:2–3, '"Honour your father and mother" (this is the first commandment with a promise), "that it may go well with you and that you may live long in the land."' In the OT, the promise relates to a long life in the Promised Land that God gave to Israel. Does it follow, then, that Paul sees no significance in the promise to live long in the land? No. Schreiner (2001: 328–329) writes, 'If we understand Paul's theology, we know that the inheritance promised to Abraham has become the world (Rom 4:13). Paul does not restrict the inheritance to the land of Palestine. He understands the inheritance to refer to the future glory awaiting believers (Rom 8:17). The promise of long life in the land, in Paul's view, relates to our heavenly inheritance. In other words, those who obey their parents will receive an eschatological reward – the inheritance promised to Abraham, Isaac, and Jacob. . . . How Paul handles the command to honor one's parents is paradigmatic. The injunction to honor parents is fulfilled rather straightforwardly in the new covenant, but the promise to live long in the land no longer relates in the same way. The land now becomes the future world that belongs to the people of God, the heavenly Jerusalem (Gal 4:26). The land promised in the Old Testament anticipates and is fulfilled in the eschatological inheritance awaiting the people of God.'

However, this conclusion does not mean that Paul is spiritualizing the Old Testament promise. For example, Louis Berkhof writes:

> The covenant with Abraham already included a symbolical element. On the one hand, it had reference to temporal blessings, such as the land of Canaan, a numerous offspring, protection against and victory over the enemies; and the other, it referred to spiritual blessings. It should be borne in mind, however, that the former were not coordinate with, but subordinate to, the latter. These temporal blessings did not constitute an end in themselves, but served to symbolize and typify spiritual and heavenly blessings.[18]

The physical–spiritual distinction is not accurate, for these promises have begun spiritually and will be consummated physically in the final new creation.[19] Though Dunn is closer to the mark in interpreting the promise, he still focuses on the spiritual aspect when he comments:

> Paul takes up the enlarged form of the promise, of course, not because it implies Israel's worldwide dominance, but presumably because it sets the narrower strand of salvation-history centering on Israel within the larger scheme of creation: the blessing promised to Abraham and his seed (including 'the nations') is the restoration of God's created order, of man to his Adamic status as steward of the rest of God's creation; over against a more nationalistic understanding of the promise, Paul's 'interpretation of the promise is a-territorial', fulfilled 'in Christ.' (Davies, *Land*, 179) Elsewhere Paul places the concept within an eschatological framework, with the Spirit as the first installment and guarantee (see further on 8:17). As with other related covenantal terms – 'promise' (Gal. 3:14) and 'seal' (see on 4:11) – Paul sees the eschatological fulfillment in terms of the Spirit given to faith.[20]

While Dunn is correct in seeing the fulfilment of God's promises in Christ within an eschatological framework, his 'a-territorial' understanding misses the mark. That is, while those who believe are sealed with the promised Holy Spirit, who is the guarantee or down payment of their inheritance until they acquire possession of it (Eph. 1:13–14), it is nevertheless a 'down payment'. What awaits them, then, is the

[18] Berkhof 1996: 296.
[19] Beale 2011: 751.
[20] Dunn 1988: 213; see also Davies 1974: 179.

ultimate fulfilment of the promise 'in a consummated order of the new heavens and the new earth' – a (physical) new creation. Hans LaRondelle notes, 'In order to understand Paul, one must view the land of Palestine as a down payment, or pledge, assuring Israel as a nation the larger territory necessary to accommodate the countless multitudes of Abraham's offspring.'[21] Indeed, Paul 'envisions a future salvation that will engulf the entire cosmos and reverse and transcend the consequences of the fall' (Rom. 8:18–25).[22]

Also important for understanding Paul's view of the promise and fulfilment of land is the concept of inheritance. For Paul, his use of this terminology is a natural extension of the meaning in the Old Testament, which commonly refers to the land allotted to Israel.[23] That is, the promise to Abraham and his offspring finds fulfilment in their inheritance of the world. This interpretation of inheritance is warranted, for in other places Paul speaks of those who will inherit the kingdom of God. George Ladd writes:

> In a number of places, God's kingdom is an eschatological blessing that is to be 'inherited' (1 Cor. 6:9, 10; 15:50; Gal. 5:21). Jesus had also spoken of the kingdom as an eschatological inheritance (Matt. 5:5). The background of this idiom is the prophetic idea of inheriting the promised land (Isa. 57:13; 60:21; 61:7; 65:9), and in the New Testament the inheritance is equated with the eschatological salvation of the Age to Come.[24]

Thus the entire world will become God's kingdom and his people's inheritance. An important link is forged, then, between inheritance, the Promised Land and the kingdom of God.[25]

---

[21] LaRondelle 1983: 139.

[22] Schreiner 1998: 437. Moo (1996: 514) notes, with the majority of commentators, that the creation (*ktisis*) here 'denotes the "subhuman" creation. Like the psalmists and prophets who pictured hills, meadow, and valleys "shouting and singing together for joy" (Ps 65:12–13) and the earth 'mourning' (Isa 24:4; Jer 4:28; 12:4), Paul personifies the subhuman creation in order to convey to his readers a sense of the cosmic significance of both humanity's fall into sin and believers' restoration to glory.' So also Schreiner 1998: 435.

[23] Moo 2008: 101. On Paul's idea of inheritance in the OT, Jewish background and the NT, see Hester 1968.

[24] Ladd 1993: 450. Also see Schnackenburg 1963: 301.

[25] Vickers (2008: 62) rightly observes that a dichotomy should not be made between Jesus, who commonly speaks of 'entering' the kingdom, and Paul, who speaks of 'inheriting' the kingdom, for (1) in the OT the Israelites both inherited and entered the land, and (2) there are examples both in the Gospels and in Paul's letters where the typical words are not used (e.g. Matt. 25:34; 1 Thess. 2:12).

However, more can be said concerning Paul's understanding of the believer's inheritance. In Colossians 1:12, Paul tells the Colossian believers that God the Father has qualified them 'to share in the inheritance of the saints in light'. Because of the combination of terms such as inheritance, deliverance and transfer, scholars have rightly read this passage against the backdrop of the exodus.[26] Moo comments:

> In a move typical of the New Testament 'christifying' of the Old Testament 'land' theme, Paul applies this language to the spiritual privilege enjoyed by God's new covenant people – including, in a particularly significant salvation-historical development, the Gentiles, such as the Colossians.[27]

Thus there is an eschatological reward for believers that has escalated from the Old Testament inheritance of the Promised Land to the New Testament inheritance of final salvation.

Another feature of inheritance in Paul is the connection with sonship. That is, Paul forges an inseparable link between adoption as sons and the believer's inheritance.[28] Of particular importance for understanding this connection is the redemptive-historical progression of sonship and inheritance, for the Old Testament demonstrates that God's son is Israel (Exod. 4:22) and the inheritance is the land. In the New Testament, however, Paul understands all God's people – both Jew and Gentile – to be sons of God through faith in Jesus Christ, and if they are Christ's then they are Abraham's offspring, inheritors according to the promise.[29] Since Christ is God's Son par excellence, those who are in Christ receive their inheritance in him as they await the final fulfilment of God's promises. Moreover, they are sealed with the promised Holy Spirit, who is the guarantee of their inheritance until they acquire possession of it (Eph. 1:13–14).[30] This calls to mind the promised Spirit to Israel.[31] Thus the Christian's inheritance looks to the not yet. Andrew Lincoln comments:

---

[26] See e.g. Pao 2012: 74; Beale 2007: 841–870.

[27] Moo 2008: 101.

[28] Ridderbos 1975: 203.

[29] Gal. 3:26, 29; cf. 4:7; Rom. 8:17.

[30] *Tēs klēronomias* is best taken as a partitive genitive, since the Spirit is the initial down payment that guarantees a much fuller set of blessings in the future. So Hoehner 2002: 243; Arnold 2010: 92.

[31] See e.g. Ezek. 36:26–27; 37:14; Joel 2:28–30.

In a down payment, that which is given is part of the greater whole, is of the same kind as that whole, and functions as a guarantee that the whole payment will be forthcoming. The Spirit then is the first installment and guarantee of the salvation of the age to come with its mode of existence totally determined by the Spirit.[32]

The consummation of the Spirit's work is cast in terms of the resurrection of the body (2 Cor. 5:5), but ultimately it will result in freeing this present creation from the effects of sin and making a new creation (Rom. 8:18–25). Dan Barber and Robert Peterson write:

The body of Christ, who is 'the firstfruits' of the resurrection (1 Cor 15:20), was not annihilated and re-created, but his own body was raised from the dead (John 2:19–22; 10:17–19). . . . Just as we will not be destroyed but renewed, so it is with God's creation. We are a microcosm of the creation. Even as we long for God's final salvation, the creation personified as an expectant mother does the same. The creation is eager to 'be set free from its bondage to corruption and obtain the freedom of the glory of the children of God' (Rom 8:21). The creation longs, so to speak, for removal of the curse (vv. 20–22). This is not destruction and re-creation but great renovation of the present cosmos.[33]

The Spirit 'connects our "already" with our "not yet," making "the hope of glory," though unseen, as certain as if it were already ours – which, in a sense, it is (cf. "glorified" in v. 30)'.[34] The inheritance, then, is future oriented and will culminate not in the annihilation of this present creation, but in the transformation of it. That is, this present corrupt earth will give way to a new heaven and new earth – the kingdom of God – as an inheritance for God's people.

Two summarizing observations can be made concerning Paul's use of inheritance. First, inheritance in the Old Testament is inextricably linked to the Abrahamic promises. The constellation of related themes became fused with other theological concepts such as union with Christ, God's presence and the temple. Thus inheritance language enables Paul to draw upon the overlap that occurs between promise and fulfilment. The second observation is that a future orientation is inherent within the idea of inheritance. Initially, this future orientation

[32] Lincoln 1990: 40.
[33] Barber and Peterson 2012: 36.
[34] Moo 1996: 530.

was present in the transmission of the promise from Abraham to his offspring. Eventually, however, the future orientation of the promised inheritance (land) is expressed through the typological correspondences that unfold within the Old Testament. Moreover, by picking up and advancing the inheritance motif in the light of the fulfilment of Christ, Paul is able to trace these typological trajectories to their ultimate fulfilment in the consummation of the eschatological promises yet to come – a new creation.

Fulfilment in Hebrews

The intersection with land in Hebrews continues the pattern of fulfilment in the New Testament with the arrival of Jesus Christ and his finished work. Perhaps the clearest presentation of the land theme is found in 3:7 – 4:13 and in chapters 11–13. This section will provide context before delving into the exegesis of these passages.

In Hebrews 1 the author presents Jesus, the radiance of the glory of God and the exact imprint of his nature (vv. 1–4), as God's final and supreme revelation. He has inherited a name that is more excellent than angels,[35] for he is superior as God's Son (vv. 5–14). Therefore the people of God must pay closer attention to the message of salvation (2:1–4) because Jesus, God's authoritative Son, is *now* the founder of a greater salvation, though his people still wait for everything to be put in subjection to him (2:5–8). Nevertheless, Jesus is seen as exalted because of his humiliation (2:9–10). Indeed, Christ assumed a human nature because the children share in flesh and blood, so that he will destroy the devil (2:14), deliver his brethren (2:15–16) and help his people by serving as their sacrificial substitute before God (2:17–18). Lindars notes, 'The real humanity of Jesus is essential for the argument of Hebrews, because the whole argument turns on the saving efficacy of his death. . . . For the solidarity of Jesus with humanity makes him a representative figure.'[36] Hence it is imperative that God's people consider Jesus, who is greater than Moses, for

---

[35] Webster (2009: 81–93) makes eight assertions about the Son, from pre-temporal eternity to glorification, that are 'expansions and reiterations' of what is contained in Jesus' more excellent name. First, God appointed him the heir of all things (1:2). Secondly, through him God created the world (1:2). Thirdly, he is the effulgence of God's glory (1:3). Fourthly, he bears the stamp of God's very nature (1:3). Fifthly, he upholds all things by his powerful word (1:3). Sixthly, he made purification for sins (1:3). Seventhly, he sat down at the right hand of the Majesty on high (1:3). And finally, he has obtained a more excellent name (1:4).

[36] Lindars 1991: 40.

Jesus is faithful over God's house as God's Son (3:1–6a). And Christians are God's house by virtue of their relation to the Messiah, which makes perseverance all the more necessary (3:6b). Now, in the light of the contrast between Moses and Jesus (3:1–6), the author of Hebrews offers a warning to Jesus' followers not to be like the wilderness generation who did not enter God's rest.

Hebrews 3:7 – 4:13 provides a warning and a promise grounded on Psalm 95:7–11. The author's use of Psalm 95 presupposes both the Abrahamic promise of land and the well-established link between the land and rest (Deut. 12:8–10).[37] The author asserts that God's people are his house if they endure to the end (3:6). This is especially important given the wilderness generation's miraculous deliverance from the Egyptians. They were delivered out of Egypt but failed to enter the Promised Land because of their unbelief and disobedience. It is astonishing that the people who were led by Moses and delivered by God out of Egypt by signs and wonders were the same ones who grumbled and rebelled (3:16–19). Thus there is an important warning to heed: to be saved *out of* bondage is incomplete unless they are saved *into* something greater. But the author does not end with a warning. Rather, he holds out a promise of hope.

The argument now shifts to the rest/land theme as the author connects his audience to the wilderness generation of the past. In contrast to the former generation, now the emphasis falls upon the Christian community as the heir to the promise of entering God's rest.[38] This promise of hope is for the present recipients. The reason the wilderness generation failed and the message did not benefit them was because it was not 'united by faith with those who listened' (4:2).[39] But now in 4:3, all who believe ('we') enter into that rest (*katapausin*).[40]

[37] Harris 2009: 176.
[38] O'Brien 2010: 156.
[39] There is some textual difficulty with this verse that concerns the participle 'joined' (*synkekerasmenous*). One textual variant that agrees better with the theme of faith throughout Hebrews has 'joined' agreeing with the 'word' (tr. 'the word/message was not joined with faith'), but the best-attested reading has the participle agreeing with 'those/them' (tr. 'they [the Israelites] were not united in faith with those who listened'). The identity of those who did listen most likely includes Joshua and Caleb, although it could also extend to the faithful remnant of future generations. On either reading the point remains the same: the good news must be accompanied with faith, for only genuine faith perseveres. For further discussion, see ibid. 162; Lane 1991a: 98; contra Guthrie 1983: 112.
[40] The present tense of *eiserchometha* has been taken several ways. Some view it as a true present, with the result that believers are already entering into that rest and enjoy the rest referred to in Ps. 95. See e.g. Lincoln 1982: 211–212; Lane 1991a; Bruce 1964: 73, n. 17. DeSilva (2000: 32) suggests that viewing it as a progressive or continuous present might be a better way to take it, for believers are 'crossing the threshold into

The author's point is understood only if his argument concerning rest is followed through the Old Testament.

The connection of rest with Canaan is given in 3:16–19 and 4:8, but the future promise of rest points to something greater. The author links Psalm 95 to Genesis 2:1–3 by the use of 'my rest' (*pausin mou*). Psalm 95 in context refers to the land of Canaan, but it also looks beyond Canaan to a future, final place of rest. Moreover, the author demonstrates this pre-existing rest by bringing in Genesis 2:1–3. O'Brien comments, 'Within a salvation-historical time frame, Psalm 95:11 and Genesis 2:2 are joined by an exegetical argument . . . to prove that the rest cannot simply be identified with the land of Canaan – it was not final (v. 8).'[41] Canaan, then, was not an end in itself; it pointed forward to something much bigger that was to come. Consequently, the conclusion is drawn in 4:6–7:

> Since therefore it remains for some to enter it, and those who formerly received the good news failed to enter because of disobedience, again he appoints a certain day, 'Today', saying through David so long afterwards, in the words already quoted,

> 'Today, if you hear his voice,
> do not harden your hearts.'

Thus centuries after the denial of the Promised Land and rest offered to the first generation, God through David appoints a new day of opportunity, 'Today'.[42] This opportunity highlights the contemporary relevance of the text and is essential to the author's argument.[43] The second generation, like the first, did not experience final rest under Joshua; for if they had, then God would not have spoken of another day later on (4:8).[44] If this were not the case, then what need was there

the "better promised land", but still must "strive earnestly to enter."' This option makes better sense of the already–not yet tension. Still others (e.g. O'Brien 2010: 165–166) take it as solely future, denoting the consummation of rest. If it is an eschatological rest that is in view, then Christians resting from their works parallels God's rest. When God completed his work of creation, he rested; so his people, having completed their service on earth, will enter into his rest. However, one is not forced to accept an either/ or decision so long as it is understood that there are *both* present *and* future aspects involved, which fits with the inaugurated eschatological nature of the NT.

[41] O'Brien 2010: 167.

[42] Lane 1991a: 100–101.

[43] Attridge 1989: 114.

[44] The assumption in Heb. 4:8 that the people under Joshua did not experience rest has presented interpretative difficulties. The statement is a second-class condition that

for the exhortation in Psalm 95? The author of Hebrews, then, demonstrates good exegesis, for he shows what was already developed within the Old Testament itself, namely the incomplete character of rest in Canaan and the future-oriented, final rest of God. The earthly land of Canaan was a type of the eternal rest that still remains. So, then, there remains a Sabbath rest for the people of God (4:9). This leads the author to conclude with a vital exhortation: 'Let us therefore strive to enter that rest, so that no one may fall by the same sort of disobedience' (4:11).

Two conclusions can be drawn from Hebrews 3:7 – 4:13. First, the rest in Canaan functions as a type of God's heavenly rest in Genesis 2 and Psalm 95; that is, entering the presence of God on the last day.[45] The rest that came with the possession of the land was achieved in some measure under Joshua. This rest reflected the rest enjoyed at creation, but it was lost in the fall. However, it still left something to be desired. This rest, then, anticipated the eschatological rest for the people of God, which David announced in Psalm 95. As the Old Testament demonstrated, rest in the land was no longer a possibility. But God's rest is available for all who believe and obey. As long as it is called today, then, God's people are not exhorted to return to the type of rest in the land of Canaan. Rather, they are exhorted to enter God's eschatological rest that comes through a newfound relationship with Christ (3:6). Secondly, the already–not yet and faith-obedience tensions seen in Deuteronomy stand parallel in important ways to the audience of Hebrews. There are both present and future realities that serve as motivations to obey and persevere, yet they stem from the unshakeable grace that is shared in Christ. Therefore the recipients must heed the message of Hebrews, for God still speaks and his word is powerful and lays open those who are accountable to him (4:12–13).

indicates 'the assumption of an untruth (for the sake of an argument)' (Wallace 1996: 694). The previous chapter demonstrated that under Joshua's leadership some level of rest was experienced. Hence one solution to this apparent problem is to make a distinction in kind when it comes to the notion of rest. That is, Joshua did not give them eternal rest but rather temporal rest. However, this proposal introduces extra-biblical categories that do not arise from the text itself. Therefore the solution opted for in the present study is to make a typological distinction in the light of later revelation, especially in the light of the other typological patterns established in the OT (e.g. rest, tabernacle/temple). The type rest under Joshua anticipated its antitype, rest under Jesus, which is made clear within the book of Joshua and later in Ps. 95 and Heb. 3 – 4. Hence there is escalation in rest from the people under Joshua to the people under Christ. See Lane 1991a: 100–101; O'Brien 2010: 169–170.

[45] Schreiner 2008: 586; Lane 1991a: 100–101; O'Brien 2010: 170.

Hebrews goes on to argue that Jesus is a greater high priest (4:14 – 7:28), a mediator of a better covenant (8:1–13), a greater tabernacle and sacrifice (9 – 10), and provides a greater redemption. The author then returns to concepts associated with land in chapters 11–12, employing terms such as *topon* ('place'; 11:8), *klēronomian* ('inheritance'; 11:8), *gēn tēs epangelias* ('the land of promise'; 11:9), *polin* ('city'; 11:10, 16), *patrida* ('homeland'; 11:14), *Siōn orei* ('Mount Zion'; 12:22), *Ierousalēm epouraniō* ('heavenly Jerusalem'; 12:22; 13:14). These chapters are consistent with the overall message of Hebrews, which present the land in the Old Testament as a type of the greater land to come.

In Hebrews 11:8–22, the author shifts the focus to Abraham the patriarch, the examplar of faith in the Old Testament. He begins by briefly recounting the story of Abraham by focusing on two events in his life. First, the author emphasizes Abraham's obedient response to God to go to a 'place' (*topon*) that he would receive as an 'inheritance' (*klēronomian*) (vv. 8–10). The second event is the faith of Abraham and his barren wife Sarah to have children (v. 11). I will, however, here examine only the focus on Abraham and the land. According to verse 9, 'by faith [Abraham] went to live in the land of promise, as in a foreign land, living in tents with Isaac and Jacob, heirs with him of the same promise'. The image of the patriarchs living in tents stresses the fact that mere entry into the land did not result in the attainment of the promised inheritance. Then immediately it says that 'he was looking forward to the city that has foundations, whose designer and builder is God' (v. 10).[46] The logical relationship between verse 9 and 10 is important to note. Abraham looked for the land of promise *because* (*gar*) he was looking to the city with foundations. The pointed contrast between 'the land of promise' and 'a foreign land' serves to show the unsettled life of Abraham. That is, 'Entrance into the promised land had brought no settlement.'[47] Hence Abraham looked beyond his present fleeting scene to the unseen blessing, for the land pointed beyond itself to a more excellent consummation. According to the author, then, the patriarchs knew that the land of promise was not the ultimate fulfilment, since they were dwelling as strangers and exiles (11:13). Lane comments:

[46] The imperfect tense form of *exedecheto* emphasizes Abraham's 'continuous expectation' (Lane 1991b: 351).
[47] Ibid. 350.

Abraham's status as an immigrant and alien in the land had the positive effect of indicating that Canaan was not, in the final sense, the promised inheritance. It served to direct his attention beyond Canaan to the established city of God as the ultimate goal of his pilgrimage [cf. 11:13–16].[48]

This point is reiterated in verse 16, 'But as it is, they desire a better country, that is, a heavenly one. Therefore God is not ashamed to be called their God, for he has prepared for them a city.'[49] Harris notes:

> Perhaps the most relevant OT passage is Isa. 54:1–17, from which the Author appears to have drawn numerous allusions. In Isa. 54:1–17, Zion, initially portrayed as a barren woman (*steira*; cf. Heb. 11:11), is exhorted to enlarge the place of her tent (*ton topon tēs skēnēs sou*, v. 2; cf. Heb. 11:8–9). The foundations (*ta themelia*, v. 11; cf. Heb. 11:10) of restored Zion (next pictured as a city) are likened to precious jewels. The indescribable beauty and security of the city are the *klēronomia* of the servants of the Lord (v. 17; cf. 11:8).[50]

The background of Hebrews 11:8–16 suggests that Isaiah 54 was important in the author's understanding of the eternal city of God to which Abraham looked.

That the land of Canaan was not ultimately the fulfilment of the promise is confirmed in that the patriarchs died there without receiving the things promised (11:13). However, the land of Canaan was not merely a rest stop. Rather, it was the Promised Land – the land Abraham and his descendants received as their inheritance. From there they continuously waited for the appearance of the city of God, of which they were already members by virtue of God's call and promise. This city is later referred to as the heavenly homeland (11:16), the city of the living God, heavenly Jerusalem (12:22), the unshakeable kingdom (12:28) and the abiding city that is to come (13:14).[51] The

---

[48] Ibid. 351. So also O'Brien 2010: 414.

[49] See Walker 1996: 214.

[50] Harris 2009: 220.

[51] Concerning the nature of the city, Lane (1991b: 467) comments, 'There has been a strong tendency to interpret the notion of the heavenly city in Hebrews from the perspective of the Platonic tradition as mediated by Philo. In Philo, however, there is no concept of a heavenly city prepared by God that will be made visible in the new age. Philo concentrates on the etymology and the symbolism of the name "Jerusalem" rather than speaking of the city itself. This is the decisive difference between the Greek

patriarchs, notes Walker, 'were looking forward, not so much to the day when their descendants would inherit the physical Land, as to the day when they themselves would inherit the heavenly country which the physical Land signified'.[52] Indeed, they looked beyond Canaan to a *new* heaven and *new* earth – a *new* Jerusalem. Again, the promise of land typologically pointed to something greater.

Two conclusions can be drawn from Hebrews 11:8–22 that contribute to the land motif in Hebrews. First, this passage underscores the relationship between the Abrahamic promises and the promised inheritance. Secondly, this passage advances the argument that the promised inheritance was not finally fulfilled in the land of Canaan, but rather in the city of God, the heavenly homeland, greeted from afar. In this way, it shows 'that the land is not only a type of promised rest, but also a type of the city of God'.[53] Thus this passage offers an important stage in the unfolding typological trajectory of the land in Hebrews.

The epilogue in Hebrews 11:39–40 provides an appropriate summary of and conclusion to the list of examples of faith in chapter 11 and a transition to the call of Hebrews 12:1–13. This conclusion is important for the entire argument in chapter 11. The author says that all those celebrated in chapter 11 were commended for their trust in God to do what he had promised. However, they *did not* obtain what was promised. This failure was not due to any fault of their own. Instead, it was due to the gracious, meticulous providence of God, 'since God had provided something better for us' (v. 40). Thus the reason given is redemptive-historical. The 'something better' is Jesus and his work. God in his providence deferred the conferral of the final reward until the advent of Christ, his sacrificial death and the enacting of the new covenant. Therefore New Testament believers are all the more exhorted to run the race with endurance, looking to Jesus (12:1–13).

The final references to 'city' are found in Hebrews 12 – 13. In 12:18–24, a contrast is made between the wilderness generation under the old covenant (18–21) and New Testament believers, specifically as they relate to Jesus the mediator of the new covenant (22–24).

philosophical treatment of the heavenly city and the biblical realism that informs the formulation of this theme in Hebrews. In Hebrews the heavenly city is a transcendent reality that faithfully reflects the realism of the Jewish apocalyptic tradition as represented in *4 Ezra* and *2 Apocalypse of Baruch*. There is nothing abstract or contingent about this city in 12:22a, which differs fundamentally from the philosophical concept in Philo.' So also O'Brien 2010: 484.

[52] Walker 1996: 212.
[53] Harris 2009: 225.

Moreover, a contrast is made between Mount Sinai and Mount Zion.[54] Attridge notes that the omission of 'Sinai' (vv. 18–21) deliberately puts the focus on Zion.[55] The seven features that describe the encounter with God at Mount Sinai are set against the seven images that create a glorious vision of Mount Zion, the heavenly city of God. New covenant believers have not come to Mount Sinai, which was a holy terror to the old covenant people. Rather, they have come to Mount Zion, the city of the living God, the heavenly Jerusalem. Believers have access to God through Jesus, the mediator of a new covenant (24a). This is a joyful, celebrative access, not a terrifying one (22), for Jesus' sprinkled blood speaks a better word than the blood of Abel (24b). Indeed, there is a better speaking, for this speech is not accompanied with judgment but with mercy. That is, this speech is to encourage believers to persevere in faith in order to obtain eschatological rest, for greater responsibility comes with greater revelation.

The last reference is found in Hebrews 13:14, where the author speaks explicitly about the earthly Jerusalem. Because Jesus suffered in order to sanctify the people with his own blood (13:12), believers are to exemplify his suffering and they are to 'go to him outside the camp and bear the reproach he endured' (v. 13). The basis (*gar*) for this exhortation is that 'we have no lasting city, but we seek *the city* that is to come' (v. 14). Whereas in other places believers are reminded of what they do have (e.g. a better sacrifice, mediator, covenant), here they are reminded of what they *do not* have. That is, it is in heaven, not *here* on earth, that they possess an enduring city. Hebrews aligns itself with the message of the Old Testament concerning land: no earthy place, land or city can provide ultimate rest and security, for the earth itself will be shaken by the voice of our fire-consuming God (12:25–29).[56] The only place that will not be shaken is the kingdom

[54] Witherington (2009: 435) notes, '[The author of Hebrews] has perhaps learned this contrast from Paul (see Galatians). It is the heavenly city, the better country that Abraham saw from afar, that they have now drawn near to. Is our author envisioning his audience being raptured into heaven, into the presence of the angels and the living God, or simply dying and going to heaven? In fact he is not. Like the author of Revelation he envisions a corporate merger of heaven and earth – or, perhaps better said, a replacement of this current world, both heavens and earth, that is wasting away, with an eternal form of heaven and earth, which when Jesus returns and the dead are raised will become heaven on earth.'

[55] Attridge 1989: 372.

[56] In contrast to 2 Peter (3:10–13) and Revelation (21:1), Hebrews does not explicitly mention a new heaven and a new earth. From this absence, interpreters such as Ellingworth (1993: 688) conclude that the created order with its materiality will be obliterated from existence and believers will inhabit a realm that is heavenly and non-material. Adams (2009: 137–138), however, rightly argues that the author of

of God (12:28). But in the present, believers follow Jesus outside the city and confidently await the place to come.[57]

In summary, Hebrews clearly picks up the Old Testament account of land and associated concepts. But for the author, the presentation of land is not unfulfilled, rejected or ignored. Rather, in the light of the coming of Christ and his greater work, God has performed a greater deliverance than that of Egypt (chs. 8–10). As a result, if they persevere in faith he will bring them into his eschatological rest, the heavenly Jerusalem, their final homeland and the unshakeable kingdom. Therefore the land theme functions as a type of what will come as a result of Christ and the blood of his perfect sacrifice. Thus the type is eclipsed by its antitype in the light of Jesus, and those trusting in him await the ultimate fulfilment of his promises.

Fulfilment in Peter

Peter also employs the language of inheritance to describe what awaits Christians.[58] Peter writes to those who are 'elect exiles' (1 Peter 1:1) of the dispersion. In other words, their status as elect of God is what accounts for their being pilgrims of this world. Furthermore, like elect

---

Hebrews looks forward to a new creation. He writes, 'In Heb. 1:2, the Son is said to be "heir of all things" (*klēronomon pantōn*), which implies that at the eschaton there will be a cosmos for him to inherit. In 2:6–8, the writer cites Ps. 8:4–6, interpreting it as a statement of Christ's (future) universal reign, in fulfilment of the destiny God intended for humanity within the created order.

'In Hebrews 2:5, the author in fact indicates that the ideal state of things envisioned in Ps. 8:4–6, to be fulfilled when Christ reigns supreme, will be manifested in "the coming world" (*tēn oikoumenēn tēn mellousan*). . . . The expectation of a new earth would fit well with the reference to "the city that is to come" (13:14; cf. 11:10). That formulation suggests a future "earthly" manifestation of the city that currently exists as a heavenly reality (12:22). In the book of Revelation, the new Jerusalem descends from heaven to take its place in the new earth (Rev. 21:9–22:5). A similar theme may be implied here. Thus, although the author does not explicitly speak of a new creation to follow the demise of the old, there is sufficient evidence to deduce that this is indeed what he expects.' See also Laansma 2008a: 125–143; 2008b: 9–18.

[57] This place is described in Hebrews as heaven (12:23), an eternal inheritance (9:15), a final resting place (4:11), a kingdom (12:28), a country (11:14), a city (11:10, 16; 12:22), Mount Zion (12:22), the heavenly Jerusalem (12:22; 13:14).

[58] Most scholars agree that Peter's recipients were mainly Gentiles. See e.g. Achtemeier 1996: 50–51; Davids 1990: 8–9; Kelly 1969: 4; Schreiner 2003: 38. E.g. they lived in ignorance (1:14) and were 'ransomed from the futile ways inherited from your forefathers' (1:18). Moreover, Peter tells them that 'the time that is past suffices for doing what the Gentiles want to do, living in sensuality, passions, drunkenness, orgies, drinking parties, and lawless idolatry. With respect to this they are surprised when you do not join them in the same flood of debauchery, and they malign you' (4:3–4).

exiles, 'dispersion' (*diasporas*) is laden with Old Testament imagery. Davids comments:

> The Jews had used the term 'dispersion' or 'diaspora' to refer to their scattered communities outside Palestine ever since the Exile (cf. the Greek form of Deut. 28:25; Neh. 1:9; and Isa. 49:6); it appears several times in the NT with this meaning (see John 7:35; 11:32). Here in Peter we find a natural transfer of one of the titles of Israel to the church, as we will frequently later (cf. 2:5, 9).[59]

The threats of dispersion (Deut. 28:15–68) were realized in the Assyrian and Babylonian exiles. Many Jews had been scattered from their homeland because of their sin and were referred to as being in the dispersion (cf. John 7:35; Jas 1:1). Here, however, Peter uses the word in a metaphorical sense and applies it to his (largely) Gentile readers throughout Asia Minor.[60] From the outset, then, Peter indicates that the church of Jesus Christ is now identified with the Israel of God, his chosen people. This identity is further confirmed in the theme of 1 Peter 2:9, where the church is called 'a chosen race'.

Peter then praises God for the Christians' certain salvation, for through the resurrection of Jesus and because of God's great mercy they have been begotten anew to a living hope (1:3; cf. 1:23),[61] to an imperishable inheritance (1:4), and by God's power are kept through faith for the salvation to be revealed (1:5). Schreiner rightly notes that Peter selects the language of 'inheritance' (*klēronomian*) to describe what awaits Christians.[62] For Peter, like Paul, the background of the idea of inheritance is the Old Testament. Schreiner comments:

> In the Old Testament the inheritance is the land God promised to his people (Num 32:19; Deut 2:12; 12:9; 25:19; 26:1; Josh 11:23;

---

[59] Davids 1990: 46.

[60] Ibid. 8–9; Schreiner 2003: 51.

[61] Achtemeier (1996: 94) comments, 'The use of the rare word *anagennaō* puts emphasis rather on rebegetting or begetting anew than on being born anew, although of course the subsequent new birth is assumed (e.g., 2:2). Such an emphasis on begetting anew means this phrase has less reference to baptism than has often been asserted. It points rather to the totally new and unique origins of the Christian community, beginning not merely with a new birth but with a new origin altogether. It is by reason of this total newness that Christians are aliens and exiles in the world, and the fact that the situation is due to God's mercy indicates clearly enough that such status is to be seen as a blessing, not a curse, a point those undergoing persecution would need to hear.'

[62] Schreiner 2003: 62.

Ps 105:11; Acts 7:5). The word is especially common in Joshua for the apportionment of the land for each tribe or family. Peter understood the inheritance, however, no longer in terms of a land promised to Israel but in terms of the end-time hope that lies before believers.[63]

In other words, Peter's use of the term is understood in the light of Christ and his fulfilment. Michaels writes:

> Peter's use of the term is most closely related to NT passages that speak of 'inheriting' either 'the kingdom' (Matt. 25:34; 1 Cor. 6:9–10; 15:50; Gal. 5:21; cf. *klēronomia* in Eph. 5:5 and *klēronomoi* in James 2:5) or 'eternal life' (Matt. 19:29; Mark 10:17; Luke 10:25; 18:18) or an equivalent (e.g., 'the earth' [Matt. 5:5], 'incorruption' [1 Cor. 15:50], 'salvation' [Heb. 1:14], 'the promise' [Heb. 6:12], 'blessing' [1 Pet. 3:9], 'these things' [Rev. 21:7]).[64]

A salvation-historical shift centred in Christ, therefore, meant that the type met its terminus in the antitype. Grudem comments:

> The 'inheritance' of the New Covenant Christian is thus shown to be far superior to the earthly inheritance of the people of Israel in the land of Canaan. That earthly land was not 'kept' for them, but was *taken from them* in exile, and later by Roman occupation. Even while they possessed the land, it produced rewards that *decayed,* rewards whose glory *faded* away. The beauty of the land's holiness before God was repeatedly *defiled* by sin (Num. 35:24; Jer. 2:7; 3:2).[65]

Such could never happen to them again in their new home in Christ's kingdom, into which they – both Jew and Gentile – have been born anew. Indeed, this promised blessing (the antitype) is imperishable, undefiled and unfading. That is, no foreign enemies can take this inheritance, because, unlike the previous symbol of God's presence in the land, this one is kept in heaven for you (1:4).

The future fulfilment of God's promise, however, should not be understood as merely spiritual. Schreiner comments, 'This hope is still physical, for we learn from 2 Peter that it will be realized in a

---

[63] Ibid. See also Davids 1990: 52; Elliot 2000: 336.

[64] Michaels 1988: 20; see also Davids 1990: 52.

[65] Grudem 1988: 58; emphases original. So also Jobes 2003: 86.

new heaven and a new earth (2 Pet 3:13; cf. Rev 21:1–22:5). But it transcends and leaves behind the land of Palestine.'[66] Again, this idea of a transformed eschatological reality is also found in Paul, who casts the same vision with different words (e.g. 1 Cor. 15:52–54; Rom. 8:18–25). Furthermore, in ways similar to the book of Revelation, Peter looks forward to the promised new heaven and new earth (3:13; cf. Rev. 21:1), which point back to Isaiah (65:17; 66:22). Indeed, God's promises will reach their fulfilment, and, in contrast with the present world filled with evil deeds (3:10), the new creation will be one in which righteousness dwells (3:13).[67]

[66] Schreiner 2003: 62.

[67] Green 2008: 335. Some scholars have drawn the conclusion from 2 Peter 3:7, 10, 12 that the present creation will be completely annihilated. See e.g. Overstreet 1980: 362–365. Barber and Peterson (2012: 37–38), however, argue that this view should be rejected for several reasons. First, such an interpretation contradicts Paul (Rom. 8:20–21) and John (Rev. 22:3), who speak of the removal of the curse, not the extinction and recreation of God's world. Secondly, Romans 8:22–23 presents humanity and creation not as annihilated, but as cleansed of sin and transformed. Thirdly, 2 Peter 3:6 says that 'the world that then existed [during the flood] was deluged with water and perished'. Perished does not speak of a literal destruction but of its cleansing through the judgment of unbelievers. In the same way, the language of burning does not entail complete destruction, but of purifying the earth by removing all wickedness. Fourthly, Peter compares the destiny of the earth and of unbelievers (3:7). The destruction of the ungodly does not mean their annihilation. Rather, it means their eternal conscious punishment (Matt. 25:41, 46; 2 Thess. 1:5–9; Rev. 20:10–15). Finally, Peter's concern is with the purifying of sinners for the new creation, resulting in new heavens and a new earth where righteousness dwells (3:13). Hence they conclude, 'For Peter, then, the governing paradigm for the new creation is the all-pervasive perfection of the cosmos, for redemption must reach as far as the damage of sin. Furthermore, Peter, the pastor, applies his message to his hearers and to us. We should live as those who will give an account to God (2 Peter 3:10), who therefore strive for godliness (v. 12), and above all who yearn for Jesus' return (vv. 12–13)' (ibid.). See also Green 2008: 334; Heide 1997: 37–56; Hoekema 1979: 280–281. 'In either case,' concludes Schreiner (2003: 392), 'it seems that we can fairly say that the future world is physical, that a new universe will be born. Believers "are looking forward" (*prosdokōmen*) to this world, to the day of God (3:12), to the fulfilment of God's promises.'

Chapter Nine

The fulfilment of the promise consummated: the eschatological kingdom in Revelation

Given the story line up to this point, it should not surprise us how it ends in Revelation 21 – 22. Moyer Hubbard writes:

> The entire biblical story, from beginning to end, can rightly be described as an epic of *new creation*. As its prologue opens with Elohim's creation of heaven and earth, so its epilogue closes with the dramatic appearance of the new heaven and new earth. . . . *Creatio originalis* gives way to *creatio nova* as the one seated upon the throne announces, 'Behold, I make all things new!' (Rev. 21:5).[1]

The final place of the kingdom, the new creation described in Revelation 21 – 22, appears as the consummation of a complex biblical continuum reaching all the way back to creation.[2] This consummation depicts the new heaven and new earth as a paradisal new Eden, new Jerusalem and cosmological temple that is, in the climax of the covenants, filled with God's presence. Moreover, the end also relates to Israel's universalized land promises that reach back to Abraham and all the way to Eden. In fulfilment of the promise to Abraham that 'in you all the families of the earth shall be blessed' (Gen. 12:3), ransomed people from every tribe, tongue, people and nation (5:9) are restored to a new creation with its new Jerusalem reminiscent of Eden. In this new creation, the geographical boundaries of 'the land' expand to the entire new creation in ways that remarkably reflect the visions of the prophets such as Isaiah, Jeremiah and Ezekiel. That is,

---

[1] Hubbard 2002: 1; emphases original.
[2] Turner 1992: 264.

Revelation 21 – 22 interprets the future fulfilment of the prophets, and the entire Old Testament, by collapsing temple, city and land into one paradisal end-time picture portraying the final reality of God's covenant presence with his people.

The new creation as Edenic paradise

Scripture is about God's restoring paradise for his glory after humanity lost it. As paradise, the new Jerusalem is the fulfilment of what Eden was designed to be. For example, both Eden and the new Jerusalem reference the waters of life (Gen. 2:10–14; Rev. 22:1–2),[3] the tree of life (Gen. 3:22–24; Rev. 22:2),[4] precious stones (Gen. 2:11–12; Rev. 22:18–21; cf. Ezek. 28:13) and God's presence with his people (Gen. 3:8; Rev. 21:3–5, 22–23; 22:4–5).[5] In contrast to Eden, however, this paradise is free from sin, securely protected from evil and the evil one, and permanently filled with God's presence. Indeed, the various correspondences and echoes of Eden, Jerusalem, the temple, the Holy

[3] Both Mounce (1998: 386) and Ladd (1972: 286) connect the 'water of life' in Rev. 22:1 to Ezek. 47:1–12 and Zech. 14:8, pointing out that it describes the reign and blessing of eternal life in the age to come. Beale and McDonough (2007: 1153–1154), however, argue that it reaches farther back than these prophecies 'to the description of the primeval garden in Gen. 2:10: "a river was going forth from Eden." In association with the first Eden's river, the "gold, the bdellium and the onyx stone" were features around one of the river's tributaries, which compares to the precious stones surrounding the river of Rev. 22:1 (cf. 21:18–21). The point is that God will make the end like the beginning, though the consummated garden will exist on an escalated scale in comparison to the first.' See also Beasley-Murray 1974: 330.

[4] D. E. Johnson (2001: 321) notes, 'The tree of life stood in the center of Eden, the garden of God (Gen 2:9), and after their foolish rebellion Adam and Eve were expelled from the garden specifically to bar them from access to the tree of life in their condition of spiritual fallenness (Gen 3:23–24). In the new heaven and earth, however, the earth's peoples will again have access to the tree of life. The seventh and final benediction will show us how this can be: "Blessed are those who wash their robes, so that they may have the right to the tree of life, and may enter the gates into the city" (Rev 22:14).'

[5] Mounce (1998: 372) comments, 'It is interesting that most recent translations have the plural, peoples ("they shall be his peoples"), rather than the singular, people. Apparently, John modified the traditional concept (Jer. 7:23; 30:22; Hos. 2:23) and substituted a reference to the many peoples of redeemed humanity. Jesus had spoken of "other sheep that are not of this fold," which must become part of the one flock (Jn. 10:16). It is with the redeemed peoples of all races and nationalities that God will dwell in glory. God himself will be with them, and he will be their God.' Beale (1999: 1047) provides further OT warrant for the change to plural 'peoples' when he points out that 'Zech. 2:10–11 anticipates Rev. 21:3 in its interpretation of the same prophecies concerning God's final communion with his people, foreseeing an ethnic expansion of the boundaries of true Israel by identifying "many nations" as "my people," a term always used elsewhere in the OT for Israel.'

of Holies and Zion 'serve to demonstrate that the present vision is the consummation of all those hopes, lest any detail of the OT should have been omitted'.[6] The divine paradisal intention of Genesis 1 – 2 is not merely recaptured in the new heaven and new earth; it is astonishingly surpassed.

The new creation as temple

Perhaps the most surprising element given the centrality of the temple in the life of Israel is that the new creation contains no temple. Revelation 21:22 declares, 'And I saw no temple in the city, for its temple is the Lord God the Almighty and the Lamb. And the city has no need of sun or moon to shine on it, for the glory of God gives it light, and its lamp is the Lamb' (Rev. 21:22–23). Though various prophets had formerly anticipated the whole city as the site of God's presence, as truly his holy mountain, John is the first to eliminate the temple altogether.[7] Instead of the temple being the exclusive place of God's presence, John declares that the entire 'paradisal city-temple of Revelation 21:1 – 22:5 encompasses the entirety of the newly created earth'.[8] The most evident sign of this city-temple is its perfectly cubic shape (21:16). This glorious description is like no other previous place on earth, but is more akin to the holy of holies (1 Kgs 6:20). Thus the new earth now serves as the place of God's presence.

In Genesis 1 – 2, Adam and Eve were to extend the geographical boundaries of the garden-temple until Eden covered the earth.[9] Over time, then, the whole earth would become a garden-temple filled with their progeny – little priest-kings – and the earth would be full of the knowledge of the Lord as the waters cover the sea. The same is true for Abraham and the nation of Israel. Revelation, however, presents as accomplished what they failed to do through the triumph of the Lamb. The Edenic imagery in Revelation 21 – 22, then, shows that the building of the temple, which began in Genesis 2, is complete in Christ, and his people will encompass the entire earth.

[6] Dumbrell 1994: 345.
[7] See e.g. Ezek. 48:35; Zech. 14:20–21; Isa. 52:1; 54:2–3.
[8] Beale 2000: 358. Beale rightly argues from the reference to Isa. 65:17 in Rev. 21:1 that it is more likely that the 'new heaven' and 'new earth' of 21:1 is defined by and equated with the paradisal city-temple of 21:2 and 21:9 – 22:5.
[9] Beale 2004b: 81–82; see also Alexander 2008: 25.

The new creation as city (new Jerusalem)

The Bible itself portrays the move from creation to the new creation as movement from a garden (Gen. 2) to a city (Rev. 21 – 22). The progression from a garden to a city symbolizes the progression and completion of God's teleological purposes. Furthermore, the symbol of a city is significant. Dumbrell writes:

> For biblical readers the city is preeminently a symbol of world government. Therefore, the New Testament asserts the fact of final Kingdom of God rule, combining people, place and divine presence. With the advent of the New Jerusalem we have moved to the end. Unlike Ezekiel 40–48 (upon which Rev. 21–22 is so much dependent), the new city does not rest upon a cosmic mountain (cf. Ezek. 40:2), but 'comes down' to earth and turns the whole earth into a paradise by his presence.[10]

Through the rich imagery of Revelation, then, John shows that redemptive history in general, and the promises of the Edenic creation in particular, are consummated in a new heaven and new earth as a paradise, temple and city. In other words, Eden has not merely been regained and the Promised Land possessed; they have been radically transformed through the life, death, resurrection and rule of the Lamb who won a new creation for his people.

In John's final vision, the Old Testament types of Eden, land, temple and city are, in the light of Christ and his work of creating a new people and place, coextensive and fulfilled in their antitype – the new heaven and new earth. And, contrary to popular belief that the consummation is merely a spiritual or ethereal place, Ladd rightly notes, 'Biblical thought always places man on a redeemed earth, not in a heavenly realm removed from earthly existence.'[11] Eden, as the new temple-city, and the land, designed to recapture and advance the idyllic conditions of Eden, now reach their terminus in the new creation. Beale notes:

> The original Eden, Israel's old temple, old land, and old city, never reached the universal goal for which they were designed. As such, they became imperfect typological realities pointing forward to a

[10] Dumbrell 1985: 31.
[11] Ladd 1972: 275.

time when these would again become eschatological realities, whose design would reach their final goal.[12]

This final picture at the end depicts a glorious return to God's people living in his place under his rule, and thereby tying together the creation and placement of humans in Eden, the redemption of Israel and, finally, God's eschatological purposes to bring blessing to the world. Indeed, the kingdom of the world will become the kingdom of our Lord and of his Christ, and he will reign for ever and ever (11:15).[13] God's people will once again dwell in the land of promise – for ever.

[12] Beale 2011: 759.

[13] Beale (ibid. 760) observes that this text is an allusion to Ps. 2:2, 8, which predicted that Israel's Messiah would inherit the whole world in fulfilment of the original intent of Israel's land promises.

A concluding summary of the New Testament

The New Testament contends that what was promised in the Old Testament is fulfilled in the New. In Matthew, God's highly anticipated Messiah arrives on the historical scene and, true to prophetic form, inaugurates the kingdom that awaits its consummation in the new earth. Thus the themes associated with land in the Old Testament are now connected to Jesus, fulfilled in the light of him and, as seen in John, enjoyed in relation to him. He performs a new exodus and saves his people out of sin and into the place of redemptive blessing – now centred in him. Moreover, he gives rest to those who come to him. Life that once abounded in the land now abounds in him, for he is the vine, the resurrection and the life. Additionally, all the nations are his and he summons his disciples to go and gather those whom he already possesses.

The fulfilment of the land theme continues throughout Hebrews, 1 and 2 Peter and Revelation. People enter God's rest through faith in the true and greater Son, Jesus Christ, and look for a better country. Though Old Testament believers looked through the land of promise to God's greater eschatological rest and city, by virtue of Christ and his work, new covenant believers now look to Jesus and confidently await their arrival in the new Jerusalem, homeland, unshakeable kingdom and abiding city that is to come, which is described in the letters of Peter and Revelation as the new heaven and new earth. In short, the land, which served as a type of this greater reality, now reaches its *telos*. And the covenant relationship for which we were created is realized in the new heaven and new earth, where our glorious triune God will dwell with us, and we will be his people, and God himself will be with us as our God (Rev. 21:3).

Chapter Ten

Theological reflections

The land promised to Abraham advances the place of the kingdom that was lost in Eden and serves as a type throughout Israel's
history that anticipates an even greater land – prepared for God's
people – that will come as a result of the person and work of Jesus
Christ. In other words, the land and its blessings (type) find their fulfilment in the new heaven and new earth (antitype) won by Christ.

As the beginning and the end show, God's cosmological purpose
is for his people to dwell in his place under his rule. That is, from
Genesis 1 through Revelation 22 God's eschatological goal is to
establish his kingdom on earth. However, due to the fall of humanity
into sin and death the accomplishment of this goal is radically marred
but not decimated, for God makes a promise that will providentially
guide his redemptive means to their divinely appointed end. That is,
future triumph over the serpent will come through the offspring of
the woman (Gen. 3:15). God will re-establish his kingdom on earth
through his graciously initiated covenants that reach their *telos* in
and through the person and work of Christ, the last Adam. As a
result, the kingdom of the world will become the kingdom of our
Lord and of his Christ, and he will reign for ever and ever (Rev. 11:15).

God's promise of land to Abraham advances God's fulfilment of
his promise in four plot movements across the Old Testament: (1)
Genesis 1 – 11, (2) the nature and scope of the Abrahamic covenant
and the promise of land, (3) the advancement and fulfilment(s) of
God's promise of land throughout Israel's history, and (4) the loss
of land in exile and the prophetic anticipation of an international and
universal restoration brought through a new covenant. In the end,
God's cosmological plan progresses from Adam through Abraham,
and is cast in terms of an Edenic land, city and temple – all of which
are coextensive. What these plot movements demonstrate, then, is that
the land is a type of a new creation that will come through Abraham's
seed and a Davidic Son, who will triumphantly bring God's new
covenant people into a new creation.

Finally, programmatic passages in the New Testament are examined,
which present the land promised to Abraham and his offspring to be

finally fulfilled in the (physical) new heaven and earth won by Christ. At this time in history, however, the fulfilment is primarily focused on Christ, who himself has inaugurated a new creational kingdom through his physical resurrection and has made new creations out of those united with him. This united people – both Jew and Gentile – now live between the inauguration and consummation of the kingdom and anticipate the final fulfilment in the new heaven and new earth (Rev. 21 – 22).

This chapter aims to apply the interpretative findings of the previous chapters to eschatology. More specifically, it will evaluate how the land promise is interpreted and fulfilled in the theological systems of dispensationalism and covenant theology in the light of the arguments presented throughout this work.

Bound for the Promised Land: some theological implications

There are various forms of dispensationalism, which makes it difficult to present a unified theology of land.[1] Nevertheless, it is possible to distil the pillars of dispensational theology into an essential core. That is, all forms of dispensational theology construct their theology of land from an interconnected set of convictions.[2] First, the sine qua non of dispensationalism is the distinction between the nation of Israel and the church.[3] Secondly, dispensationalists believe that God's unconditional promise of land in the Abrahamic covenant must be fulfilled to the nation of Israel in the future, which 'includes at least

---

[1] See e.g. Bateman 1999; Feinberg 1988: 63–86; Blaising 1992: 13–34; 1993a: 9–56; Ryrie 2007; Saucy 1993.

[2] I have adapted these points from Stephen Wellum in Gentry and Wellum 2012: 704.

[3] Ryrie 2007: 46; Blaising 1992: 23. Feinberg (1988: 72–73) rightly notes that most theological systems, even covenant theology or systems that most allegorize the OT, distinguish Israel from the church. Therefore it is the kind of distinction that distinguishes dispensationalism. For Feinberg, 'what is distinctive of dispensational thinking is recognition' of the four distinct senses of seed ([1] biological, ethnic, national; [2] political; [3] spiritual; [4] typological) 'as operative in both Testaments coupled with a demand that no sense (spiritually especially) is more important than any other, and that no sense cancels out the meaning and implications of the other senses. The more one emphasizes the distinctness and importance of the various senses, the more dispensational and discontinuity-oriented his system becomes, for the distinct senses necessitate speaking of Israel ethnically, politically, and spiritually, as well as speaking of the church' (ibid.). Ware (1992: 92) defines this distinction when he writes, 'Israel and the church share theologically rich and important elements of commonality while at the same time maintaining distinct identities.'

the millennial reign of Christ and for some dispensationalists, extends into the eternal state as well'.[4] Feinberg writes, 'If an OT prophecy or promise is made unconditionally to a given people and is still unfulfilled to them even in the NT era, then the prophecy must still be fulfilled to them.'[5] Thirdly, and building on the second point, is a hermeneutical concern: the New Testament does not reinterpret or spiritualize the land promise to Israel.[6] Again, Feinberg writes, 'Lack of repetition in the NT does not render an OT teaching inoperative during the NT era so long as nothing explicitly or implicitly cancels it.'[7] Feinberg's contention applies to types and antitypes and leads to the fourth point, which Wellum says is often not argued but is assumed. Wellum writes:

> For dispensational theology, the 'land' must *not* be viewed as a type or pattern of something greater. . . . Instead, it is a straightforward ('literal') promise that reaches its fulfillment only with Christ ruling and reigning in the millennium in the land of Israel. To view the land as a divinely given pattern which looks back to the creation and forward to the greater reality of the new creation is rejected.[8]

This point is demonstrated by Feinberg when he states:

> My contention is that understanding that both type and antitype must have their own meaning even while bearing a typological relation to the other, understanding the implications of NT reinterpretation of the OT, and realizing that progress of revelation only renders earlier truth inoperative if God says so leads one to see that the meaning of both OT and NT passages must be maintained.[9]

As a result, dispensationalists reject the idea that the land promised to Abraham and given to Israel serves as a type of the new creation won by Christ for all God's people. How, then, does the present study differ from the dispensational view? To answer this question is to

---

[4] Blaising 1993a: 21; cf. Feinberg 1988: 68. Kaiser (1981: 311) writes, 'The mark of God's new measure of grace, not only to Israel as a nation but also to all the nations and Gentiles at large, will be Israel's return to the land and enjoyment of it in the millennium.' See also Ware 1992: 93–96.

[5] Feinberg 1988: 76. See also Blaising 1993b: 132–134.

[6] Saucy 1993: 30–31.

[7] Feinberg 1988: 76.

[8] Gentry and Wellum 2012: 704.

[9] Feinberg 1988: 79.

summarize the biblical-theological arguments set forth in the previous chapters across the three horizons (textual, epochal and canonical) of Scripture.

To begin, appeal to the unconditional nature of the Abrahamic covenant does not prove that the promise of land must be exclusively fulfilled to the nation of Israel in the future. As chapter 3 demonstrated, the common distinction between unconditional and conditional covenants is not quite accurate. On the one hand, Genesis 15 forcefully shows that God will unilaterally fulfil the promise and conditions of the covenant even if it means taking the curse upon himself. However, this unconditional emphasis does not remove the necessity of Abraham's obedience. Genesis 17:2 and 22:17–18 (cf. 26:4–5) show that God requires an obedient partner in the covenant relationship. He promises the covenant blessings to Abraham, but these blessings are reserved for people who trust and obey him. In other words, the ultimate fulfilment of the covenant is grounded on God's promises, but the means of fulfilment will come through Abraham's (and his descendants') obedience. This conditionality, therefore, is instrumental to the reception and fulfilment of the promises. The tension between God's promise and the necessity of obedience in the covenant relationship becomes clearer and stronger as the story line progresses, and is crucial for understanding the nature and progression of the covenants as they reach their *telos* in Christ, who inaugurates a new and better covenant in his own blood. That is, when the larger canonical story line is considered, the conditions are met by God himself when he sends his obedient Son – the true seed of Abraham (Gal. 3) – to fulfil the demands of the covenant.

Furthermore, appeal to the Abrahamic covenant supports the view that the land promise is finally fulfilled in a greater way than in the geographical boundaries of Canaan. That is, the Abrahamic covenant itself has *both* national and international *and* regional and global dimensions, which are later confirmed through the progress of God's revelation. This point must be traced across the three horizons of Scripture. First, the calling of and promise to Abraham recovers the universal purpose of Adam in terms both of offspring and land. In other words, the universal scope of Eden temporarily narrows to the land of Canaan, which then expands with the proliferation of Abraham's offspring.

Secondly, when Genesis 22:17–18 and 26:3–4 are taken together, the immediate context of the Abrahamic covenant already points to a universal expansion of the territorial promise. In other words, the propagation of Abraham's offspring will result in inheriting the world (cf. Rom. 4:13). This interpretation is not reinterpreting or spiritual-izing the Old Testament promise. Rather, it establishes the type or pattern that the ultimate fulfilment of the promise will encompass the entire world.

Thirdly, after the exodus from Egypt, Deuteronomy depicts Israel's imminent entrance into the Promised Land as a return to Edenic conditions, for they will multiply, subdue and enjoy blessing in the land. Moreover, when Israel – God's son – inherits the land, rest will follow. Securing their inheritance of the Promised Land, then, presents a pattern, or type, of Israel's entering into God's eternal rest, of which Canaan is the beginning.

Fourthly, Joshua demonstrates initial fulfilment of the Abrahamic promise and at the same time anticipates a greater fulfilment that will bring Eden-like rest. However, the end of Joshua points to Israel's future failure and further need for subsequent repossession.

Fifthly, a significant advance of God's promise to plant his people in the land comes with the arrival of David and his son Solomon. David and Solomon, respectively, enjoy expansive and international reigns, and the nation enjoys rest from its enemies. The construction of the temple and subsequent rest represent a new Eden, for God once again dwells with his people 'in a more intensive sense'.[10] However, while Solomon typifies a return to Edenic conditions, he is responsible through his disobedience for the second expulsion from the sanctuary-land and the end of the monarchy.[11] Subsequently, the united kingdom is divided and exiled. In the midst of judgment, however, the prophets resound with the eschatological hope of restoration that will bring the universal purposes of Eden, Abraham and David back into focus.

Finally, the prophets advance the pattern of God's promise by portraying the return from exile in various ways and stages, including both a physical and spiritual return with national and international results. That is, through the new covenant God will make a new people – composed of both believing Jews and Gentiles – and make a new place for them to live. This restoration describes incredible realities that expand the original forms: the return is so glorious that it is described as an Edenic city-temple-land, coextensive with the new creation and filled with an international people. Therefore, as the Old Testament progresses and escalates towards God's fulfilment of his

---

[10] Poythress 1991: 70.
[11] Davis 2011: 40.

promises, at each stage of redemptive history the numerous textual and historical correspondences present the Promised Land as a type that will ultimately be fulfilled when the rule of the king will extend to the entire creation (Ps. 72:8–11, 17–19).

Before moving to the New Testament, an important observation must be made concerning an Old Testament theology of land. There are exegetical grounds both in the immediate context of the Abrahamic covenant and across the entire Old Testament to argue that God's original intention for the land was not *merely* to be limited to the specific geographical boundaries of Canaan. In other words, when situated within the biblical covenants and viewed diachronically, the land functions as a type or pattern of something greater that will recapture God's original design for creation.[12] This point is important, for non-dispensationalists have been charged with not sufficiently developing a theology of the land on Old Testament terms.[13] Feinberg writes:

> Dispensational and nondispensational thinkers agree that the NT fulfills the OT and is a more complete revelation of God. But there is disagreement as to what that means for the priority of one Testament over the other. Nondispensationalists begin with NT teaching as having priority, and then go back to the OT. Dispensationalists often go back to the OT, but wherever they begin they demand that the OT be taken on its own terms rather than reinterpreted in the light of the NT.[14]

While this charge is debatable,[15] there is some warrant that confirms Feinberg's point.[16] For example, Louis Berkhof writes:

> The covenant with Abraham already included a symbolical element. On the one hand it had reference to temporal blessings, such as the land of Canaan, a numerous offspring, protection against and

---

[12] Gentry and Wellum 2012: 706.
[13] Feinberg 1988: 75.
[14] Ibid.
[15] E.g. Wellum (Gentry and Wellum 2012: 117–118) contends, 'ironically . . . dispensational *and* covenant theology actually follow the *same* hermeneutic in appealing to the Old Testament, yet they do so *in different areas* which are central to their theological system' (emphases original). For dispensationalism, the area of contention is the Israel–church relationship, particularly concerning the land promise. For covenant theology, the area of contention is also the Israel–church relationship, particularly the genealogical principle 'you and your children' (ibid.).
[16] Notable exceptions include Hoekema 1979: 274–287; Johnston and Walker 2000: 15–50; C. J. H. Wright 2004: 184–186; Beale 2011: 750–772; Storms 2013: 344–348.

victory over the enemies; and the other, it referred to spiritual blessings. It should be borne in mind, however, that the former were not coordinate with, but subordinate to, the latter. These temporal blessings did not constitute an end in themselves, but served to symbolize and typify spiritual and heavenly blessings.[17]

Similarly, Francis Andersen notes:

> The prophets who give warning of threatened deportation from Palestine also hold out hopes of redemption by restoration to the promised land. But in the New Testament such a matter is wholly spiritualized; the land of promise is 'a better heavenly city' (Heb 11:10, 16), a thought in line with Paul's teaching that Sarah, as the mother of us all, is 'Jerusalem which is above' (Gal 4:26). The promised rest continues to remain, then, to the people of God and those who believe in Jesus enter into it (Heb 4).[18]

Bruce Waltke contributes a substantial chapter developing an Old Testament theology of land, but then argues:

> [T]he New Testament redefines Land in three ways: first, *spiritually,* as a reference to Christ's person; second, *transcendentally,* as a reference to heavenly Jerusalem; and third, *eschatologically,* as a reference to the new Jerusalem after Christ's second coming. By 'redefine' we mean that whereas 'Land' in the Old Testament refers to Israel's life in Canaan, in the New Testament 'Land' is transmuted to refer to life in Christ.[19]

As a result, dispensationalists such as Blaising and Bock write:

> Is it possible that covenantalist approaches to the question of the relationship of Old Testament and New Testament hope are already

---

[17] Berkhof 1996: 296.
[18] Andersen 1960: 243–244.
[19] Waltke with Yu 2007: 560; emphases original. Beale (2011: 769), also a non-dispensationalist, rightly criticizes this definition for sounding 'a bit too close to allegorization or undue spiritualization, even though Waltke contends that Christ has the authority to redefine the OT divine authorial intent in this manner'. In its place, Beale (ibid.) elaborates on Waltke's definition in this way: 'that the land was a type of the new creation in that its true design was for Israel (as a corporate Adam) to be faithful and expand the land's borders to encompass the whole earth. Since Israel failed in this, its old land still pointed to this unfulfilled universal consummated expansion into a new creation at some point in the future.'

determined by a traditional structure framed within the linguistic dimensions of the New Testament before the biblical theology of the Old Testament has been properly understood in its historical setting?[20]

While this question is disputable, the present study is in basic agreement with them in that covenant theology tends to move from the Old Testament to the New too quickly before comprehensively developing the land theme across the Old Testament, both in its historical and epochal horizons. When this process is accomplished, the New Testament demonstrates both *when* and *how* the Old Testament is brought to fulfilment in Christ, though in a way that does not reinterpret, spiritualize or contravene the earlier texts.[21]

The New Testament demonstrates that what was promised in the Old Testament is fulfilled through the person and work of Christ, the son of David, the son of Abraham, the son of Adam, the son of God. Jesus – the true Israel – inaugurates the kingdom through his death and resurrection and finally delivers his people from the exile of sin. He interprets the eschatological land promises through the lens of the many typological and universalized texts in the Old Testament (Matt. 5:5). He makes a new covenant people – described as new creations and a new temple – with those united to him, the true temple. This new people, the church of Jesus Christ made up of both Jew and Gentile, await their final home, the new heaven and new earth that is cast in terms of a paradisal garden-temple-city.[22] In other words, the variegated realities of the Old Testament promises – the expansive city, temple and land – overlap with the new creation won by Christ (Rev. 21 – 22). Thus Israel's land promises reach the fulfilment of their original design when redeemed people from every tribe, tongue, nation and people fill and inhabit the whole earth.[23] In this sense, then, what believing Israel obtains is far greater than the land of Canaan, for they – along with the nations – will inherit the whole earth in fulfilment of God's gracious and irrevocable promises.

[20] Blaising and Bock 1992: 393.
[21] Gentry and Wellum 2012: 116.
[22] That the church of Jesus Christ is composed of both Jew and Gentile (e.g. Galatians) does not eliminate a future salvation for ethnic Israel (Rom. 9 – 11). However, this future salvation is obtained only through faith in Jesus Christ as a surprising display of God's faithfulness and grace.
[23] Contrary to the notion that this fulfilment is merely ethereal or spiritual, George Ladd (1972: 275) is correct when he writes, 'Throughout the entire Bible, the ultimate destiny of God's people is an earthly destiny.'

The issue of the fulfilment of the land promise in the New Testament presents a crucial issue for a particular view of typology within dispensationalism. Dispensationalists agree that if the land promised to Israel is unconditional, then the ultimate fulfilment must be to the nation of Israel in the future regardless of how the New Testament applies the Old Testament texts.[24] As a result, Edward Glenny notes that progressive dispensationalists, who agree with revised dispensationalists but go beyond them in their understanding of typology, allow some of the Old Testament promises for Israel to find typological fulfilment in the church. However, this initial fulfilment does not annul the original Old Testament meaning for Israel.[25] That is, 'Even though the church fulfils these Old Testament prophecies, it does not exhaust them.'[26] When applied to the issue of land, then, this view maintains that, although some spiritual aspects are applied to the church, the territorial aspects of God's promise to the nation of Israel will be fulfilled in the future.[27] In other words, although the antitype is in a real sense a fulfilment of the type, the fulfilment is only a partial one. Therefore the original promises to the nation of Israel will still be kept, even if they have partial application to the church.[28]

So what are we to make of this approach to the typological fulfilment of the land promise? Although this view should be commended for attempting to apply the inaugurated eschatological nature of the kingdom to its interpretation of the land promise, it does not do full justice to the New Testament presentation of the already–not yet character of the kingdom or the nature of typological fulfilment in Scripture. First, the application of inaugurated eschatology is not accurate *at this point*. That is, while there is an already–not yet nature to the kingdom in the New Testament, this eschatological perspective does not *merely* mean that part of the kingdom is present now in the church and part of it will be present later in the nation of Israel.

[24] See e.g. Feinberg 1988: 77–83.

[25] Glenny 1997: 627–638.

[26] Ibid. 634–635. Though Feinberg's (1988: 77) overall position more closely resembles revised dispensationalism, his view of typology is similar to progressive dispensationalism. E.g. he writes, 'Double fulfilment is necessitated by the NT's application of the passage to the church and by maintaining the integrity of the OT's meaning, especially in view of the unconditional nature of the promises to Israel.'

[27] Ware 1992: 94.

[28] This both–and approach is tied to the inaugurated eschatology embraced by progressive dispensationalists. That is, the kingdom of God has come partially (spiritually) in the arrival of Christ, and, derivatively, his church, but the final establishment of his kingdom on earth awaits its consummation upon Christ's final return.

Instead, the New Testament shows that *all* of God's saving promises have *already* been fulfilled in Christ and that these promises are expanding where Christ is present – in the church now and finally in the new heaven and new earth in the age to come.

Secondly, Scripture presents the New Testament antitype to fulfil the Old Testament type, for in and through the person and work of Christ all of God's promises have reached their *telos*. This point is what distinguishes the view of this book from replacement theology. In other words, it is not that the church replaces Israel and inherits her blessings. Rather, Israel finds its fulfilment not in a community but in an individual Son of God.[29] Richard Davidson demonstrates this typological pattern by examining every New Testament use of 'type' and its cognates.[30] The Bible's use of typology is consistently characterized by an eschatological escalation, or intensification, in the progression from type to antitype and from promise to fulfilment. Furthermore, biblical typology is *Christotelic*.[31] In other words, Old Testament types do not merely correspond ana-logically to New Testament types, but were designed by God to be 'a shadow of the good things to come' (Heb. 10:1).[32] Mark Karlberg writes:

> To be sure, there is still to be at the consummation an antitypical fulfillment of the land promise, a cosmic antitype to typological Canaan-land, such as does not obtain in the present Church-age stage of the new covenant. But genuine typological interpretation rules out any additional literal fulfillment of the land promise in a future restoration of national Israel subsequent to or alongside the messianic fulfillment.[33]

Indeed, all of God's promises find their ultimate terminus in the person and work of Christ as the culmination of God's revelation and redemptive plan, which will end in nothing less than a new creation for all of his people *in Christ*.

---

[29] France 1989: 208.

[30] Davidson 1981.

[31] This term comes from Enns 2005. While I do not accept many of Enns's con-clusions concerning the NT's use of the OT, this particular term is helpful because it reminds the reader that Scripture has an eschatological purpose and goal that are realized in and through Christ and his work.

[32] E.g. the sacrificial system, temple and priesthood.

[33] Karlberg 1988: 259–260.

Conclusion

Here, at the end, let us be reminded that our great and glorious triune God fulfils his promises. In his ministry, Jesus announced that God was working to fulfil his ancient promises of restoration from exile and the establishment of his universal and international kingdom. In this age, however, we live as sojourners and exiles who seek the city that is to come, whose designer and builder is God (1 Peter 2:11; Heb. 11:10; 13:14). We should in faith, therefore, live with this eschatological anticipation in our minds and hearts, and in our words to others until *that* day (1 Thess. 4:13 – 5:11).

> Then I saw a new heaven and a new earth, for the first heaven and the first earth had passed away, and the sea was no more. And I saw the holy city, new Jerusalem, coming down out of heaven from God, prepared as a bride adorned for her husband. And I heard a loud voice from the throne saying, 'Behold, the dwelling place of God is with man. He will dwell with them, and they will be his people, and God himself will be with them as their God. He will wipe away every tear from their eyes, and death shall be no more, neither shall there be mourning nor crying nor pain any more, for the former things have passed away.'
>
> And he who was seated on the throne said, 'Behold, I am making all things new.' (Rev. 21:1–5)

Amen. Come, Lord Jesus.

Bibliography

Achtemeier, Paul J. (1996), *1 Peter*, Hermeneia, Minneapolis: Fortress.

Adam, Peter (2008), *Written for Us: Receiving God's Words in the Bible*, Nottingham: Inter-Varsity Press.

Adams, Edward (2009), 'The Cosmology of Hebrews', in Richard Bauckham, Daniel R. Driver, Trevor A. Hart and Nathan MacDonald (eds.), *The Epistle to the Hebrews and Christian Theology*, Grand Rapids: Eerdmans, 122–139.

Alexander, T. Desmond (1997), 'Further Observations on the Term "Seed" in Genesis', *TynB* 48.2: 363–367.

——— (1998), *The Servant King: The Bible's Portrait of the Messiah*, Vancouver: Regent College.

——— (2000a), 'Beyond Borders: The Wider Dimensions of Land', in Philip Johnston and Peter Walker (eds.), *The Land of Promise: Biblical, Theological, and Contemporary Perspectives*, Leicester: Apollos; Downers Grove: InterVarsity Press, 35–50.

——— (2000b), 'Seed', in *NDBT*, 769–773.

——— (2008), *From Eden to the New Jerusalem: Exploring God's Plan for Life on Earth*, Nottingham: Inter-Varsity Press.

——— (2012), *From Paradise to the Promised Land: An Introduction to the Pentateuch*, 3rd ed., Grand Rapids: Baker.

Allison Jr., Dale C. (2005), *Studies in Matthew: Interpretation Past and Present*, Grand Rapids: Baker.

Andersen, Francis (1960), 'The Scope of the Abrahamic Covenant', *Chm* 74.4: 239–244.

Anderson, Bernhard W. (1986), *Understanding the Old Testament*, 4th ed., Englewood Cliffs, N.J.: Prentice-Hall.

——— (1999), *Contours of Old Testament Theology*, Minneapolis: Fortress.

Arnold, Clinton E. (2010), *Ephesians*, ZECNT, Grand Rapids: Zondervan.

Ateek, Naim (1989), *Justice and Only Justice: A Palestinian Theology of Liberation*, Maryknoll, N.Y.: Orbis.

——— (2000), 'Zionism and the Land: A Palestinian Christian Perspective', in Philip Johnston and Peter Walker (eds.), *The Land of Promise: Biblical, Theological and Contemporary Perspectives*, Leicester: Apollos; Downers Grove: InterVarsity Press, 201–214.

——— (2008), *A Palestinian Christian Cry for Reconciliation*, Maryknoll, N.Y.: Orbis.

Attridge, Harold W. (1989), *The Epistle to the Hebrews*, Hermeneia, Philadelphia: Fortress.

Baker, David L. (1994), 'Typology and the Christian Use of the Old Testament', in G. K. Beale (ed.), *The Right Doctrine from the Wrong Text? Essays on the Use of the Old Testament in the New*, Grand Rapids: Baker, 313–330.

——— (2010), *Two Testaments, One Bible: The Theological Relationship Between the Old and New Testaments*, 3rd ed., Leicester: Apollos; Downers Grove: InterVarsity Press.

Barber, Dan C., and Robert A. Peterson (2012), *Life Everlasting: The Unfolding Story of Heaven*, Phillipsburg: P. & R.

Barclay, J. M. G. (ed.) (2004), *Negotiating Diaspora: Jewish Strategies in the Roman Empire*, London: T. & T. Clark.

Barker, Kenneth L. (1992), 'The Scope and Center of Old and New Testament Theology and Hope', in Craig A. Blaising and Darrell L. Bock (eds.), *Dispensationalism, Israel and the Church: The Search for Definition*, Grand Rapids: Zondervan, 293–328.

Barnett, Paul (2009), *Messiah: Jesus – The Evidence of History*, Nottingham: Inter-Varsity Press.

Barr, James (1999), *The Concept of Biblical Theology: An Old Testament Perspective*, Minneapolis: Fortress.

Bartholomew, Craig G. (2007), 'The Theology of Place in Genesis 1–3', in J. G. McConville and Karl Möller (eds.), *Reading the Law: Studies in Honour of Gordon J. Wenham*, New York: T. & T. Clark, 173–195.

——— (2011), *Where Mortals Dwell: A Christian View of Place for Today*, Grand Rapids: Baker.

Bartholomew, Craig G., and Michael W. Goheen (eds.) (2004), *The Drama of Scripture: Finding Our Place in the Biblical Story*, Grand Rapids: Baker.

Bass, Derek Drummond (2008), 'Hosea's Use of Scripture: An Analysis of His Hermeneutics', PhD diss., Louisville: Southern Baptist Theological Seminary.

Bateman IV, Herbert W. (ed.) (1999), *Three Central Issues in Contemporary Dispensationalism: A Comparison of Traditional and Progressive Views*, Grand Rapids: Kregel.

Bateman IV, Herbert W., Darrell L. Bock and Gordon H. Johnston (2012), *Jesus the Messiah: Tracing the Promises, Expectations, and Coming of Israel's King*, Grand Rapids: Kregel.

Bauckham, Richard (1993a), *The Climax of Prophecy: Studies on the Book of Revelation*, New York: T. & T. Clark.

——— (1993b), *The Theology of the Book of Revelation*, Cambridge: Cambridge University Press.

——— (2008), *Jesus and the God of Israel: God Crucified and Other Studies on the New Testament's Christology of Divine Identity*, Grand Rapids: Eerdmans.

Beale, G. K. (1994), 'Did Jesus and His Followers Preach the Right Doctrine from the Wrong Texts? An Examination of the Presuppositions of Jesus' and the Apostles' Exegetical Method', in G. K. Beale (ed.), *The Right Doctrine from the Wrong Text? Essays on the Use of the Old Testament in the New*, Grand Rapids: Baker, 387–404.

——— (1997), 'The Eschatological Conception of New Testament Theology', in Kent E. Brower and Mark W. Elliot (eds.), *Eschatology in Bible and Theology: Evangelical Essays at the Dawn of a New Millennium*, Downers Grove: InterVarsity Press, 11–52.

——— (1999), *The Book of Revelation*, NIGTC, Grand Rapids: Eerdmans.

——— (2000), 'Revelation (Book)', in *NDBT*, 356–363.

——— (2002), 'The New Testament and New Creation', in Scott J. Hafemann (ed.), *Biblical Theology: Retrospect and Prospect*, Downers Grove: InterVarsity Press, 159–173.

——— (2004a), 'The Final Vision of the Apocalypse and Its Implications for a Biblical Theology of the Temple', in T. Desmond Alexander and Simon Gathercole (eds.), *Heaven on Earth: The Temple in Biblical Theology*, Waynesboro, Ga.: Paternoster, 191–209.

——— (2004b), *The Temple and the Church's Mission: A Biblical Theology of the Dwelling Place of God*, NSBT 17, Leicester: Apollos; Downers Grove: InterVarsity Press.

——— (2005), 'Eden, the Temple, and the Church's Mission in the New Creation', *JETS* 48.1: 7–12.

——— (2007), 'Colossians', in G. K. Beale and D. A. Carson (eds.), *Commentary on the New Testament Use of the Old Testament*, Grand Rapids: Baker; Nottingham: Apollos, 841–870.

——— (2008), *The Erosion of Inerrancy in Evangelicalism: Responding to New Challenges to Biblical Authority*, Wheaton: Crossway.

———— (2011), *A New Testament Biblical Theology: The Transformation of the Old Testament in the New*, Grand Rapids: Baker.

———— (2012a), *Handbook on the New Testament Use of the Old Testament: Exegesis and Interpretation*, Grand Rapids: Baker.

———— (2012b), 'The Use of Hosea 11:1 in Matthew 2:15: One More Time', *JETS* 55.4: 697–715.

Beale, G. K., and Sean M. McDonough (2007), 'Revelation', in G. K. Beale and D. A. Carson (eds.), *Commentary on the New Testament Use of the Old Testament*, Grand Rapids: Baker; Nottingham: Apollos, 1081–1161.

Beasley-Murray, George R. (1974), *The Book of Revelation*, London: Marshall, Morgan & Scott.

———— (1992), 'The Kingdom of God in the Teaching of Jesus', *JETS* 35.1: 19–30.

———— (1999), *John*, WBC 36, 2nd ed., Nashville: Thomas Nelson.

Berkhof, Louis (1996), *Systematic Theology*, Grand Rapids: Eerdmans.

Betz, Hans Dieter (1995), *The Sermon on the Mount*, Hermeneia, Minneapolis: Fortress.

Birch, Bruce C., Walter Brueggemann, Terence E. Fretheim and David L. Peterson (1999), *A Theological Introduction to the Old Testament*, Nashville: Abingdon.

Blackburn, W. Ross (2012), *The God Who Makes Himself Known: The Missionary Heart of the Book of Exodus*, NSBT 28, Nottingham: Apollos; Downers Grove: InterVarsity Press.

Blaising, Craig A. (1992), 'Dispensationalism: The Search for Definition', in Craig A. Blaising and Darrell L. Bock (eds.), *Dispensationalism, Israel and the Church: The Search for Definition*, Grand Rapids: Zondervan, 13–34.

———— (1993a), 'The Extent and Varieties of Dispensationalism', in Craig A. Blaising and Darrell L. Bock (eds.), *Progressive Dispensationalism* (eds.), Grand Rapids: Baker, 9–56.

———— (1993b), 'The Structure of the Biblical Covenants: The Covenants Prior to Christ', in Craig A. Blaising and Darrell L. Bock (eds.), *Progressive Dispensationalism* (eds.), Grand Rapids: Baker, 128–173.

Blaising, Craig A., and Darrell L. Bock (eds.) (1992), *Dispensationalism, Israel and the Church: The Search for Definition*, Grand Rapids: Zondervan.

———— (1993), *Progressive Dispensationalism*, Grand Rapids: Baker.

Blocher, Henri (2006), 'Old Covenant, New Covenant', in A. T. B. McGowan (ed.), *Always Reforming: Explorations in Systematic Theology*, Nottingham: Apollos; Downers Grove: InterVarsity Press, 240–270.

Block, Daniel I. (1998), *The Book of Ezekiel 25–48*, NICOT, Grand Rapids: Eerdmans.

——— (2012), *Deuteronomy*, NIVAC, Grand Rapids: Zondervan.

Blomberg, Craig L. (1992), *Matthew*, NAC 22, Nashville: Broadman & Holman.

——— (2000), 'The Unity and Diversity of Scripture', in *NDBT*, 64–72.

Bock, Darrell L. (1987), *Proclamation from Prophecy and Pattern: Lucan Old Testament Christology*, Sheffield: JSOT Press.

——— (1999), 'Covenants in Progressive Dispensationalism', in Herbert W. Bateman IV (ed.), *Three Central Issues in Contemporary Dispensationalism*, Grand Rapids: Kregel, 169–203.

——— (2001), 'The Kingdom of God in New Testament Theology', in David W. Baker (ed.), *Looking into the Future: Evangelical Studies in Eschatology*, Grand Rapids: Baker, 28–60.

Brown, Raymond E. (1970), *The Gospel According to John XIII–XXI*, Garden City, N.Y.: Doubleday.

Bruce, F. F. (1964), *The Epistle to the Hebrews*, NICNT, Grand Rapids: Eerdmans.

Brueggemann, Walter (1977), *The Land: Place as Gift, Promise, and Challenge to Biblical Faith*, Philadelphia: Fortress.

Burge, Gary M. (1994), 'Territorial Religion, Johannine Christology, and the Vineyard of John 15', in Joel B. Green and Max Turner (eds.), *Jesus of Nazareth: Lord and Christ: Essays on the Historical Jesus and New Testament Christology*, Grand Rapids: Eerdmans, 384–396.

——— (2004), *Whose Land? Whose Promise? What Christians Are Not Being Told About Israel and the Palestinians*, Cleveland: Pilgrim.

——— (2010), *Jesus and the Land: The New Testament Challenge to 'Holy Land' Theology*, Grand Rapids: Baker.

Byrne, Brendan (1996), *Romans*, SP, Collegeville, Minn.: Liturgical.

Calvin, John (1998), *Commentaries on the Epistle of the Apostle Paul to the Romans*, tr. and ed. John Owen, Grand Rapids: Baker.

Caragounis, C. C. (1992), 'Kingdom of God/Heaven', in *DJG*, 417–430.

Carson, D. A. (1984), *Matthew*, EBC 8, ed. Frank E. Gaebelein, Grand Rapids: Zondervan, 1–599.

—————— (1991), *The Gospel According to John*, PNTC, Grand Rapids: Eerdmans.

—————— (1992), 'Unity and Diversity in the New Testament: The Possibility of Systematic Theology', in D. A. Carson and John D. Woodbridge (eds.), *Scripture and Truth*, Grand Rapids: Baker, 65–95.

—————— (1996), *The Gagging of God: Christianity Confronts Pluralism*, Grand Rapids: Zondervan; Leicester: Apollos.

—————— (1998), 'NT Theology', in R. P. Martin and P. H. Davids (eds.), *Dictionary of the Later New Testament and Its Developments*, Downers Grove: InterVarsity Press; Leicester: Inter-Varsity Press, 796–814.

—————— (2000), 'Systematic Theology and Biblical Theology', in *NDBT*, 89–104.

—————— (2004), 'Atonement in Romans 3:21–26', in Charles E. Hill and Frank A. James III (eds.), *The Glory of the Atonement: Biblical, Theological, & Practical Perspectives*, Downers Grove: InterVarsity Press; Leicester: Apollos, 119–139.

Carson, D. A., and John D. Woodbridge (1986), *Hermeneutics, Authority, and Canon*, Grand Rapids: Zondervan, 1986; repr. Eugene, Ore.: Wipf & Stock.

—————— (1992), *Scripture and Truth*, Grand Rapids: Baker.

Childs, Brevard S. (1992), *Biblical Theology of the Old and New Testaments: Theological Reflection on the Christian Bible*, Minneapolis: Fortress.

Clarke, T. A. (2010), 'Complete v. Incomplete Conquest: A Re-Examination of Three Passages in Joshua', *TynB* 61.1: 89–104.

Clements, Ronald E. (2004), 'Law and Promise', in Ben C. Ollenburger (ed.), *Old Testament Theology: Flowering and Future*, Winona Lake: Eisenbrauns, 156–173.

Clines, D. J. A. (1997), *The Theme of the Pentateuch*, 2nd ed., Sheffield: JSOT Press.

Clowney, Edmund (1961), *Preaching and Biblical Theology*, Grand Rapids: Eerdmans.

Collins, Jack (1997), 'A Syntactical Note (Genesis 3:15): Is the Woman's Seed Singular or Plural?', *TynB* 48.1: 139–148.

—————— (2006), *Genesis 1–4: A Linguistic, Literary, and Theological Commentary*, Phillipsburg: P. & R.

Cranfield, C. E. B. (1975), *A Critical and Exegetical Commentary on the Epistle to the Romans: Introduction and Commentary on Romans I–VIII*, ICC, London: T. & T. Clark.

Davids, Peter H. (1990), *The First Epistle of Peter*, NICNT, Grand Rapids: Eerdmans.

Davidson, Richard (1981), *Typology in Scripture: A Study of Hermeneutical ΤΥΠΟΣ Structures*, *AUSDDS* 2, Berrien Springs, Mich.: Andrews University.

Davies, W. D. (1974), *The Gospel and the Land: Early Christianity and Jewish Territorial Doctrine*, Berkeley: University of California Press.

———— (1982), *The Territorial Dimension of Judaism*, Minneapolis: Fortress.

Davies, W. D., and Dale C. Allison Jr. (2004), *Matthew 1–7*, ICC, London: T. & T. Clark.

Davis, John A. (2011), 'Discerning Between Good and Evil: Solomon as a New Adam in 1 Kings', *WTJ* 73: 39–57.

Dempster, Stephen G. (2003), *Dominion and Dynasty: A Theology of the Hebrew Bible*, NSBT 15, Leicester: Apollos; Downers Grove: InterVarsity Press.

———— (2008), 'Exodus and Biblical Theology: On Moving into the Neighborhood with a New Name', *SBJT* 12.3: 4–23.

Derrett, J. D. M. (1984), '*Palingenesia* (Matthew 19:28)', *JSNT* 20: 51–58.

deSilva, David A. (2000), 'Entering God's Rest: Eschatology and the Socio-Rhetorical Strategy of Hebrews', *TrinJ* 21: 25–43.

De Vries, Simon J. (2004), *1 Kings*, 2nd ed., WBC 12, Nashville: Nelson.

Dodd, C. H. (1935), *The Parables of the Kingdom*, London: Nisbet.

Duguid, Ian M. (2000), 'Exile', in *NDBT*, 475–478.

Dumbrell, William J. (1984), *Covenant and Creation: A Theology of the Old Testament Covenants*, Carlisle: Paternoster.

———— (1985), *The End of the Beginning: Revelation 21–22 and the Old Testament*, Eugene, Ore.: Wipf & Stock.

———— (1994), *The Search for Order: Biblical Eschatology in Focus*, Eugene, Ore.: Wipf & Stock.

———— (2002), *The Faith of Israel: A Theological Survey of the Old Testament*, Grand Rapids: Baker; Leicester: Apollos.

Dunn, James D. G. (1988), *Romans 1–8*, WBC 38, Nashville: Thomas Nelson.

———— (2004), 'The Problem of "Biblical Theology"', in Craig Batholomew, Mary Healy, Karl Möller and Robin Parry (eds.), *Out of Egypt: Biblical Theology and Biblical Interpretation*, SHS 5, Grand Rapids: Zondervan, 172–184.

Ellingworth, Paul (1993), *The Epistle to the Hebrews*, NIGTC, Grand Rapids: Eerdmans.

Elliot, John H. (2000), *1 Peter: A New Translation with Introduction and Commentary*, AB, New York: Doubleday.

Enns, Peter E. (2000), 'Exodus (Book)', in *NDBT*, 146–152.

––––––– (2005), *Inspiration and Incarnation: Evangelicals and the Problem of the Old Testament*, Grand Rapids: Baker.

Feinberg, John S. (ed.) (1988), 'Systems of Discontinuity', in John S. Feinberg (ed.), *Continuity and Discontinuity: Perspectives on the Relationship Between the Old and New Testaments*, Wheaton: Crossway, 63–86.

––––––– (2001), *No One Like Him: The Doctrine of God*, Wheaton: Crossway.

Fenton, J. C. (1977), *The Gospel of St. Matthew*, rev. ed., Philadelphia: Westminster.

Frame, John M. (1987), *The Doctrine of the Knowledge of God*, Phillipsburg: P. & R.

––––––– (2010), *The Doctrine of the Word of God*, Phillipsburg: P. & R.

France, R. T. (1989), *Matthew: Evangelist and Teacher*, Eugene, Ore.: Wipf & Stock.

––––––– (1998), *Jesus and the Old Testament*, Vancouver: Regent.

––––––– (2007), *The Gospel of Matthew*, NICNT, Grand Rapids: Eerdmans.

––––––– (2008), 'Matthew and Jerusalem', in Daniel M. Gurtner and John Nolland (eds.), *Built upon the Rock: Studies in the Gospel of Matthew*, Grand Rapids: Eerdmans, 108–127.

Gentry, Peter J. (2007), 'Rethinking the "Sure Mercies of David" in Isaiah 55:3', *WTJ* 69: 279–304.

––––––– (2008), 'Kingdom Through Covenant: Humanity as the Divine Image', *SBJT* 12.1: 16–33.

Gentry, Peter J., and Stephen J. Wellum (2012), *Kingdom Through Covenant: A Biblical-Theological Understanding of the Covenants*, Wheaton: Crossway.

Glenny, W. Edward (1997), 'Typology: A Summary of the Present Evangelical Discussion', *JETS* 40.4: 627–638.

Golding, Peter (2004), *Covenant Theology: The Key of Theology in Reformed Thought and Tradition*, Fearn, Scotland: Mentor.

Goldingay, John (2003), *Old Testament Theology*, vol. 1: *Israel's Gospel*, Downers Grove: InterVarsity Press.

––––––– (2006), *Old Testament Theology*, vol. 2: *Israel's Faith*, Downers Grove: InterVarsity Press.

Goldsworthy, Graeme (1991), *According to Plan: The Unfolding Revelation of God in the Bible*, Leicester: Inter-Varsity Press; Downers Grove: InterVarsity Press.

———— (2000), *The Goldsworthy Trilogy*, Carlisle: Paternoster.

———— (2006), *Gospel-Centered Hermeneutics: Foundations and Principles of Evangelical Biblical Interpretation*, Nottingham: Apollos; Downers Grove: InterVarsity Press.

———— (2012), *Christ-Centered Biblical Theology: Hermeneutical Foundations and Principles*, Nottingham: Apollos; Downers Grove: InterVarsity Press.

Goppelt, Leonhard (1982), *Typos: The Typological Interpretation of the Old Testament in the New*, tr. Donald H. Madvig, Grand Rapids: Eerdmans.

Green, Gene L. (2008), *Jude and 2 Peter*, BECNT, Grand Rapids: Baker.

Grenz, Stanley J., and John F. Franke (2001), *Beyond Foundationalism: Shaping Theology in a Postmodern Context*, Louisville: Westminster John Knox.

Grudem, Wayne (1988), *1 Peter: An Introduction and Commentary*, TNTC, Leicester: Inter-Varsity Press; Downers Grove: InterVarsity Press.

Grüneberg, Keith N. (2003), *Abraham, Blessing, and the Nations: A Philological and Exegetical Study of Genesis 12:3 in Its Narrative Context*, Berlin: Walter de Gruyter.

Guthrie, Donald (1983), *Hebrews*, TNTC, Leicester: Inter-Varsity Press.

Habel, Norman C. (1995), *The Land Is Mine: Six Biblical Land Ideologies*, Minneapolis: Fortress.

Hafemann, Scott J., and Paul R. House (eds.) (2007), *Central Themes in Biblical Theology: Mapping Unity in Diversity*, Nottingham: Apollos; Grand Rapids: Baker.

Hagner, Donald A. (1993), *Matthew 1–13*, WBC 33A, Dallas: Word.

Hamilton Jr., James M. (2005), 'God with Men in the Prophets and the Writings: An Examination of the Nature of God's Presence', *SBET* 23.2: 166–193.

———— (2006a), 'The Center of Biblical Theology: The Glory of God in Salvation Through Judgment', *TynB* 57.1: 57–84.

———— (2006b), 'The Skull-Crushing Seed of the Woman: Inter-Biblical Interpretation of Genesis 3:15', *SBJT* 10.2: 30–54.

———— (2010), *God's Glory in Salvation Through Judgment: A Biblical Theology*, Wheaton: Crossway.

Hamilton, Victor P. (1990), *The Book of Genesis: Chapters 1–17*, NICOT, Grand Rapids: Eerdmans.

Hanson, K. C. (ed.) (2005), *From Genesis to Chronicles: Explorations in Old Testament Theology*, Minneapolis: Fortress.

Harris, Dana M. (2009), 'The Eternal Inheritance in Hebrews: The Appropriation of the Old Testament Inheritance Motif by the Author of Hebrews', PhD diss., Deerfield: Trinity Evangelical Divinity School.

Hasel, Gerhard (1991), *Old Testament Theology: Basic Issues in the Current Debate*, 4th ed., Grand Rapids: Eerdmans.

——— (2003), *New Testament Theology: Basic Issues in the Current Debate*, Grand Rapids: Eerdmans.

Hays, Richard B. (1997), '*ΠΙΣΤΙΣ* and Pauline Theology: What Is at Stake?', in E. Elizabeth Johnson and David M. Hay (eds.), *Pauline Theology, Looking Back, Pressing On*, vol. 4, Atlanta: Scholars Press, 35–40.

Heide, Gale Z. (1997), 'What Is New About the New Heaven and the New Earth? A Theology of Creation from Revelation 21 and 2 Peter 3', *JETS* 40.1: 37–56.

Hester, James D. (1968), *Paul's Concept of Inheritance: A Contribution to the Understanding of Heilsgeschichte*, Edinburgh: Oliver & Boyd.

Hoehner, Harold (2002), *Ephesians: An Exegetical Commentary*, Grand Rapids: Baker.

Hoekema, Anthony A. (1979), *The Bible and the Future*, Grand Rapids: Eerdmans.

Holwerda, David E. (1995), *Jesus and Israel: One Covenant or Two?* Grand Rapids: Eerdmans.

Horner, Barry E. (2007), *Future Israel: Why Christian Anti-Judaism Must Be Challenged*, NACSBT, Nashville: Broadman & Holman.

Horton, Michael S. (2002), *Covenant and Eschatology: The Divine Drama*, Louisville: Westminster John Knox.

——— (2006), *God of Promise: Introducing Covenant Theology*, Grand Rapids: Baker.

Hoskins, Paul M. (2006), *Jesus as the Fulfillment of the Temple in the Gospel of John*, Eugene, Ore.: Wipf & Stock.

House, Paul R. (1998), *Old Testament Theology*, Downers Grove: InterVarsity Press.

——— (2002), 'Biblical Theology and the Wholeness of Scripture', in *Biblical Theology: Retrospect and Prospect*, Downers Grove: InterVarsity Press, 2002.

Howard Jr., David M. (1998), *Joshua: An Exegetical and Theological Exposition of Holy Scripture*, NAC 5, Nashville: Broadman & Holman.

Hubbard, Moyer V. (2002), *New Creation in Paul's Letters and Thought*, SNTSMS 119, Cambridge: Cambridge University Press.

Huey Jr., F. B. (1993), *Jeremiah, Lamentations*, NAC 16, Nashville: Broadman & Holman.

Inge, John (2003), *A Christian Theology of Place*, Explorations in Practical, Pastoral and Empirical Theology, Burlington, Vt.: Ashgate.

Jewett, Paul (2007), *Romans: A Commentary*, Hermeneia, Minneapolis: Fortress.

Jobes, Karen H. (2003), 'The Syntax of 1 Peter: Just How Good Is the Greek?', *BBR* 13.2: 159–173.

Johnson, Dennis E. (2001), *The Triumph of the Lamb: A Commentary on Revelation*, Phillipsburg: P. & R.

Johnson, Luke Timothy (1982), 'Romans 3:21–26 and the Faith of Jesus', *CBQ* 44: 77–90.

Johnston, Philip, and Peter Walker (eds.) (2000), *The Land of Promise: Biblical, Theological, and Contemporary Perspectives*, Leicester: Apollos; Downers Grove: InterVarsity Press.

Jónsson, Gunnlauger A. (1988), *The Image of God: Genesis 1:26–28 in a Century of Old Testament Research*, ConBOT 26, Lund: Almqvist & Wiksell.

Kaiser Jr., Walter C. (1970), 'The Eschatological Hermeneutics of "Epangelicalism": Promise Theology', *JETS* 13: 91–99.

——— (1973), 'The Promise Theme and the Theology of Rest', *BSac* 130: 135–150.

——— (1978), *Toward an Old Testament Theology*, Grand Rapids: Zondervan.

——— (1981), 'The Promised Land: A Biblical-Historical View', *BSac* 138: 302–312.

——— (2008), *The Promise-Plan of God: A Biblical Theology of the Old and New Testaments*, Grand Rapids: Zondervan.

Karlberg, Mark W. (1988), 'The Significance of Israel in Biblical Typology', *JETS* 31.3: 257–269.

Kelly, J. N. D. (1969), *The Epistles of Peter and of Jude*, BNTC, London: Hendrickson.

Kidner, Derek (1973), *Psalms 73–150*, TOTC, Leicester: Inter-Varsity Press; Downers Grove: InterVarsity Press.

——— (1987), *The Message of Jeremiah*, BST, Leicester: Inter-Varsity Press; Downers Grove: InterVarsity Press.

Kim, Joon-Sik (2001), 'Your Kingdom Come on Earth: The Promise of the Land and the Kingdom of Heaven in the Gospel of Matthew', PhD diss., Princeton: Princeton Theological Seminary.

Kline, Meredith G. (2006), *Kingdom Prologue: Genesis Foundations for a Covenantal Worldview*, Eugene, Ore.: Wipf & Stock.

Klink III, Edward W., and Darian R. Lockett (2012), *Understanding Biblical Theology: A Comparison of Theory and Practice*, Grand Rapids: Zondervan.

Koorevar, H. J. (1990), *De Opbouw van het Boek Jozua*, Heverlee: Centrum voor Bijbelse Vorming België.

Köstenberger, Andreas J. (2009), *A Theology of John's Gospel and Letters*, BTNT, Grand Rapids: Zondervan.

——— (2012), 'The Present and Future of Biblical Theology', *Them* 37.3: 445–464.

Köstenberger, Andreas J., and Peter T. O'Brien (2001), *Salvation to the Ends of the Earth: A Biblical Theology of Mission*, NSBT 11, Leicester: Apollos; Downers Grove: InterVarsity Press.

Laansma, Jon (2008a), 'The Cosmology of Hebrews', in Jonathan T. Pennington and Sean M. McDonough (eds.), *Cosmology and New Testament Theology*, LNTS 355, London: T. & T. Clark, 125–143.

——— (2008b), 'Hidden Stories in Hebrews: Cosmology and Theology', in Richard Bauckham, Daniel R. Driver, Trevor A. Hart and Nathan MacDonald (eds.), *A Cloud of Witnesses: The Theology of Hebrews in Its Ancient Context*, LNTS 355, London: T. & T. Clark, 9–18.

Ladd, George Eldon (1959), *The Gospel of the Kingdom*, Grand Rapids: Eerdmans.

——— (1972), *A Commentary on the Revelation of John*, Grand Rapids: Eerdmans.

——— (1993), *A Theology of the New Testament*, rev. ed., Grand Rapids: Eerdmans.

——— (1998), *Crucial Questions About the Kingdom of God*, Eugene, Ore.: Wipf & Stock.

Lane, William L. (1991a), *Hebrews 1–8*, WBC 47A, Dallas: Word.

——— (1991b), *Hebrews 9–13*, WBC 47B, Dallas: Word.

LaRondelle, Hans K. (1983), *The Israel of God in Prophecy: Principles of Prophetic Interpretation*, Berrien Springs, Mich.: Andrews University Press.

Leder, Arie C. (2010), *Waiting for the Land: The Story Line of the Pentateuch*, Phillipsburg: P. & R.

Lee, Pilchan (2001), *The New Jerusalem in the Book of Revelation: A Study of Revelation 21–22 in the Light of Its Background in Jewish Tradition*, WUNT 2.129, Tübingen: Mohr Siebeck.

Levenson, Jon D. (1984), 'The Temple and the World', *JR* 64.3: 275–298.

——— (1985), *Sinai and Zion: An Entry into the Jewish Bible*, New York: HarperCollins.

Lillback, Peter A., and Richard B. Gaffin (eds.) (2013), *Thy Word Is Still Truth: Essential Writings on the Doctrine of Scripture from the Reformation to Today*, Phillipsburg: P. & R.

Lincoln, Andrew T. (1982), 'Sabbath, Rest, and Eschatology in the New Testament', in D. A. Carson (ed.), *From Sabbath to Lord's Day*, Eugene, Ore.: Wipf & Stock, 197–220.

——— (1990), *Ephesians*, WBC 42, Nashville: Thomas Nelson.

Lindars, Barnabas (1991), *The Theology of the Letter to the Hebrews*, Cambridge: Cambridge University Press.

Lints, Richard (1993), *The Fabric of Theology: A Prolegomenon to Evangelical Theology*, Grand Rapids: Eerdmans.

Lister, John Ryan (2010), '"The Lord Your God Is in Your Midst": The Presence of God and the Means and End of Redemptive History', PhD diss., Louisville: Southern Baptist Theological Seminary.

Lohfink, Norbert, and Erich Zenger (2000), *The God of Israel and the Nations: Studies in Isaiah and the Psalms*, tr. Everett R. Kalin, Collegeville, Minn.: Liturgical Press.

Luz, Ulrich (1993), *The Theology of the Gospel of Matthew*, Cambridge: Cambridge University Press.

——— (2007), *Matthew 1–7: A Commentary*, Hermeneia, Minneapolis: Fortress.

Mabie, F. J. (2005), 'Geographical Extent of Israel', in *DOTHP*, 316–328.

McComiskey, Thomas Edward (1985), *The Covenants of Promise: A Theology of the Old Testament Covenants*, Grand Rapids: Baker.

——— (1992), 'Hosea', in Thomas Edward McComiskey (ed.), *The Minor Prophets: An Exegetical and Expository Commentary*, vol. 1, Grand Rapids: Zondervan, 1–237.

McConville, J. Gordon (1993), *Grace in the End: A Study in Deuteronomic Theology*, Grand Rapids: Zondervan.

——— (2001), 'Restoration in Deuteronomy and the Deuteronomic Literature', in James M. Scott (ed.), *Restoration: Old Testament, Jewish, and Christian Perspectives*, Leiden: Brill, 11–40.

—— (2005), 'Prophetic Writings', in *DTIB*, 628–632.

McKenzie, J. L. (1974), *A Theology of the Old Testament*, Garden City, N.Y.: Doubleday.

McKeown, James (2003), 'Land, Fertility, Famine', in *DOTP*, 487–491.

Marshall, I. Howard (1988), 'An Assessment of Recent Developments', in D. A. Carson and H. G. M. Williamson (eds.), *It Is Written: Scripture Citing Scripture*, Cambridge: Cambridge University Press, 1–21.

Martens, Elmer Arthur (1997), *Old Testament Theology*, IBR Bibliographies 13, Grand Rapids: Baker.

—— (1998), *God's Design: A Focus on Old Testament Theology*, 3rd ed., N. Richland Hills, Tex.: BIBAL Press.

—— (2004), 'Land and Lifestyle', in Ben C. Ollenburger (ed.), *Old Testament Theology: Flowering and Future*, Winona Lake: Eisenbrauns, 222–241.

—— (2009), 'O Land, Land, Land: Reading the Earth Story in Both Testaments', in Jon Isaak (ed.), *The Old Testament in the Life of God's People: Essays in Honor of Elmer A. Martens*, Winona Lake: Eisenbrauns, 223–244.

Martin, Oren R. (2013), 'Bound for the Kingdom: The Land Promise in God's Redemptive Plan', PhD diss., Louisville: Southern Baptist Theological Seminary.

Mathews, Kenneth A. (1996), *Genesis 1–11:26*, NAC 1A, Nashville: Broadman & Holman.

—— (2000), 'Genesis', in *NDBT*, 140–146.

—— (2005), *Genesis 11:27–50:26*, NAC 1B, Nashville: Broadman & Holman.

Merrill, Eugene H. (2006), *Everlasting Dominion: A Theology of the Old Testament*, Nashville: Broadman & Holman.

Michaels, J. Ramsey (1988), *1 Peter*, WBC 49, Waco: Word.

Millar, Gary J. (1998), *Now Choose Life: Theology and Ethics in Deuteronomy*, NSBT 6, Leicester: Apollos; Downers Grove: InterVarsity Press.

—— (2000), 'Land', in *NDBT*, 623–627.

Miller, Patrick D. (1969), 'The Gift of God: The Deuteronomic Theology of Land', *Int* 23: 451–465.

Moo, Douglas J. (1996), *Romans*, NICNT, Grand Rapids: Eerdmans.

—— (2008), *The Letters to the Colossians and to Philemon*, PNTC, Grand Rapids: Eerdmans; Nottingham: Apollos.

Morgan, Christopher W., and Robert A. Peterson (eds.) (2013), *Fallen: A Theology of Sin*, Wheaton: Crossway.

Morris, Leon (1965), *The Apostolic Preaching of the Cross*, 3rd ed., Grand Rapids: Eerdmans.

——— (1983), *The Atonement: Its Meaning and Significance*, Leicester: Inter-Varsity Press; Downers Grove: InterVarsity Press.

——— (1988), *The Epistle to the Romans*, Grand Rapids: Eerdmans; Leicester: Inter-Varsity Press.

——— (1995), *The Gospel According to John*, rev. ed., NICNT, Grand Rapids: Eerdmans.

Motyer, J. Alec (1993), *The Prophecy of Isaiah: An Introduction & Commentary*, Leicester: Inter-Varsity Press; Downers Grove: InterVarsity Press.

——— (1999), *Isaiah*, TOTC, Leicester: Inter-Varsity Press; Downers Grove: InterVarsity Press.

Mounce, Robert H. (1998), *The Book of Revelation*, 2nd ed., NICNT, Grand Rapids: Eerdmans.

Murray, John (1965), *Epistle to the Romans*, NICNT, Grand Rapids: Eerdmans.

——— (1988), *The Covenant of Grace: A Biblico-Theological Study*, Phillipsburg: P. & R.

Nelson, Richard D. (1987), *First and Second Kings*, IBC, Nashville: Westminster John Knox.

Niehaus, Jeffrey J. (1995), *God at Sinai: Covenant and Theophany in the Bible and Ancient Near East*, Grand Rapids: Zondervan.

——— (2008), *Ancient Near Eastern Themes in Biblical Theology*, Grand Rapids: Kregel.

——— (2009), 'Covenant: An Idea in the Mind of God', *JETS* 52.2: 225–246.

Nolland, John (2005), *The Gospel of Matthew: A Commentary on the Greek Text*, NIGTC, Grand Rapids: Eerdmans.

O'Brien, Peter T. (2010), *The Letter to the Hebrews*, PNTC, Grand Rapids: Eerdmans; Nottingham: Apollos.

Osborne, Grant R. (2006), *The Hermeneutical Spiral: A Comprehensive Introduction to Biblical Interpretation*, 2nd ed., Downers Grove: InterVarsity Press.

Oswalt, John N. (1986), *The Book of Isaiah: Chapters 1–39*, NICOT, Grand Rapids: Eerdmans.

——— (1998), *The Book of Isaiah: Chapters 40–66*, NICOT, Grand Rapids: Eerdmans.

Overstreet, R. L. (1980), 'A Study of 2 Peter 3:10–13', *BSac* 137: 354–371.

Pao, David W. (2012), *Colossians and Philemon*, ZECNT, Grand Rapids: Zondervan.

Pate, C. Marvin, J. Scott Duvall, J. Daniel Hays, E. Randolph Richards, W. Dennis Tucker Jr. and Preben Vang (2004), *The Story of Israel: A Biblical Theology*, Downers Grove: InterVarsity Press; Leicester: Apollos.

Pennington, Jonathan T. (2007), *Heaven and Earth in the Gospel of Matthew*, Grand Rapids: Baker.

Plummer, Robert L. (2010a), *40 Questions About Interpreting the Bible*, Grand Rapids: Kregel.

―――― (2010b), 'Righteousness and Peace Kiss: The Reconciliation of Authorial-Intent and Biblical Typology', *SBJT* 14.2: 54–61.

Poythress, Vern Sheridan (1991), *The Shadow of Christ in the Law of Moses*, Phillipsburg: P. & R.

Preuss, H. D. (1996), *Old Testament Theology*, 2 vols., tr. L. G. Purdue, Louisville: Westminster John Knox.

Rad, Gerhard von (1965), *The Message of the Prophets*, New York: Harper & Row.

―――― (1966), *The Problem of the Hexateuch and Other Essays*, tr. E. W. Trueman Dicken, London: Oliver & Boyd.

―――― (2005), *Old Testament Theology*, 2 vols., tr. D. M. G. Stalker, Peabody: Prince.

Reichenbach, Bruce R. (2003), 'Genesis 1 as a Theological-Political Narrative of Kingdom Establishment', *BBR* 13.1: 47–69.

Rendtorff, Rolf (2005), *The Canonical Hebrew Bible: A Theology of the Old Testament*, tr. David E. Orton, Leiden: Deo.

Ribbens, Benjamin J. (2011), 'Typology of Types: Typology in Dialogue', *JTI* 5.1: 81–96.

Ridderbos, Herman (1962), *The Coming of the Kingdom*, Phillipsburg: P. & R.

―――― (1975), *Paul: An Outline of His Theology*, tr. John Richard De Witt, Grand Rapids: Eerdmans.

―――― (1997), *The Gospel of John: A Theological Commentary*, tr. John Vriend, Grand Rapids: Eerdmans.

Robertson, O. Palmer (1980), *The Christ of the Covenants*, Phillipsburg: P. & R.

―――― (2000), *The Israel of God: Yesterday, Today, and Tomorrow*, Phillipsburg: P. & R.

Rogland, Max (2008), 'Abram's Persistent Faith: Hebrew Verb Semantics in Genesis 15:6', *WTJ* 70: 239–244.

Rosner, B. S. (2000), 'Biblical Theology', in *NDBT*, 3–11.

Ross, Allen P. (1997), 'Exile', in *NIDOTTE* 4: 595–601.

Routledge, Robin (2008), *Old Testament Theology: A Thematic Approach*, Nottingham: Apollos; Downers Grove: InterVarsity Press.

Rushdoony, Rousas John (1994), *Systematic Theology*, 2 vols., Vallecito, Calif.: Ross House.

Ryrie, Charles C. (2007), *Dispensationalism*, rev. ed., Chicago: Moody.

Sailhamer, John H. (1992), *The Pentateuch as Narrative: A Biblical-Theological Commentary*, Grand Rapids: Zondervan.

Saucy, Robert L. (1993), *The Case for Progressive Dispensationalism: The Interface Between Dispensational and Non-Dispensational Theology*, Grand Rapids: Zondervan.

Schnabel, Eckhard J. (2000), 'Scripture', in *NDBT*, 34–43.

Schnackenburg, Rudolph (1963), *God's Rule and Kingdom*, New York: Herder & Herder.

Schreiner, Thomas R. (1998), *Romans*, BECNT, Grand Rapids: Baker.

——— (2001), *Paul, Apostle of God's Glory in Christ: A Pauline Theology*, Downers Grove: InterVarsity Press; Leicester: Apollos.

——— (2003), *1, 2 Peter, Jude*, NAC 37, Nashville: Broadman & Holman.

——— (2008), *New Testament Theology: Magnifying God in Christ*, Grand Rapids: Baker; Nottingham: Apollos.

——— (2013), *The King in His Beauty: A Biblical Theology of the Old and New Testaments*, Grand Rapids: Baker.

Schreiner, Thomas R., and Ardel B. Caneday (2001), *The Race Set Before Us: A Biblical Theology of Perseverance and Assurance*, Downers Grove: InterVarsity Press; Leicester: Inter-Varsity Press.

Schultz, Richard L. (2012), 'Hearing the Major Prophets: "Your Ears Are Open, but You Hear Nothing" (Isa. 42:20)', in Craig G. Bartholomew and David J. H. Beldman (eds.), *Hearing the Old Testament: Listening for God's Address*, Grand Rapids: Eerdmans, 332–355.

Schweitzer, Albert (1914), *The Mystery of the Kingdom of God*, New York: Schocken.

Scobie, C. H. H. (1991), 'The Structure of Biblical Theology', *TynB* 42.2: 163–194.

——— (2003), *The Ways of Our God: An Approach to Biblical Theology*, Grand Rapids: Eerdmans.

Seifrid, Mark A. (2000), *Christ, Our Righteousness: Paul's Theology of Justification*, Leicester: Apollos; Downers Grove: InterVarsity Press.

Seitz, Christopher R. (2007), *Prophecy and Hermeneutics: Toward a New Introduction to the Prophets*, Grand Rapids: Baker.

Sim, David C. (1993), 'The Meaning of *palingenesia* in Matthew 19:28', *JSNT* 50: 3–12.

Sizer, Stephen (2007), *Zion's Christian Soldiers? The Bible, Israel and the Church*, Nottingham: Inter-Varsity Press; Downers Grove: InterVarsity Press.

Storms, Sam (2013), *Kingdom Come: The Amillennial Alternative*, Fearn, Scotland: Mentor.

Swain, Scott R. (2011), *Trinity, Revelation, and Reading: A Theological Introduction to the Bible and Its Interpretation*, New York: T. & T. Clark.

Taylor, John B. (2004), 'The Temple in Ezekiel', in T. Desmond Alexander and Simon Gathercole (eds.), *Heaven on Earth: The Temple in Biblical Theology*, Waynesboro, Ga.: Paternoster, 59–70.

——— (2009), *Ezekiel*, TOTC, Nottingham: Inter-Varsity Press; Downers Grove: InterVarsity Press, 1969; repr.

Terrien, Samuel (1978), *The Elusive Presence: Toward a New Biblical Theology*, New York: Harper & Row.

Thomas, Matthew A. (2011), *These Are the Generations: Identity, Covenant, and the 'Toledot' Formula*, New York: T. & T. Clark.

Thompson, Alan J. (2011), *The Acts of the Risen Lord: Luke's Account of God's Unfolding Plan*, NSBT 27, Nottingham: Apollos; Downers Grove: InterVarsity Press.

Thompson, J. A. (1963), 'The Significance of the Ancient Near Eastern Treaty Pattern', *TynB* 13: 1–6.

——— (1980), *The Book of Jeremiah*, NICOT, Grand Rapids: Eerdmans.

Turner, David L. (1992), 'The New Jerusalem in Revelation 21:1–22:5: Consummation of a Biblical Continuum', in Craig A. Blaising and Darrell L. Bock (eds.), *Dispensationalism, Israel and the Church: The Search for Definition*, Grand Rapids: Zondervan, 264–292.

——— (2008), *Matthew*, BECNT, Grand Rapids: Baker.

Van Aselt, Willem J. (2000), *The Federal Theology of Johannes Cocceius (1603–1689)*, tr. Raymond A. Blacketer, Leiden: Brill.

VanGemeren, Willem A. (1988), *The Progress of Redemption: The Story of Salvation from Creation to the New Jerusalem*, Grand Rapids: Baker.

——— (1990), *Interpreting the Prophetic Word: An Introduction to the Prophetic Literature of the Old Testament*, Grand Rapids: Zondervan.

Vanhoozer, Kevin J. (1998), *Is There a Meaning in This Text? The Bible, The Reader, and the Morality of Literary Knowledge*, Grand Rapids: Zondervan; Leicester: Apollos.

Venema, Cornelis P. (2000), *The Promise of the Future*, Edinburgh: Banner of Truth.

——— (2008), *Christ and the Future: The Bible's Teaching and the Last Things*, Carlisle: Banner of Truth.

Vickers, Brian J. (2008), 'The Kingdom of God in Paul's Gospel', *SBJT* 12.1: 52–67.

Vogt, Peter T. (2009), *Interpreting the Pentateuch: An Exegetical Handbook*, Grand Rapids: Baker.

Vos, Geerhardus (2004), *Biblical Theology: Old and New Testaments*, Carlisle: Banner of Truth.

Waldow, H. E. von (1974), 'Israel and Her Land: Some Theological Considerations', in H. N. Bream, R. D. Heim and C. A. Moore (eds.), *A Light unto My Path: Old Testament Studies in Honor of Jacob M. Myers*, Philadelphia: Temple University Press, 475–492.

Walker, P. W. L. (ed.) (1994), *Jerusalem Past and Present in the Purposes of God*, rev. ed., Grand Rapids: Baker.

——— (1996), *Jesus and the Holy City: New Testament Perspectives on Jerusalem*, Grand Rapids: Eerdmans.

——— (2000), 'The Land in the Apostles' Writings', in Philip Johnston and Peter Walker (eds.), *The Land of Promise: Biblical, Theological and Contemporary Perspectives*, Leicester: Apollos; Downers Grove: InterVarsity Press, 81–99.

Wallace, Daniel B. (1996), *Greek Grammar Beyond the Basics: An Exegetical Syntax of the New Testament*, Grand Rapids: Zondervan.

Waltke, Bruce K. (2001), 'The Kingdom of God in Biblical Theology', in David W. Baker (ed.), *Looking into the Future: Evangelical Studies in Eschatology*, Grand Rapids: Baker, 15–27.

Waltke, Bruce K., with Charles Yu (2007), *An Old Testament Theology: An Exegetical, Canonical, and Thematic Approach*, Grand Rapids: Zondervan.

Walton, John H. (2009), *The Lost World of Genesis One: Ancient Cosmology and the Origins Debate*, Downers Grove: InterVarsity Press.

Ward, Timothy (2009), *Words of Life: Scripture as the Living and Active Word of God*, Leicester: Inter-Varsity Press; Downers Grove: InterVarsity Press.

Ware, Bruce A. (1992), 'The New Covenant and the People(s) of God', in Craig A. Blaising and Darrell L. Bock (eds.), *Dispensationalism, Israel and the Church: The Search for Definition*, Grand Rapids: Zondervan, 68–97.

Watts, Rikki E. (2000), 'Exodus', in *NDBT*, 478–487.

Webb, Barry G. (1990), 'Zion in Transformation: A Literary Approach to Isaiah', in D. J. A. Clines, S. E. Fowl and S. E. Porter (eds.), *The Bible in Three Dimensions*, JSOTSup 87, Sheffield: JSOT Press, 65–84.

Weber, Timothy (2004), *On the Road to Armageddon: How Evangelicals Became Israel's Best Friend*, Grand Rapids: Baker.

Webster, John (2009), 'One Who Is Son: Theological Reflections on the Exordium to the Epistle to the Hebrews', in Richard Bauckham, Daniel R. Driver, Trevor A. Hart and Nathan McDonald (eds.), *The Epistle to the Hebrews and Christian Theology*, Grand Rapids: Eerdmans, 69–94.

Weinfeld, Moshe (1970), 'The Covenant of Grant in the OT and in the Ancient Near East', *JAOS* 90: 184–203.

———— (1993), *The Promise of the Land: The Inheritance of the Land of Canaan by the Israelites*, Berkeley: University of California Press.

Weiss, Johannes (1971), *Jesus' Proclamation of the Kingdom of God*, Philadelphia: Fortress.

Wellum, Stephen J. (2006), 'Baptism and the Relationship Between the Covenants', in Thomas R. Schreiner and Shawn D. Wright (eds.), *Believer's Baptism: Sign of the New Covenant in Christ*, Nashville: Broadman & Holman, 97–162.

Wenham, Gordon J. (1987), *Genesis 1–15*, WBC 1, Waco: Word.

———— (1994), 'Sanctuary Symbolism in the Garden of Eden Story', in Richard S. Hess and David Toshio (eds.), *I Studied Inscriptions from Before the Flood: Ancient Near Eastern, Literary, and Linguistic Approaches to Genesis 1–11*, Winona Lake: Eisenbrauns, 399–404.

———— (2003), *Exploring the Old Testament: A Guide to the Pentateuch*, Downers Grove: InterVarsity Press.

Westermann, Claus (1972), *Beginning and End in the Bible*, tr. Keith Crim, Philadelphia: Fortress.

Wheaton, Byron L. (2006), 'Focus and Structure in the Abraham Narratives', *TrinJ* 27.1: 143–162.

Williamson, H. G. M. (1985), 'The Old Testament and the Material World', *EvQ* 57.1: 5–22.

Williamson, Paul R. (2000a), 'Covenant', in *NDBT*, 419–429.

———— (2000b), 'Promise and Fulfillment: The Territorial Inheritance', in Philip Johnston and Peter Walker (eds.), *The Land of Promise: Biblical, Theological, and Contemporary Perspectives*, Leicester: Apollos; Downers Grove: InterVarsity Press, 15–34.

———— (2003), 'Covenant', in *DOTP*, 139–155.

——— (2007), *Sealed with an Oath: Covenant in God's Unfolding Purpose*, NSBT 23, Nottingham: Apollos; Downers Grove: InterVarsity Press.

Willis, Wendell (ed.) (1987), *The Kingdom of God in 20th-Century Interpretation*, Peabody: Hendrickson.

Willitts, Joel (2007), *Matthew's Messianic Shepherd-King: In Search of 'The Lost Sheep of the House of Israel'*, Berlin: Walter de Gruyter.

Witherington III, Ben (2009), 'The Conquest of Faith and the Climax of History (Hebrews 12:1–4, 18–29)', in Richard Bauckham, Daniel R. Driver, Trevor A. Hart and Nathan McDonald (eds.), *The Epistle to the Hebrews and Christian Theology*, Grand Rapids: Eerdmans, 432–437.

Wolters, Al (2004), 'Zechariah 14 and Biblical Theology', in Craig Bartholomew, Mary Healy, Karl Möller and Robin Parry (eds.), *Out of Egypt: Biblical Theology and Biblical Interpretation*, SHS 5, Grand Rapids: Zondervan, 262–285.

Woodbridge, John D. (1982), *Biblical Authority: A Critique of the Rogers/McKim Proposal*, Grand Rapids: Zondervan.

Wright, Christopher J. H. (1984), *Living as the People of God*, Leicester: Inter-Varsity Press; Downers Grove: InterVarsity Press.

——— (1990), *God's People in God's Land: Family, Land, and Property in the Old Testament*, Grand Rapids: Eerdmans.

——— (1993), 'Biblical Reflections on Land', *ERT* 17.2: 153–167.

——— (2004), *Old Testament Ethics for the People of God*, Leicester: Inter-Varsity Press; Downers Grove: InterVarsity Press.

Wright, N. T. (1992), *The New Testament and the People of God*, in Christian Origins and the Question of God 1, Minneapolis: Fortress.

Index of authors

Index of Scripture references